CW00502469

The Trust F

Essays on the current political crisis and hope for the future

Trust is essential for our democracy. We trust our political leaders and institutions to put the public interest before their personal or partisan advantage. We trust each other to work and live together. No system is perfect and there is rarely one right answer to the big challenges faced, but we expect leaders to be honest, competent and compassionate – and punish any breaches harshly in the polls or at the ballot box.

But not any longer. Now is a time of political crisis that's fuelled by a lack of trust in government and the mainstream. This carries significant and damaging consequences for the future of our democracy fragmenting and polarising our communities. While election results from Brexit to Trump shocked political pundits on both sides of the Atlantic, the roots of an alienated and divided public who increasingly do not trust public figures to put the public interest first have causes that run deep. The absence of trust creates a political shift akin to a new kind of revolution putting at risk our democracy's future health. Awareness and action have never been needed more urgently.

For over two decades, Thom Brooks has been a leading voice in exposing this crisis in trust and challenging its foundations. This provocative collection of new and recent reflections brings together his work as a freelance columnist and essayist covering Brexit, British values, citizenship and immigration, Scotland's independence referendum, tackling the Covid-19 pandemic, education policy and legal reform. These essays highlight his substantial contributions to some of the leading political issues of our day. How deep is our current crisis – and what can we do about it to rebuild trust in our politicians, public institutions and each other? Brooks provides clear insights into these issues and more with his 'realistic optimism' for the future and why we can be the solution to our political crisis.

Thom Brooks is Professor of Law and Government, the Dean of Durham Law School, Executive Member of the Fabian Society and policy advisor to the Labour Party. He is a regular contributor to the *Daily Telegraph*, *The Guardian*, *The Independent*, *New Statesman*, *The Times* and frequent broadcast commentator for BBC News, CNN, ITV News, Sky News and international media.

Thom Brooks is an award-winning author, public speaker, the UK's only Professor of Law and Government and senior policy advisor to the Labour Party. He is the Dean of Durham University's Law School, President of the Society of Legal Scholars and sits on the Executive Committees of both the Fabian Society and the Society of Labour Lawyers. Brooks has visited at the universities of Chicago, Columbia, Harvard, NYU, Nice, Oxford, Penn, St Andrews, Uppsala and Yale.

A leading advocate for the academic voices in public debates and for the public understanding of UK immigration law and policy for two decades, he has made over two thousand media appearances since 2013 regularly speaking on BBC One, BBC News, ITV News, Sky News and international broadcasters including Al Jazeera, CNN, Deutsche Welle and France 24. His freelance columns are published in the *Daily Telegraph*, *The Guardian*, *The Independent*, *New Statesman*, *The Times* and many others.

Brooks is quoted by the Electoral Commission in support of its recommendation to change the wording of the EU Referendum. His research is cited by the Connecticut Supreme Court in *Santiago II* finding the death penalty unconstitutional in that US state. His work was recognised by Research Councils UK in its report about the top 100 big ideas in British universities. He lives in County Durham.

The Trust Factor

Essays on the current political crisis and hope for the future

Thom Brooks

methuen

This collection of essays first published in Great Britain in paperback and ebook by
Methuen & Co 2022

1

Methuen & Co
Orchard House
Railway Street
Slingsby, York, YO62 4AN
www.methuen.co.uk

Copyright in the collection © 2022 Professor Thom Brooks

Professor Brooks has asserted his moral rights in accordance with the
Copyright, Designs and Patents Act 1988

Methuen & Co. Limited Reg. No. 5278590

A CIP catalogue record for this title is available from the British Library

ISBN (paperback): 978 0 413 77848 2
ISBN (ebook): 978 0 413 77859 8

Typeset (for paperback and ebook) in Great Britain by
SX Composing DTP, Rayleigh, Essex
Printed and bound in Great Britain by Clays Ltd, Elcograf S.p.A.
Cover design: Brill

This paperback edition is sold subject to the condition that it shall not,
by way of trade or otherwise be lent, resold, hired out or otherwise
circulated in any form of binding or cover other than that in which it is
published and without a similar condition, including this condition,
being imposed on the subsequent purchaser.

For Bhikhu Parekh

Contents

Acknowledgements

These essays have appeared across a number of newspapers, magazines, blogs and websites. My thanks to all of them for publishing the original pieces – and also to the many contacts I have had the pleasure of working with over the years, including Rebecca Attwood, Asa Bennett, Jamie Burton, Elliot Chappel, Matt Chorley, Harry de Quetteville, Joel Dimmock, Laurence Dodds, Peter Edwards, Hannah Fearn, Mark Ferguson, Will Gore, Kathryn Hearn, Laura Hood, Matthew Jenkin, Paul Jump, Richard Kirkman, Hannah McGrath, Sarah Pine, Conor Pope, Rachael Revesz, Anna Rhodes, Sienna Rodgers, Kuba Shand-Baptiste and Chris Stevenson among many others.

While always interested in current affairs and politics, my interest in UK developments owe much to one of my first students – Luke Sullivan – and my guru, the professor of professors Bhikhu Parekh to whom I dedicate this book. I am grateful for conversations about the above topics with a wide range of friends and colleagues in Parliament, including Diane Abbott, Hilary Benn, Roberta Blackman-Woods, Tony Blair, Nick Bowes, Graham Brady, Gordon Brown, Robert Buckland, Michael Burke, Gavin Callaghan, Alan Campbell, Shami Chakrabarti, Jenny Chapman, Charles Clarke, Jeremy Corbyn, Kate Green, Dominic Grieve, David Hanson, Emma Hardy, Andrew Harrop, Roy Kennedy, Afzal Khan, Emma Lewell-Buck, Afzal Khan, Sadiq Khan, Holly Lynch,

Ian Mearns, Ed Miliband, David Miliband, Chi Onwurah, Bridget Phillipson, Angela Rayner, Harvey Redgrave, Rachel Reeves, Bell Ribeiro-Addy, Roger Roberts, Richard Rosser, Angela Smith, Jacqui Smith, Keir Starmer, Marc Stears, Jo Stevens, Lachlan Stuart, Nick Thomas-Symonds, Clare Williams, Phil Wilson and a great many others with apologies for anyone left out – with all responsibility for views expressed resting with me alone.

'It is mutual trust, even more than mutual interest, that holds human associations together.'

H. L. Mencken

Introduction

Trust is fundamental to our everyday lives. We trust others to not attack us walking to work. We trust other drivers to keep to their side of the road. We trust bus drivers to stay on the road and not veer off a cliff. We trust our schools to keep our children safe from harm. We trust that our salaries get paid into our accounts on time and trust it will remain in the bank until it's spent. We trust a contract for employment or owning a house is worth the paper it's written on. We trust that when someone breaks the law and gets caught that he or she will be punished.

A world without trust is a world too chaotic and frightening to imagine. Every passer-by is a potential threat, no one is truly safe and law is an ideal rather than reality. We would have anarchy instead of community, alienated separation instead of working together and most of what we take for granted everyday would give way a more difficult and unjust life for all.

Trust is also essential for our democracy. It's its life's blood. We trust our political leaders and institutions to put the public interest before their own personal or partisan advantage. We know no system is perfect and that our big challenges rarely have only one right answer, but we expect our leaders to be honest, competent and compassionate to a considerable degree – and above what we expect in each other at our workplaces. We can easier tolerate a mistake at the office than an error at the Home Office, especially when the former is running late for a group meeting and the latter is failing to protect our national borders. When our political leaders make mistakes, we normally expect such breaches to be punished harshly either in the polls or at the ballot box. Retaining public confidence is more important than doing a good job honestly.

But perhaps not any longer. We can now see clear signs of a deepening political crisis that's fuelled by a lack of trust in government and all things mainstream, including news media. This carries significant and damaging consequences for the future of our democracy as it hastens the fragmentation and polarisation of our communities.

The usual examples used to show this crisis has started are Brexit and Trump. It's important to understand why these events are not the main issue so we can focus more attentively on the root causes which have run deep and growing in recent years.

The UK's Brexit and America's election of Trump took pundits on both sides of the Atlantic by surprise. I know this well as I'm originally American and I've been a British citizen since 2011 with continuing interest in studying the politics of my native and adopted countries. When shock results happen, it raises questions about how the experts could get it so wrong. Was the public honest in responding to opinion polls? Were pundits hopelessly out of touch with the public mood? Is this a sign of a turn to populism? Commentators clutched desperately for plausible excuses about getting their predictions wrong, but not about getting right what was happening beneath the surface.

Britain went to the polls in June 2016 in a referendum over whether to remain in the European Union or leave it. For most voters, this had not been a top three or even top ten issue. For most of the campaign, remaining in the EU was in a comfortable lead. This status quo was endorsed by leading politicians from Labour, the Conservatives and others, such as former Prime Ministers John

Major and his successor Tony Blair. Much of the campaign focused on how leaving the EU would damage the UK. Yet again the public surprised, choosing to leave the EU in a close, but decisive, victory.

Across the pond, Hillary Clinton's bid to become the first female US President was successful in every way except the final result. She was endorsed by leading Democrats and Republicans alike remaining ahead in the polls from start to finish. Much of the campaign focused on how her opponent, Donald Trump, was unfit for office. Clinton also won the most popular votes, but fell short on Electoral Colleges which determine the outcome. Despite being the favourite and most popular candidate nationally, Clinton lost to Trump, a political novice that most had written off as an impossibility.

It's impossible to overlook commonalities. Both Brexit and Trump are events where the frontrunner held a commanding lead, but built on the soft foundation of a safer bet than the more risky rival. Victory was won by appealing to voters who felt by and large they had little more to lose – and had a deep mistrust of established conventional voices on the political right and left. Queues of former presidents and Prime Ministers lined up on only one side helped maintain the view that the usual options had little difference between them in standing with an unpopular status quo. With no one arguing a positive case for life unchanged, trying something different in a sea of malaise and distrust had sufficient appeal to bring new voters out for a change. The rest is history.

A common mistake is to see singular events like Brexit or Trump as 'the crisis.' They aren't. Nor will I argue that voters made mistakes.

On the contrary, the main concern is what lies underneath the whole political framework – namely, the growing decline of trust in politicians and public bodies of both right and left. Let me be clear. There is no crisis in movements for political change nor challenging the mainstream. Instead, the problem lies in our current climate where trust has broken down to new lows that create problems for politicians and public bodies of any kind from functioning effectively. Democracies hold elections with winners and losers. But their future health depends on all sides accepting and respecting results with trust in the process being fair. Justice must be done, but it must also be seen to be done. We do not secure justice by doing one and not the other. When people lack trust in leaders and institutions, this is a recipe not of populism, but of alienation mixed with desperation as ideas and 'solutions' previously off the table as ill-thought out and unworkable take centre stage.

Declining trust can shake the very foundations of our political system. This is not new. The fact is that trust has been under attack for many years. The public's distrust of our politicians or institutions to defend the public good is matched only by the public's distrust of journalists as their best source of information and commentary about the world around them fuelling interest in alternative media. It creates a vicious circle where the distrust is so strong that only narratives that confirms some preconceived view counts as trustworthy with an increasing number of outlets and voices to cater to virtually any ideology. What brings people together is no longer a shared public good held in common, but smaller groups based on shared partisanship. We are becoming islands of 'us' versus 'them' where only we can be right and it's increasingly difficult to find new common ground.

The increasing absence of trust has created a kind of political revolution. You won't see burning Molotov cocktails in the streets or mass occupation, but here the revolution is very much more hidden in plain sight. The signs are all around us from how many see the mainstream news as only propaganda, the global scientific consensus in support of climate change is dismissed as partisan and, in extreme cases, the existence of a deadly pandemic considered no more than fake news. This did not happen overnight. Nor is there any simple fix.

The revolution has rung in a political crisis. It is a crisis where the public does not trust its leaders, institutions or even each other. Without trust, victory becomes defeat. Several years after the EU Referendum result and claims to 'Get Brexit Done' in December 2019, the UK was trying to renegotiate its agreement within weeks of signing it. This was to avoid a customs border in the Irish Sea between Great Britain and Northern Ireland that the Prime Minister promised would not happen, but was written into his Brexit deal.

Instead of getting Brexit done and over, the work has only just begun. Trust is at the heart of it. 'Brexit means Brexit' meant very different things to different supporters as it was never defined. One key campaigner revealed to me that this was key to the strategy during the campaign: the fewer the details, the less that could be a target for opponents. Keeping the campaign about broad cross-cutting principles for the future was important to build a wider coalition that would only come apart if any one view of Brexit became the only goal.

And it goes a lot further than Brexit itself. As the public became more divided, it also became more divisive. Differences mattered more than what was shared. Getting the best Brexit deal became less important than one side putting down the other. This worked both ways, too. What started as a debate about the UK's place in Europe quickly turned into an existential crisis about British identity, history and values. This wasn't about reasserting Britain in the world, but a looking inward rethinking what is Britishness.

An example of this is the long litany of troubling policies under the Government's 'hostile environment.' Their goal was not primarily to reduce numbers, but to feed the 'us' versus 'them' narrative. The hope was that by scapegoating immigrants – and giving at least an appearance of tough enforcement – the Government could bring more of 'us' together where 'us' meant British citizens with a right to be in the UK. The policy was a disaster. Not only did it fail to identify anybody new in the UK unlawfully, it led to deportation orders against individuals entitled to permanent residency or citizenship. While meant to reinforce a particular view of Britishness, the hostile environment was counterproductive and contrary to British values, including fair play. But it unleashed a general mistrust of belonging. The community became a place where the Government wanted each individual to prove their right to remain here – encouraging everyone to be suspicious about everybody. This doesn't bring people closer together, but breeds a lack of trust that pulls people apart further fracturing solidarity.

Across the Atlantic, Trump cultivated a brand that only he could be trusted appealing directly to supporters through social media by-passing mainstream news to get his messages heard unfiltered. For his fans, alternative voices were not to be trusted – whether or not criticisms about Trump were factually correct. What mattered most was allegiance and challenging a status quo to 'drain the swamp.' Trust in Trump was everything. This helps explain why the Republican Party has struggled in Trump's absence as a support system built around one individual cannot be transferred to anybody else. The fate of Trump and Republicans is intertwined. Their future is part of a wider narrative concerning the decline of trust in politicians and public bodies turning individuals to reject conventional politics and news media charting an uncertain path.

This *Trust Factor* is hugely important for understanding how we got to where we are and the obstacles to overcome if we are to break out of our current crisis. For over two decades, I have explored these issues in over four hundred columns, essays and blogs for news outlets like the *Daily Telegraph*, *The Guardian*, Huffington Post, *The Independent*, *LabourList*, *New Statesman*, *The Times* and many more. This book brings together some of my best read and widely commented upon work on why Brexit is still not done, the lessons to learn from Trump's election, the problem of trust and hope in British politics for Tories and Labour, the search for 'British' values, the challenges in combating the Covid-19 global pandemic and major changes in our universities. All are mostly in their original form with only minor changes, and mostly typographical.

As a law professor and Dean of Durham's Law School, I've written widely about law and legal reform. Much of this focuses on citizenship and immigration, as I have been advising the Labour Party for many years in this area. My work has exposed serious problems with how our immigration system works from how it's funded, its rules enforced and how much it departs from public expectations.

I have included an autobiographical piece that I wrote about my coming to the UK and North East of England from the United States that touches further on points of similarity and contrast between my former and current homes.

But I could not write a book – even if mostly a collection of previously published essays – detailing the soft revolution fuelled by the absence of trust without commenting on why I hope for the future. A new essay to conclude this book is offered there. Its message of my realistic optimism has perhaps never been needed more urgently which I hope will resonate widely.

Together, the essays bring out various themes that are summarized at the start of each chapter. These themes can reappear and are reamplified like returning to a refrain, but each time adding some new layer of meaning. These pieces cover my contributions from 2003 to the present and so offer some insights into key political issues as they happened – with several key predictions coming true – and, taken as a whole, I hope provide some useful glimpse into why the Trust, not Trump, Factor defines our present – and our future. If we want a different (and better) politics, it requires a new foundation of trust between the public, its institutions, the media and our political leaders. They must work together to achieve the next revolution out of our current malaise. It could not come soon enough.

A Very British 'Brexit'

In 2015, Prime Minister David Cameron – remember him? – promised voters that he would deliver an in/out referendum on the UK's EU membership if he won a majority in the General Election. At that time, 'Brexit' was not yet a word and nor was the British public much concerned about it. The EU was not a top three or even top five election issue. Most people weren't asking to leave the European Union. Cameron didn't want to either.

The main reason for a referendum on the EU was never to leave it, but to kill off UKIP as a political threat to future Conservative majorities. Nigel Farage's UKIP's key contribution was not electoral success, but splitting the political right and taking votes away from the Tories. This was enough in 2010 to cost Cameron's Conservatives a majority and force an uneasy Coalition Government with the Liberal Democrats.

Cameron wanted no such repeat in 2015. He needed to neutralize UKIP and promising the possibility of exiting the EU through a referendum seemed the perfect ticket. Or at least it did to him at the time. The strategy was a great short-term success. UKIP's vote share collapsed and Cameron won a majority. In his almost unexpected triumph, he moved swiftly to hold the referendum he didn't much want about an issue few cared about that risked leaving the EU which he desperately wanted to avoid. He must not have thought anything would go wrong.

The essays in this chapter run from 2015 to the present. They chart the various mistakes in how the referendum was held. One such problem was in advocating not for the benefits of EU membership, but that a vote *for* the EU was for a *reformed* EU. Few seemed to grasp the nuances of the institutional changes that would happen if the UK voted Remain (and have not happened since the vote for Leave). It left no side advocating for membership at that time – a huge gift for Leave.

My primary contribution to the Brexit vote was recommending to the Electoral Commission that the original EU referendum question and answer be changed. The original question had asked if voters agreed on remaining and this was objectionable because it was not neutral. If Remain won, it could be challenged and undermine the finality the referendum was supposed to provide. The options of 'yes' or 'no' broke conventions. In previous referenda on Scotland's independence or alternative voting, a vote for yes was a vote for change – and no meant no change. But Cameron had wanted yes to mean yes to staying in the EU. I advised the Commission accept a more neutral form of words which they accepted – and I am quoted in support of their recommendation to government. The rest is history.

Before the first vote was cast, I believed that a genuine Brexit – now referred to as a 'No Deal' outcome – would never happen in two years and any break would be less decisive than supporters promised. My reasoning was not that the establishment would never allow it, as I don't accept conspiracy-like theories. It was simple pragmatism. There are many thousands of legal regulations that were never going to be tied up and sorted into 'keep as is,' 'reform' and 'throw in the bin' within two years or less. And this was especially not going to happen without any clear roadmap for how such decisions would be made.

One of the more insightful remarks I heard at the time of the vote came from someone senior in the Vote Leave camp. After a good-natured public debate, we spoke over a drink about the strategy. I pointed out that what Vote Leave needed was a blueprint – something like the *Scotland's Future* white paper used to promote Scotland's independence – that would clarify more specifically what a vote for Brexit would deliver.

I was told that the team had learned from Scotland's failed vote and the lesson was to provide no such details. The strategy was to focus on a core message based around values like 'Take Back Control' and freedom which were more open-textured. They could then shift position when under fire and strike back without giving away any clear target.

My reply seemed innocent at the time. 'But if you only do that', I said, 'then "Brexit" will mean something very different to each voter. If you win the vote, it will lead to a civil war with no one satisfied that whatever is called "Brexit" is the Brexit they wanted.'

I heard only a laugh and then 'we can cross that bridge when we get there.' At the time, Leave was far behind in the polls. And my prediction of a civil war came true. Just ask Theresa May who endured more problems from her own backbenches than she did across the despatch box.

Four years later, Brexit has started, but far from done. Northern Ireland remains in the customs union and separated from the rest of the United Kingdom by a customs border as a compromise to keep the land border open with the Republic of Ireland. This breaks promises made by the Prime Minister that this would not happen and its political repercussions are only just starting to be felt with three different DUP leaders this year and more uncertainty ahead.

In August 2016, literally everyone thought Brexit was a matter of time and it would be over on schedule. I was a lone voice during those first months making the argument that the deadline simply could not be met, delays were inevitable, our leaving would not be a full break given the main reasons for wanting a vote on Brexit was never to actually leave the EU, but for the Tories to consolidate their majority in Parliament. Not all of my predictions came true, but much else did.

These essays chart the problems of this so very British 'Brexit' as it unfolded. Trust takes centre stage: Cameron offered a referendum he never wanted, May promised to deliver a Brexit she originally opposed and voters rejected the establishment from celebrity politician endorsements to mainstream media. The loss of trust – and political trustworthiness – is at the heart of how this event happened. Any change of direction in future will require this to be rebuilt.

If Cameron wants EU reforms, he should look closer to home[1]

David Cameron is in a crisis of his own making. He promised a referendum on Britain's membership of the EU and his government is delivering it next year.

But Cameron added a twist. He did not want this to be a vote on the UK's existing relationship with Brussels. Instead, the Prime Minister made clear this would be a decision for or against the reforms that his government delivers. The referendum was always really about Cameron's influence in Europe than Britain's place in it.

After much delay, the Government set out four simple EU reforms it would demand from Brussels: protecting the single market for Britain and other non-euro countries, boosting competitiveness by setting targets for reducing red tape, exempting

1 'If Cameron wants EU reforms, he should look closer to home', *LabourList* (17 December 2015).

Britain from 'ever-closer union' to bolster national parliaments and restricting in-work benefits like tax credits to EU migrants.

The rationale for this list is it can be delivered – but critics rightly point out these reforms as window dressing making little fundamental change to Britain's relationship with the EU. It is doubtful that many will rally to the call 'what do we want? – less red tape!', 'when do we want it? – in due course!'

Are such points worth making? Yes. Do they require any fundamental reform of existing treaties? Not at all.

This has heaped pressure on Cameron to deliver on restricting in-work benefits to EU migrants. This policy has strong popular appeal and would go some way to showing his government can yield fundamental EU reforms.

It did not take long for the Prime Minister to realise that having one rule for British citizens and another for all other EU nationals on benefits is more difficult than he first thought. This has faced stiff opposition from other European leaders with little to no ground to give.

The result leaves Cameron in a difficult position. He wants to show his government can deliver on very modest tweaks to Britain's place in the EU, but a failure to make good on the most prominent of his four reforms may undermine his case opening the door for a Brexit that Cameron is keen to avoid.

The good news is there is a way out of this. But the bad news is how. Cameron wants to point the finger at Europe. He wins when it changes – Brussels is the problem that Britain must fix. It is certainly a popular view for many of his backbenchers.

In fact, the Government can do something about restricting EU migration if it wanted to – and without forcing any EU treaty changes. But instead of blaming Europe, Cameron's government should blame its own inaction to do what it can. Solving the problem may come uncomfortably too close to home for some at his top table.

The 'free' movement of EU nationals is not what it appears. EU migrants can be subject to border controls and even deported. Like all legal rights, there are specific conditions to be satisfied. There is also judicial precedent of EU nationals crossing borders expecting to be paid benefits from their new country of residence without contributing where these have been denied and the individual removed.

The problem for Cameron is not the lack of EU regulations on migration, but the failure of his government to enforce the rules already in place. Blaming others for your problem is easy, cheap and possibly effective until the facts become clear that with rights come responsibilities – namely those of the Government – to police these rights.

Border control on the cheap might be good for freeing up funds for other important areas, but decisions taken here in Britain by a government that can act should not be masked by ministers unwilling to take responsibility where they can.

If Cameron wanted the EU referendum to really be a vote of confidence in his Government's ability to deliver his four point plan, he might get just that and risk a Brexit. The tragedy is it might all be avoided – not by cancelling the ballot – by refusing to act within his Government's existing powers whether for lack of knowledge or resolve.

Is the 'persona' veiling issues?[2]

The EU referendum on whether Britain will remain or leave is one of the most important many of us will make in our lifetimes. If only it was that simple. What should be a decision about our shared political future is being twisted into a verdict on the personal legacy of one person: David Cameron.

2 'Is the "persona" veiling issues?' *The Northern Echo* (2 March 2016): 14.

Cameron's real aim for the EU referendum is clear from the start. In 2013, he promised a vote on the EU if the Conservatives won the next General Election. He said the country would debate the arguments 'in favour and against the arrangement we negotiate' – and not the arrangement Britain has already.

Cameron remains on message more than two years later. He made clear in announcing his proposals that: 'It will be your decision whether to remain in the EU on the basis of the reforms we secure, or whether we leave.' For Cameron, this isn't a referendum about Europe, but about his political leadership.

To be fair, he knew this was never going to be easy and claimed to have 'no illusions about the scale of the task ahead.' Finding meaningful changes that all other twenty-seven EU leaders and the EU Parliament can accept is more difficult than finding a needle in a large haystack. Cameron has done well to have any proposal on the table at all.

But if he succeeds – and there is every possibility that he won't – Cameron's EU reforms increase the risks that the UK will Brexit. We only need to look at the deal on offer. Neither friend nor foe can deny that Cameron's new deal is a complex mix of ifs, ands and buts intelligible to a few beyond seasoned Eurocrats and civil servants. If you confuse voters, you lose elections – and Cameron's EU reforms become more obscure the closer you look.

Cameron's 'emergency brake' is a key part of his new EU deal. The Prime Minister said recently that 'people coming to Britain from the EU must live here and contribute for four years before they qualify for in-work benefits or social housing.'

This tough sounding rhetoric is divorced from the reality – and its workings about as clear as North Korean rocket science. Cameron's brake can only be used if the EU gives a green light. The UK must convince other members that a stop on benefits is 'necessary' because of the pressures from specifically EU migration with data Britain does not have. An emergency brake will be only a temporary measure.

Cameron's brake is not only short-term but 'proportionate.' The EU can agree an emergency brake is used in the UK or some other member state limiting it to just a year or two – four years is the maximum and not the mandatory time frame. If EU leaders agreed to this reform, the brake would likely be used rarely and perhaps only a year or two at most – while migrants receive a growing share of benefits during this period. Not quite what Cameron led many to believe.

Cameron's brake is meant to put a stop to child benefits for EU migrants, too. He said: 'We should end the practice of sending child benefit overseas.' But now we learn that any cap would not apply to any of the 150,000 or more EU migrants already in Britain – not one. Another clear statement that is anything but when you see the fine print.

Another key part of the EU reforms is a 'red card' for unwanted laws. But his proposal is more like a red card that does not always get players off the pitch. All twenty-eight EU countries have twelve weeks to get fifty-five per cent or more 'of the votes allocated to national Parliaments' to stop it. This is as difficult to achieve as it is to understand. But it gets worse.

Each Parliament that votes against a law must state its 'reasoned opinions' for it. Rejecting a proposed EU law is not enough – and a point missed by everyone thus far. The European Council can then either let the bill die or it can 'accommodate the concerns expressed' through amending the bill so it can then become law.

Cameron's two flagship reforms can be summarised as an 'emergency brake' only operated by other drivers that doesn't bring cars to a stop – and a 'red card' that doesn't throw all players off the pitch. Reforms they are; meaningful or readily intelligible they are not. The initial polls post-EU deal are not looking good.

When first announcing a referendum, Cameron said: 'It is hard to argue that the EU would not be greatly diminished by Britain's departure.' The big problem he faces is that we might say the same about him.

Cameron wanted a referendum about his legacy, as well as the UK's place in Europe. In tying them together, he risks losing both. Cameron's best hope of seeing the UK remain in the EU is to recognise its future does not depend on his new deal. Perhaps he can better achieve his future legacy by dropping the reforms that were to be its foundation. But this may be an act of statesmanship too much.

The 'Brexodus' effect is not what you might think[3]

Net migration has fallen slightly by 29,000 to 244,000 in the year ending September 2017 according to the latest figures published by the Office for National Statistics. This level is similar to early 2014, but still more than twice the Government's target of 100,000 or less. Net migration is a composite statistic, adding together all persons coming to the UK over the last year minus those leaving.

While we've moved on from record highs, all under a Tory-led government, the Prime Minister remains a long way off from her campaign pledge to reduce annual migration. When we look closely at the latest data, three things become clear that are surprising:

First, what Diane Abbott called 'the Brexodus effect' last week is real. While more EU citizens come to the UK than leave, they are arriving in much smaller numbers and choosing elsewhere to work.

3 The Brexodus effect is not what you might think', *LabourList* (2 March 2018).

Secondly, the Brexodus effect includes more than EU citizens – but British citizens, too. About 52,000 more Brits left than came back. It's regularly overlooked that UK citizens are included in the net migration statistics. If they were removed, the net migration of non-UK citizens would be 296,000 and remain at historic highs.

Pessimism about the UK's future post-Brexit is a possible factor in this surprising phenomena. This should be causing some alarm in 10 Downing Street, if highly skilled British workers see now as a time to leave rather than rebuild. Most people choosing to leave do so for work-related reasons. The Government needs to improve confidence in our economy fast – and there is no sign of that happening.

Thirdly, it's entirely in the Government's power to achieve its arbitrary net migration target if it really wanted to. Most net migration – estimated at 205,000 – is made up of non-EU citizens. This is more than twice the number of European citizens. Visas for non-EU citizens for work, study or other streams are controlled by the Home Office. The numbers here cannot be blamed on the EU or free movement. The ONS states that much of the rise was from foreign students, predominantly from Asia. This is entirely under the Government's control yet it chooses not to do what it so often promises.

There are many reasons to keep Britain open to highly skilled migration, welcoming the best and brightest foreign students, and ensure immigration rules don't break up families unfairly or unreasonably. Diane Abbott articulated that view last week – and Labour has consistently opposed the use of arbitrary targets that only seem to damage the economy, divide communities and separate families. It's high time we moved on to a new immigration system that is fair and reasonable, replacing the *ad hoc* patchwork causing so much chaos, confusion and problems now.

Theresa May's government could meet her net migration target – an election manifesto pledge – by this Christmas if she wanted to. If she does not, then either her government is unaware of its own immigration powers, which is very unlikely, or it is saying one thing about the target while doing another in wilfully choosing to ignore it.

There are good reasons to reject this approach and I've urged before for net migration targets to be scrapped in favour of a focus on migration-related impact. Labour has been right to reject it from the start. The latest figures make absolutely certain that any failure by the Tories to meet May's target is the sole fault of her government – and they should be held to account for their incompetence or choice to mislead the public (and maybe both) in handling immigration so badly. Continuing to treat the public with such contempt is bad not only for British businesses and immigrants themselves, but also public confidence in our democracy.

We can counter the claim that Brexit means taking back control of the UK's borders[4]

The EU Referendum is finally here. By the end of the week we will know whether Britain will Remain or Leave. Any Remain supporter will be concerned about polls in recent days showing each side by side or with Brexit edging ahead – although we should recall our bitter memories last year of how polls did anything but predict the outcome.

A key issue in the debate remains immigration. While the economy is Remain's greatest strength, there is little doubt that immigration has been its weakness. Brexiteers continue to make the case for Leave around the idea that Britain can better control its borders outside the EU than remaining within it.

4 We can counter the claim that Brexit means taking back control of the UK's borders', *LabourList* (20 June 2016).

This is a simple pitch for a complex area. The UK's immigration rulebook is currently over two thousand pages long. The rules cover everything from student visas and marriage to non-EU workers and British citizenship. And that's before we have the extensive case law.

Migration does not have simple answers. If the aim is to deny entry to anyone born abroad, then leading Leave campaigners from South East MEP Dan Hannan (born in Peru) to dual US and UK citizen Boris Johnson (born in New York) become issues. Or if denying entry to non-British spouses were an aim, then there's Nigel Farage's German wife.

My point is that keeping non-British or foreign-born citizens out to 'take back control' isn't a simple matter – and leading Leave campaigners don't support it anyway for reasons both political and perhaps personal.

Their case is that Brexit means taking back control of Britain's borders. So is it true? We must counter this central argument better if we want to win the vote on Thursday.

But we can do this – and from our progressive Labour values. Let me explain.

Vote Leave claims that if Britain left the EU we could launch an Australian-styled points-based system of immigration control. Britain could keep its doors open to the most talented and highly skilled benefiting economically, but without exposing us to unlimited migration.

The problem is that this is not how the points-based system works in Australia. Their aim was to increase immigration – if any migrant met set criteria, the door was wide open to admit as many that wanted to come settle in Australia. Even Migration Watch – yes, even them – are opposed to setting up Australia's system in the UK because it would likely lead to even more migration than less.

A more sensible approach is to have controls on the skills and work that Britain wants to attract – such as nurses, university lecturers and other highly skilled workers – but subject to a cap. The good news is Britain already has this, at least for non-EU citizens. And we've had it in place for over a decade thanks to a Labour government. I know – I had to satisfy it in order to settle in Britain before becoming a British citizen in 2011. Vote Leave also claims exiting the EU would mean the end of the free movement of EU citizens. The key point here is 'free' movement isn't free – there are controls. The issue is enforcing existing rules better and not that no such rules exist.

For example, 'free' movement is for workers, not benefit claimants. No EU citizen arriving in Britain can claim benefits for the first three months – and if there is no job or realistic prospect of work, they can be deported within six months. Or in other words, they may be required to leave in six months just like any other tourist must. Simple as that – and this has been upheld by the courts... in Europe, too. Perhaps these rules could be enforced better. But we have them – and we have past Labour Governments to thank in establishing much of the system now in place.

Labour Governments did something else. Britain has an opt-out of EU migration policies, but we opted in to the so-called Dublin Regulation coming into force four months into Tony Blair's first term. The Dublin deal is an EU-wide agreement on refugees: if anyone sets foot first in Greece or Italy and makes a claim for asylum in Britain later, he or she can be returned to the first EU country entered. This is a policy with wide support from across the political spectrum.

If Britain left the EU, we leave the Dublin deal altogether. We're out and on our own. Britain could not return every asylum seeker to other EU countries as it would be outside the EU deal. This would increase the number of asylum cases heard – and supported – in the UK. It might also attract more cases to Britain as they would be considered here without possibility of return to other parts of the EU.

The UK is also a part of EU-wide intelligence on counterterrorism, as highlighted by Labour's Shadow Immigration Minister and former DPP Keir Starmer. No doubt, the UK would remain a part of some shared system, but it might no longer be part of the same regulatory framework for tackling terrorists if outside EU system. This would inevitably raise issues over time about how intelligence can and should be shared with the UK as a non-member.

Vote Leave thinks we can take more control of Britain's borders outside the EU and reduce net migration.

Yet the closer we look, migration would likely increase under the migration-promoting points-based policy of Australia; EU migration controls exist and 'free', uncontrolled movement does not; the UK could see more asylum seekers making their way to Britain without being returned to other EU countries entered first; and our EU-wide counterterrorism efforts would be needlessly complicated for no clear benefit to Britain or the EU.

Labour can make these points – and forcefully – as the engine behind much of the system and key agreements that made these controls possible. If the public wants better controls, we can do this better remaining in the EU – and thanks to the hard work of Labour Governments.

While the Tories continue their civil war and David Cameron thinks his 'deal' more important than the public interest, it's not too late for Remain to win the day. Labour supporters making a Labour-rooted case can make the difference.

This campaign won on lies has created a poisonous atmosphere[5]

Britain is in a crisis of its own making. It started with a plan to win the last election. David Cameron was concerned that support for UKIP might deny the Tories seats in Parliament – and hand the keys to 10 Downing Street to Labour's Ed Miliband.

Cameron promised to hold a referendum on whether the UK should remain in the EU if – and only if – the Tories won the 2015 general election. Perhaps he thought it was a good idea at the time. The polls had the Tories neck and neck with Labour with the expected outcome of another Coalition Government. In other words, Cameron's referendum pledge was a promise he might not have expected to keep.

We know what happened next. In hindsight, Cameron's Tory party won an outright majority, UKIP lost one of its two MPs in a national humiliation – and the promise of a referendum would have made no real difference to the result.

And so Britain embarked on a referendum that the public didn't ask for and the Tories didn't need. A perfect recipe for an Eton-educated mess.

The campaigns for and against centred on two issues. Remain supporters highlighted the risks of damaging Britain's fragile economy: the pound would lose value and jobs would be lost. Voting to leave the EU was to choose an unnecessary and avoidable recession.

These claims were dubbed 'project fear' by Leave campaigners – and they countered by focusing on the issue of immigration, and so scaring the public much more. All part of a 'positive' image of, well, a Britain with less scary foreigners.

5 'This campaign won on lies has created a poisonous atmosphere', *The Journal* (Newcastle) (1 July 2016): 25.

The Vote Leave campaign had one other claim plastered all over the side of their tour bus. It boldly claimed that if Britain left the EU they would put £350m extra into the NHS each week. While virtually every media organisation claimed this figure was a fiction, Leave campaigners from Boris Johnson to Michael Gove said again and again it was true and would be spent on the NHS.

Then there was the vote count. To the surprise of everyone – and not least campaigners for leaving the EU – the Leave side won it. Jubilant scenes starting in Sunderland started to appear on our television screens. Yet it would all be short-lived.

Leave's great victory began to unravel within hours of its success. Early Friday morning the U-turns began – not least by Nigel Farage, of all people. There is no £350m per week to spend and definitely not on the NHS. After claiming during the campaign that substantial cuts to net migration – getting it under 100,000 per year – were impossible within the EU, we were told within hours that no such target will be met – and no new target offered. In fact, there might not be cuts to migration or restrictions on EU free movement after all.

It all gets worse. After months of their opponents arguing that Leave had no plan, Leave now admitted – only after their win – that they had no plan. They never made a plan to have a plan for what would happen next. This shows how genuinely serious they were about the vote and their lack of any regard for the potential consequences. They blamed Cameron for being on the wrong side of the argument – and then criticised him for not doing their homework for them.

I don't blame the voters for the mess we're in. Much fault lies at the feet of David Cameron. He should have campaigned like his career depended on it – because it did. He should have thought twice about calling for a referendum that the public was not asking for. It was a mistake to pin high hopes on his securing some new deal with the EU to woo voters giving himself only a few weeks to pull it off. And for such a major decision there should have been more than a few months to consider it, for a more informed decision like in Scotland's independence referendum.

But substantial fault also lies at the feet of the Leave campaign. Elections are contested on the basis of promises. When the Liberal Democrats broke a central pledge against raising tuition fees, they were rightly stung for it.

It is beyond comprehension to find Leave campaigners denying every significant promise they made to the public – within hours of winning the vote. They tried to sell us something and didn't deliver what it says on the tin. All voters – whether for Leave or Remain – should be furious that such a momentous decision and exercise of individual conscience could be manipulated like this.

Some will argue we have our democracy back. But, in fact, it never went away. Parliament has always remained sovereign. As every lawyer knows, EU laws have the status they do in Britain because of an Act of Parliament. And it is clear that scrapping primary legislation is a task for Parliament alone. There will be another vote before any Brexit happens, at least in Westminster.

And there's something deliciously ironic in seeing elected MEPs, like Nigel Farage, shouting about the lack of democracy. After seventeen years in politics, maybe he should look in the mirror instead of a television camera and think about that. He's become the career politician he likes to demonise.

This brings me to my last point. A campaign won on lies that stoked fears of non-white immigrants, such as UKIP's poster of refugees, has created a poisonous atmosphere. Racist hate crimes have spiked across Britain as foreigners are told that a vote for leaving the EU means our fellow citizens and neighbours should be deported. Welcome to post-Brexit Britain.

I'm fairly certain a *complete* EU exit will not happen with so many details to fill in and so much to do. Britain has too much to lose and the legal difficulties are unprecedented. But I also predict the damage to Britain – at home and abroad – will take many months, if not years, to heal. The Tories and Farage have much to answer for. Let's hold them to account. The future of our democracy is at potential risk.

The Remainers already feel let down. Soon everybody else will[6]

So what is Brexit?

Prime Minister Theresa May repeats again and again that 'Brexit means Brexit.' It doesn't explain anything at all. Little wonder the public is growing increasingly impatient.

The EU Referendum was not an election campaign. Last year, our political parties ran on manifestos. If they won the election, they had a programme their government would attempt to make happen.

When David Cameron won a surprise majority, his Conservative government moved swiftly to implement a manifesto commitment to holding a referendum on Britain's membership of the European Union. We all know now what happened next.

But few realise what the future holds. The Government's commitment to holding a referendum was only that – there would be a public vote, but there is no manifesto pledge to do anything about the result.

In law, a referendum result is advisory on Parliament but not binding. Parliament need do nothing at all legally. But, of course, there will be real political pressure – manifesto or not – to act on

---

6 'The Remainers already feel let down. Soon everybody else will', *The Journal* (Newcastle) (9 September 2016): 27.

behalf of how the public had voted. And this is where Theresa May is beginning the test the public's patience.

There is nothing new about campaign promises that are hard to believe or don't happen. This problem of promising more than will be delivered has damaged public trust.

I do not doubt that *both* Remain and Leave made promises that are problematic. It would have been much better if we had some clear picture about what Brexit would be – like in the referendum over Scotland's independence. In that vote, the public could see a plan for what independence would look like. Each side could contest whether this plan was worth having, but at least there was something on the table.

A leading figure in the Students for Leave campaign made clear to me that Leave learned its lessons from Scotland's vote. There would be no manifesto or plan so that criticisms would have no substance to pick apart. Better to keep the conversation about whether or not the public wants more control than actually specify what this really look like.

We were all sold bottles of bitter snake oil by pipe dream, pro-Brexit merchants.

Remember the pledge of an extra £350m each week to the NHS? Not £3.50 extra has been promised since. It didn't take Nigel Farage twenty-four hours to say this big investment was not going to happen after all. Then again he also conceded defeat before Leave was in fact declared the winner. Yes, this is the kind of political 'judgement' we've come to expect from the twice former UKIP leader.

But let's not focus on the made up number of £350m for the NHS. If there will be any savings – and it looks like a big 'if' – from leaving the European Union, then where will be this new investment? Thus far much has been said and nothing delivered. If this is the Brexit recipe for success, it won't get far on the Great British Bake Off any time soon with these damp cakes.

Some Leave campaigners promised us 'more' control on immigration. We never knew much about how this would happen beyond bringing to Britain an Australia-inspired points-based system.

Yet there are more problems here. Points-based systems are designed to increase immigration – and this is why Australia started one. They award points for qualifications, salary, language fluency and other desirable factors. You add them up and if you have the right total or more then you can get a visa to work and live in the country easily. And that's why Migration Watch has long opposed this system: it encourages immigration from those who can qualify rather than deter migrants from coming over.

Now points-based immigration does not have to lead to more immigrants. You can limit the numbers that can qualify by capping the number of visas. Sound like an obvious compromise? Well, that is what Britain already does.

You read that here first: all those Brexit campaigners arguing for a points-based system didn't know (or didn't care) that Britain already has a points-based system – and with caps on the number of visas available. You can thank the Labour Party for launching the system. Whoever knew Boris, Gove and Farage were pinching ideas on immigration from Labour that have been in place for years? (I know – I had to pass this test to stay here.)

If this looks like Brexit campaigners don't actually know how Britain's immigration system has been working for years – why else promote a 'new' policy already in place? – then you're catching on to how little substance is behind 'Brexit means Brexit.'

And that's what we thought we knew. Now we learn from May that her government won't support a points-based immigration post-Brexit. Somehow Brexit seems to actually mean something less 'Brexit.'

If anything shouts danger ahead, it must be a Cabinet meeting for a 'Brexit Brainstorm' without any visible agreement about what will be different for Brexit Britain.

Some believe that Brexit is simple: all we need do is leave and the future is ours. But the question is not only about what deal we'll have for trade with the EU. This should be difficult enough – and the evidence suggests forging a deal outside the EU and EEA will take more than the two years available. That means we'll be trading on similar terms as North Korea. Is that what getting freedom is going to look like? Doesn't appear like a great leap forward to me.

Finally, Britain must do much more than leave – it must figure out what it will be. Not every EU law is bad. No Brexit campaigner thinks maternity rights should end, or many other rights and protections guaranteed to EU citizens. We've been promised the good laws will stay – but be made British – and the bad ones will go. But no one made a list beyond a few soundbites about which of the 17,000 or more regulations we want to keep, amend or bin. This must all be agreed before Brexit happens – otherwise, we're walking into chaos on purpose.

And so the more May's government looks at Brexit, the more complicated and thorny this path looks – and the less likely it will ever really happen. Already Brexit doesn't mean what its supporters promised.

It's unfortunate enough that Remainers feel let down. Soon we all will.

The meaningless mantra of 'Brexit means Brexit'[7]

The public is right to be confused about what their government is doing about this constitutional crisis. During the EU referendum, there were multiple voices making different claims about Brexit

7 'The meaningless mantra of "Brexit means Brexit"', *E!Sharp* (29 October 2016).

means. Parliament would regain its sovereignty from Europe, Britain would control borders using a points-based system and the NHS would receive £350 million per week were only three of the big promises made to voters.

Each of these promises is unravelling. Within twenty-four hours, Brexit campaigners denied there would be extra funding for the NHS – even those who had spent weeks in a bus promising the controversial £350 million per week figure most critics claimed would not materialize. These critics have been proven right.

Next came immigration. Theresa May has given little away about what Brexit Britain's immigration policy will be – but she did make clear what it is not when she ruled out a points-based system. If Britain is to 'take back control', then it will not be doing probably the one thing that about every pro-Brexit voter wanted.

The decision against a points-based system took me by surprise. I'm originally from the United States. I came to Britain in 2001 and later had to satisfy the points-based immigration system already in place now for several years for non-EU migrants like me. There is no such system to launch or create from scratch – it is up and running.

I know a thing or two about immigration. I'm a law professor specializing in immigration policy, but I am also a British citizen – and received my naturalization when Theresa May was Home Secretary with a welcome letter from her. She should know how immigration works too. If a points-based system with a cap worked for migrants like me, then why can't it work for others as well? Or is there another explanation?

This is where the third promise about Parliament reclaiming its sovereignty from Brussels comes in. Most Brexit voters wanted Parliament to have its powers back – and sovereignty was the big motivating campaign issue. To leave the EU, Parliament must remove the European Communities Act 1972 from its statutes.

Abolishing an Act of Parliament is not in the gift of any minister – even the Prime Minister. And as just about every lawyer will tell you. Every lawyer, that is, except the Prime Minister's.

Theresa May has said that she will trigger Article 50 starting the road to Brexit in two years or less no later than the end of March 2017. She believes that she has the (prerogative) power to do this – although this is disputed by quite literally every lawyer I have spoken to whatever their politics.

On the one hand, this could be seen as an extraordinary act. The Prime Minister moving quickly to start a process before she or anyone else knows how it will end up. She can claim some veneer of democracy – the public did vote for leaving the EU, but did not give consent to any plan or manifesto for it. This is all a veneer because no one voted for a government led by May either – and a referendum is legally advisory, but does not change the law.

On the other hand, this is very much a richly, political act. In moving against an unrealistic timetable, this will hasten a judgement by the courts that may stop the Government in its tracks and require that they seek Parliament's approval. If this means postponing beyond March, then May can claim that she's on the people's side and don't blame her if 'the plan' doesn't happen. And I strongly suspect – still – that it won't.

May's decision to make Boris Johnson the Foreign Secretary led to gasps and amazement, but I thought it a brilliant strategic move for ensuring Brexit means something less than Brexit. Who better than a lead campaigner for Leave to tell the country what Brexit – at last – really does mean? The many fabulous trade deals with America, China, Australia and others have thus far come to nothing. No one is talking until after the UK is out and the terms and conditions for trade are known.

And there is a sizeable legal mess to wade through in addition to trade deals with the EU and the rest of the world. Some estimate

17,000 or more rules to divide into laws worth keeping as is, laws worth reforming and laws worth nothing that could take many years to fix.

With nothing to show – not even a definition for what Brexit 'means' – May has put her hopes on the courts doing the right thing and requiring Parliament's consent which could deflect criticism from her to it. May is also banking on it being Boris – and not her – that will have to look straight at the cameras and claim Brexit is something different than heard on the campaign trail.

So will Brexit happen? Something called Brexit might – but probably not what most will expect.

I'm known as the Brexit expert who said it would never actually happen – after Article 50, my opinion hasn't changed[8]

Last year's EU referendum result was a big surprise followed by bigger questions about when Brexit would start and what it might look like. A few months later, after being quoted in *The Independent*, I became known worldwide as the 'expert' who claimed 'Britain will never leave the EU.'

Now that Theresa May has triggered Article 50 and negotiations will start shortly, I've been asked many times whether I've changed my mind. Isn't it time that Remain supporters stopped being Remoaners?

The short answer is no, although it mostly depends on what you mean by that elusive term 'Brexit.' If Brexit is about the UK severing all ties to the EU to reclaim our sovereignty and take back control of our borders, then this isn't likely.

8 'I'm known as the Brexit expert who said it would never actually happen,' *The Independent* (9 April 2017).

The problem is that often when people talk about leaving 'the EU' they confuse it with leaving the EEA (European Economic Area) and its single market – but not all EEA states are in the EU. It may be possible for the UK to leave the EU but remain in the EEA and follow the Norway model, an option many people think is preferable.

This EU versus EEA distinction is important in principle because leaving the EU doesn't mean ending free movement, as this is connected to EEA membership, but voters were only asked about the EU in last year's referendum.

In practice though, it doesn't matter too much. The Prime Minister has said free movement for Europeans will continue for years post-Brexit as part of an extended 'transition', and how long this will last is anyone's guess.

Likewise, there will be no substantive change in most other areas either. The misnamed 'Great Repeal Bill' is neither great nor a repeal – it will only keep existing EU laws in a holding pattern until the UK decides what to do with them. All 83,000 or more.

It will be an enormous task for the Government to wade through them in their many thousands deciding which to keep, amend or scrap. And that's without contemplating the poor parliamentary aides having to produce risk assessments for possible consequences for each decision. Taking back control never looked so time-consuming. It's difficult to see future governments spending much time on anything more than what Britain should keep or kick out on Brexit Day – while EU states focus on moving forward.

What we know now is that we won't have a clear break with any of it. The Prime Minister has even voiced her interest in Britain remaining a part of shared counterterrorism and security arrangements. Brexit will not mean Britain cuts the cord with Europe to go it alone. Instead, we'll be keeping what we like and revising what we don't – or at least we'll try.

May has triggered Brexit, but Britain hasn't left the EU yet. I still strongly doubt a full break is on the cards, however unpopular such an outcome might be for Brexit supporters.

I accept the country voted to leave the EU. I even criticised the Government for its original referendum question being biased in favour of Remain demanding a change – which the Electoral Commission agreed and government accepted. So this isn't a case of sour grapes.

But I'm also not the one who made promises that can't or won't be kept. The Government has much to answer for. The sooner it acknowledges the realities, the better.

Theresa May just quietly made a sinister deal about EU citizens which puts us on the fast track to a bad Brexit[9]

After dragging her leopard print shoes for too long, Theresa May has finally made public her plans for 'safeguarding the position of EU citizens living in the UK' – and it raises far more questions than it answers.

For example, will the UK guarantee the rights of all EU nationals already here? The answer is we don't know because May hasn't said. It all boils down to technicalities that only lawyers can appreciate. Not the way to win public confidence at a crucial time on such a fundamental issue.

Only those here during an as-yet-unspecified qualifying period will count. This will range from 29 May 2017 to 29 May 2019 – and it raises the possibility of the UK Government retrospectively

9 'Theresa May just quietly made a sinister deal about EU citizens which puts us on a fast track to a bad Brexit', *The Independent* (26 June 2017).

stripping EU nationals of their existing rights. Not everyone who should be safe is safe. This won't be decided later – perhaps two years from now. But we do know that Irish citizens will be unaffected thanks to an agreement forged in the 1940s. Confused? It gets worse.

If we knew the cut-off point for qualifying – which we don't – would all EU nationals here at that time be allowed to stay? The answer is probably not. May is only considering qualifying EU nationals (not all EU nationals) currently here. Some out of work or in study will require proof of comprehensive health insurance to have residency in the UK as an EU national.

While many speak of free movement, there are restrictions like this to ensure migrants are not a burden on public services – and the UK Government is not very good at checking to see if every EU national in the UK is properly exercising their free movement rights. Many don't find out they've not followed the rules correctly until it is almost too late and they're having their application for residency rejected. They will be some of the EU citizens who may be forced to exit in 2019.

Any EU citizen not here for five years on Brexit day will have up to two years to acquire – and pay for – temporary residency. But no one knows when this is or how much this will be.

The questions don't stop there. Theresa May told the House of Commons that the new rules won't split up any families. But how can she know this when we don't know who qualifies to stay and who doesn't?

Not all spouses will meet May's test. If a non-EU spouse joins his EU spouse in the UK and they break up within five years, what will happen to them both and their children? Would it matter if the children were born and bred in Britain?

We're told that the Government 'will tailor the eligibility criteria', but not what the new criteria is likely to be. The Government provides an illustration showing how many arriving after the unknown cut-off date will face future immigration controls described as 'depends on rules in place at the time' – in other words, the Government doesn't seem to have a firm grasp of where it is going.

So is this about treating EU nationals like non-EU citizens? Not quite. There's no requirement to pass an English exam or a citizenship test, but these will be required for temporary residents post-Brexit who want to stay permanently. In other words, it's a complicated maze that doesn't quite simplify the rules to make them knowable to anyone but the lawyers – and even they will be wading through the new regulations, if agreed, wondering at times what to do next.

EU nationals here and UK citizens abroad need certainty about their rights to work, live or study wherever they are currently in the UK. Instead of providing certainty and stability, Theresa May is serving up caveats and creating chaos.

And it will probably get worse. A key sticking point is the jurisdiction of the European Court of Justice (ECJ). If there is some dispute about the enjoyment of residency rights by a EU national in the UK, which body should have a say?

The EU has made clear it may be unwilling to compromise on the ECJ – and the PM has said only British courts should have a say. Both sides seem quiet on whether they would be willing to agree some kind of international tribunal with representation from each side but chaired by some third party – but how exactly such a body would work is not yet even up for discussion.

It's like May is making it all up as she goes along, as if she never thought ahead to actually having to deliver on the details of what 'Brexit means Brexit' is about. This is no way to run negotiations and it makes for a fast path to a bad deal – at a huge cost to the country and our global reputation.

Saying 'Brexit means Brexit' was the easy part[10]

Theresa May promised voters a strong and stable leadership that would push for the best Brexit deal but her negotiations are going as poorly as her election campaign. She has given an early sign of her Government's negotiation abilities and strategic planning.

There was no preparation for anything but a landslide victory in the general election. When that did not happen, her team was caught off guard and made it up as they went along, unsure when the Queen's Speech would be delivered, what would be in it and how they could continue to be in government without having won a parliamentary majority. Backed into a corner, they found their elusive magic money tree paying out big and upfront in a deal with the DUP. If this small party in Northern Ireland can extract £1.5 billion so easily, it is difficult to see things going any better against a well-organised EU team of highly experienced negotiators.

The Prime Minister was even criticised by her supporters for being too automated and repeating the same answers to different questions, leading some to call her 'Maybot.' While we live in an age of soundbites, Mrs May had not received the memo that the soundbites should not always be the same ones all the time.

The issue here is that there is a limit to how long saying 'Brexit means Brexit' is sustainable before it begins to mean little more than gobbledygook. Throughout the election voters were offered precious little about what Brexit would mean for them. It now appears that Mrs May's government might not have had much more to say.

Negotiations have a standard operating procedure. Each side presents an outline, sometimes referred to as a skeleton argument, about how they view the situation and what outcomes they want

10 'Saying "Brexit means Brexit" was the easy part', *The Times* (3 July 2017).

to achieve. This provides all parties to talks with a kind of starting place to begin agreeing next steps. The EU had this written up in advance and made it public upfront.

However, the UK has yet to produce its outline proposal even after talks have started, managing only to produce a paper on the rights of EU citizens. This strongly suggests to observers like me that the Government is still working out what its position is — they seem to lack a settled view of where they want to go. If they know where, then they should say.

While some may argue that negotiators will want to keep their powder dry, now is not the time for that. There is a tight timetable made shorter by Mrs May's decision to hold a snap election she did not need to and, if anything, has made her work more difficult.

Later this year, the UK and EU must reach some broad consensus on basic principles for how Brexit will work. This would leave about a year, and it will take at least six months, for all member states and relevant EU bodies like its Parliament to ratify it. In eighteen months the more focused talks about how the Brexit principles will be worked out in detail will start, and this explains why a long transition period is likely but also why a deal must be struck fairly quickly if there is to be one at all.

What we have seen thus far has not been promising. Mrs May's 'offer' on rights for EU citizens raises more questions than it answers. While she wanted to provide certainty, she created confusion. We do not know when the cut-off date will be for EU citizens to stay in the UK but know the date might have passed although the Government has yet to decide. We know that some EU nationals here before that date will qualify, but Mrs May has not guaranteed it for all who have been here. She has said that families will not be split by any change in the rules but we do not know how these rules would handle routine immigration matters.

Leavers like Boris Johnson harm their Brexit cause more than its critics[11]

He's at it again. The publicity-craving Foreign Secretary has been largely silent and offline for much of his poor start as Foreign Secretary. While he has failed to deliver anything new of substance as a senior minister, Boris tries to make up for it in a 4,200 word rant for the *Daily Telegraph* on what 'Brexit means Brexit' should really mean.

It raises a key question: so why did he do it? It appears to be a clear attempt to bully a weak PM to deliver on his undeliverable promises made over the course of the EU Referendum campaign. Boris has reportedly been stung by criticisms that he lied during the campaign and his piece was an act of self-defence aimed at salvaging some part of his reputation.

It hasn't worked. Especially damaging to his credibility was the frequent claim that leaving the EU would mean £350 million extra per week for the NHS. The ONS has been clear through the EU Referendum campaign that the figure was a 'misuse' of official statistics. Britain does not pay that amount to Brussels and within hours of the Brexit win it was confirmed no new money to the NHS was forthcoming Brexit or no Brexit. Making it worse for Boris, the ONS chief has again called him out for peddling a porky in repeating the false £350m claim.

While May appears too weak to sack a disloyal senior member of her Cabinet, Johnson's influence is so poor he must take to the papers to find the support he clearly lacks in the Cabinet. With Number 10 so keen to micromanage, Boris must be feeling hamstrung as Foreign Secretary with such limited discretion.

11 'Leavers like Boris Johnson harm their Brexit cause more than their critics', *Huffington Post* (18 September 2017).

We must wonder why anyone sitting at the top table must resort to the papers to let the PM know his views. A strong sign that he has been marginalised and left out to pasture – and that Boris feels May is too weak to sack him for any apparent disloyalty.

For all the many attacks on Brexit sceptics for how they talk down Britain's potential, this very public spat at the heart of government is even worse for weakening the Government's already poor hand. If the PM thought she had a difficult time before, it's only worse now. Ironically, it's mostly because of meddling by pro-Brexit ministers like Boris rather than criticisms from pro-Remain sceptics.

Yes, EU negotiators are likely to continue highlighting the split among the British public for what they want out of Brexit. But a split at the Cabinet table is much more damaging. It is almost beyond comprehension that Theresa May triggered Brexit without any clear, specific plans for what she wanted, how she would get it or how it could be delivered – and without a Cabinet fully in support. If she can't carry them, why think she can carry the country?

Then again a Prime Minister who thought she could take the public for granted in calling a snap election – leading to her losing a majority in Parliament – might also be taking her own ministers for granted. We're all the worse off for it.

If Brexit can be stopped, why won't the PM consider it? [12]

Yesterday, Prime Minister Theresa May updated Parliament on her Government's Brexit negotiations as the next round begins shortly in Brussels.

12 'If Brexit can be stopped, why won't the PM consider it?' *Huffington Post* (10 October 2017).

By all accounts, talks have not gone well. While May has been desperate to begin discussions on a future trade deal, the European Union has stood firm on wanting agreement on the divorce bill and rights for EU citizens.

Each day marks a slow march off the cliff's edge of No Deal and land's end is nearly in sight. Brexit's champions like Liam Fox claimed a deal with EU would be 'one of the easiest in human history' – and completed by *this* month. What a difference a year makes: instead, we're nearly halfway to exiting the European Union without either a deal or an alternative to fall back on. It's like jumping out of an airplane without a parachute.

The current impasse should make Remain and Leave supporters alike very nervous. Neither side argued for a result that would leave Britain worse off.

Evidence is growing that the public doesn't approve of how Brexit talks are going with increasing support for changing course. So if Brexit can be stopped, why won't the PM consider it?

It's not too late to hit the brakes before sending the country off the tracks. When the Prime Minister triggered Article 50, the UK sent notification to the EU of our intention to leave – which we can withdraw at any time before March 2019.

In fact, there are reports that this is the legal advice that May received with an attempt to get this information in the public domain.

May can halt Britain's exit for now by withdrawing notification of the UK's intention to leave. No doubt some Leavers would see this as betrayal, but they would be wrong.

May's team has been hopelessly outflanked by the EU. The Government needs time to get the details of our future strategy right – hitting the brakes now with a view to restarting the engine later does not disrespect the EU Referendum result. Voters were not promised Brexit at any cost, but a deal that would benefit Britain.

The more this seems unlikely to be achieved, the more May's government should rethink their plans to respect the Referendum result more, not less.

Whatever 'Brexit' people voted for, they will get something very different. To that effect, Brexit looks increasingly unlikely to happen. (I'm not the only one who thinks this.) No £350 million per week for the NHS, no end to free movement from Brexit day, no new points based immigration system – the list grows of promises (made to win votes) broken from within hours of the referendum result.

But I doubt the PM will give this option much thought. After starting talks by clearing the table of most options for negotiating, May has left little to bargain with – and so finds her ministers walking around Brussels empty-handed with little to show for nearly a year of their efforts. To change course now would be yet another U-turn undermining once more her claim to offer 'strong and stable' leadership that looks more weak and wobbly by the day.

After trying to blame the judiciary for delaying the start of Brexit talks, her ministers blame the EU for not caving into any of her minority Government's demands. Her Brexit strategy seems little more than hoping we retain full benefits of EU membership without paying the club's fee, and if we don't have any clear contingency plan the EU won't let a departing member feel much pain. In other words, a game of political chicken that could leave a lot of broken eggs on our shores.

Brexit also gives May a sense of purpose. She can and does continually refer to keeping her Cabinet and backbenchers united on delivering Brexit whatever else their many deep divisions might be.

Being on side with an idea is easier when we don't know exactly what it means – and as the details of what Brexit really will deliver versus what was promised becomes clearer we can expect any veneer of unity to come away. We see it now as the Foreign Secretary Boris Johnson and chief Brexiteer has gone to some lengths to dictate to the Prime Minister what the terms of Brexit should be.

May is too weak to sack her senior minister who is popular among backbenchers needing their support – and if she acts now only after increasingly vocal calls for Boris to go, she would show her leadership as weak as well in a classic Catch-22.

So we have a Prime Minister on a slow march to Brexit and off a cliff edge without a deal who is able to hit the brakes, but either too politically weak or naïve to call for time and get the best deal for Britain's EU exit by delaying the date we leave. The simple explanation for this is she must not envisage having a genuine political future after year's end – and so is giving little thought to the UK's thus far non-existent deal with the EU she doesn't expect to see through and is leaving for her successor.

But as the Tories return to Westminster with WhatsApp coup plans and secretive leadership plots underway, it is increasingly clear that Conservative Party divisions over Europe that led to the referendum are damaging Britain's opportunities for making a success from the referendum result.

Bringing Labour into a grand coalition team would give May new options in Brexit talks[13]

Each round of Brexit talks begins as the last ends: progress stalling with time running out to agree a deal. Like a scratched album – remember those? – stuck in the same groove, the Prime Minister's team strike a similar note repeating the same mantras about the

13 'Bringing Labour into a grand coalition team would give May new options in Brexit talks', *The Times* (9 November 2017).

great deal they'd reach if only the European Union would give them their cake and let them eat it.

Nearly one year in and little to show for it. How much will the divorce be exactly? Will there be a transitional period or not? And if so, will the UK be allowed to start trade talks outside the EU? Will an end to freedom of movement 'as we know it' mean imposing existing restrictions on EU nationals coming here or something altogether different? Does 'settled status' mean EU citizens become second-class? And what might become of British nationals abroad? There are few answers with Brexit, only new questions. No wonder there is continuing uncertainty.

But this sixth round of Brexit talks is different from the others. Yesterday Simon Stevens, the chief executive of NHS England, wanted the Government to commit more money to the health service after Brexit, referring to Vote Leave's famous red bus promising an extra £350 million per week. Otherwise, there would be a worrying disconnect between what people were promised about Brexit and what they would get, damaging public trust.

Mr Stevens has a point. While true that not every Brexit supporter voted to leave the EU because of the promise of additional funding, it is also true that many did do so and that this was repeatedly promised by Vote Leave campaigners like Boris Johnson, the foreign secretary. Theresa May frequently invokes that Brexit must honour the referendum result, but she is selective in what honouring this result entails for the Brexit negotiations. Keir Starmer, Labour's Shadow Brexit Secretary, frequently criticises Mrs May for sweeping too much off the table for talks, leaving little to bargain with.

However, it's actually worse than that. She works within a tight space of red lines drawn partly by her and the rest by Boris's red bus. The Prime Minister can no more honour the Brexit result by leaving the EU than she can increase significantly money for public services such as the NHS.

Brexit was expected to be Britain's biggest challenge since the Second World War. That early prediction has turned out to be true. Such an occasion requires the full commitment of any government to make it a success. That is not the happy situation that Mrs May finds herself in.

Weeks of sexual harassment allegations and investigations exposing many years of bad behaviour and potential criminality leading to the resignation of a key cabinet minister is bad enough. Now a second cabinet minister is likely to resign over unauthorised meetings with Israeli officials. In the meantime, the Foreign Secretary has become embroiled in a new row after an extraordinary gaffe in erroneous testimony to Parliament that risks increasing a British mother's time in an Iranian jail by five years. It's impossible to rule out more departures before the holidays at this stage.

If this isn't a government in crisis, then I don't know what is. That it is all unravelling at the most critical crunch time for Brexit negotiations makes an enormously difficult job much harder. Theresa May needs more than extra time or a scandal-free cabinet, but a new option. While suspending talks by temporarily withdrawing our notification to leave the EU from March 2019 might be too unpalatable for the Tory backbenches and more committed Brexit supporters, her next best alternative is to make a significant concession and bring Labour into a grand coalition-styled team.

This changed dynamic would help bring Parliament to work together much better and gain more confidence from our EU counterparts. Perhaps Labour would want Mrs May to lie in her own bed now that she's made it. Making the offer does Mrs May no harm if rebuffed.

However, the risks for Mrs May are two-fold. The first is that the Brexit delivered by a coalition might depart significantly from what she set out at the start. This would be a welcome change because it could bring more flexibility into the negotiations and help make progress more quickly. The second is the brave act of statesmanship – putting the country ahead of party – which may not be available for much longer.

Every Prime Minister thinks about his or her legacy. Now is the time for Mrs May to do some serious reflection about how to turn things around fast. Time won't stand still for her to choose a new direction or the keep with the current bus crash in painfully slow motion.

Theresa May won't win a penalty shoot-out with the EU by treating its citizens like a political football[14]

Theresa May has faced heavy criticism at home and in Europe for her handling of Brexit talks. From the start, her government was accused of treating EU citizens like a bargaining chip to win new trade deals. There's good reason why this has stuck.

May has introduced so many red lines and conditions on EU negotiations it's little surprise they have not progressed much. We know far more what Brexit is not than what it means. For example, the Prime Minister has vetoed staying in the single market, remaining in a customs union, having a points-based immigration system or allowing continued free movement of EU citizens.

The new joke doing the rounds much better than May's plans was summed up by German Chancellor Angela Merkel commenting that Theresa May says she wants Brexit, but doesn't say what Brexit might be like. When asked what Britain wants, May asks Merkel to make her an offer – which clearly puts the horse before the cart. Cue belly laughs from Brussels. It's like ending a relationship to

14 'Theresa May won't win a penalty shoot-out with the EU by treating its citizens like a political football', *Huffington Post* (18 February 2018).

start seeing other people but asking your ex-lover for advice on how to be more than friends. No wonder Eurocrats are confused.

May's government repeatedly denies using EU citizens like a political football – giving them a kicking as they play the game of Brexit in Europe – claiming that no guarantees should be offered to EU citizens here until there is certainty for UK nationals there. Only problem with that denial is the EU made clear its support for permanent rights for UK nationals. So the issue isn't the failure of the EU to secure rights of UK nationals, but of May's government to extend the reciprocal agreement to EU citizens in the UK. Like a football player blaming the opposing team for unfair play while trying to foul their players when they think the referee isn't watching.

Now we learn that May's tough talk is more soundbite than reality. She might want registration schemes to cover EU nationals already here and for those coming during the transition, but it turns out persistent lack of resources and understaffing – much of it on her watch as then Home Secretary – has left the Home Office unable to cope with high expectations set for it. Nor does it help there is no clear idea about how many EU nationals are here either.

These dire straits are a shambles. The decision to pull the trigger on Article 50 was clearly done before there was any substantive plan for what kind of Brexit would be delivered and how to do it. More a cynical gimmick to win quick favour with right-wing tabloids in a surprise attack on Labour through a snap election. Yet the Prime Minister who declared only she could deliver 'strong and stable leadership' has only done the opposite as her plot backfired spectacularly in what was called the worst manifesto launch and campaign in living memory.

The problem here is – to quote May during the campaign – 'nothing has changed.' She says much, but delivers so little. Not even phase one of the Brexit talks has actually been completed. The proof? Continuing confusion about how May's red line on leaving any form of a customs union with her pledge to keep an open border in Northern Ireland – not to mention her view that nothing is agreed until everything is agreed. So each phase of the talks is incomplete until it's all approved. It doesn't stop her ministers from saying phase one is complete, but this is only another example of their saying one thing and the reality being different.

This is not simply a problem of Brexit talks going much slower than government politicians say although time is running out and it is increasingly alarming how much remains to settle. The elephant in the room is the damage to our democracy such empty promises made repeatedly will have in perhaps Brexit's most bitter legacy. Not a good scorecard.

Leaving the EU was fuelled by many things from a desire to reassert British sovereignty to concerns about immigration, but a key driver was a sense of alienation and distrust of the political classes. Voters who felt left behind by globalisation made their voices heard unmistakably. Pro-Brexit politicians made promises their critics said they couldn't keep. Now this is being tested and looks increasingly certain that any Brexit we get will be far from what was promised.

If talks do not improve soon – or if there is no new option on the table that is deliverable and has public support, the damage done will be much more than to Theresa May's personal fortunes (she's already on borrowed time) but to the system overall that risks harming all sides at a critically important time.

As Brexit talks inch closer to full-time, May is betting on a high stakes gamble taking on the EU in a penalty shoot-out-like situation. We all know how well this usually turns out. The risk to all parties is not only that May might miss the goal and leave Britain worse off, but the public will want some new national game. Politics as we know it may change whether or not those in power want it to with consequences yet to be seen.

If Theresa May wants to deliver a workable Brexit plan, she should swallow her pride and ask for more time [15]

A weekend, let alone a week, can be a long time in politics. After nearly two years, Theresa May saw the time was right last Friday to gather her full cabinet to form a collective view on what 'Brexit means Brexit' actually stood for. Agreement seemed to have been reached but only forty-eight hours later the two key Brexiteer ministers resigned, claiming May's plan betrayed the EU Referendum vote.

The current debacle throws the Prime Minister's Brexit strategy into chaos, increasing the risk of Britain getting No Deal and the worst possible outcome. It's clear therefore that the Prime Minister must change course – acting like 'nothing has changed' didn't work for the snap election she called in which she lost her majority in Parliament, and it won't save us from falling off the Brexit cliff edge either.

Losing Boris Johnson's support for her plans is so damaging precisely because he led the successful Vote Leave campaign that May tried to defeat. Whatever political cover she had for her Brexit strategy by keeping him in government is now gone and with it key public support. Fewer than one in ten think May's Brexit plans are going well.

After feeling slighted by May's reliance on civil servant Olly Robbins to discuss details of the Government's position with negotiators in Brussels, David Davis's resignation is harmful for the prime minister for the message it sends to the EU. Let's not forget that any deal must be agreed by the two sides by October so that each can confirm its acceptance before the March 2019 deadline.

15 'If Theresa May wants to deliver a workable Brexit plan she should swallow her pride and ask for more time', *The Independent* (11 July 2018).

This leaves new Brexit secretary Dominic Raab a hundred days (supposedly) to conclude a nearly two-year negotiation he has not been involved in previously. It's not how any country should conduct such seriously important talks; it makes Britain appear either unable, unwilling or ill-prepared to take back the control the public voted for.

Such a mess at home and abroad might be excusable if it brought success of course. Yet May's deal, which has evidently divided her cabinet and the country, will be dead on arrival when it reaches Brussels. Its cherry-picked benefits and costs, complete with an unworkable blueprint for overcoming customs checks and a proposal for free movement of goods but not services (which the EU has already ruled out) can make any observer wonder what exactly was the point in piecing together such a political Frankenstein that both Leavers and Remainers want to run out of town.

But the truth is that with only a few months left to go the Government has finally, if amateurishly, produced a collective(ish) view about what their vision of Brexit means after all. This should have happened eighteen months ago and didn't, but we are here now. It's a first step towards developing something more serious.

Remember too that Brexit going badly is in not in the EU's interests either. While both sides will want to come out stronger, each is critically important to the future success of the other. Both Britain and the EU need an agreement that works.

Does this mean there should be a 'People's Vote' or re-run of the referendum? Not necessarily. The main problem right now is time, which the Government does not have. As such, it needs to ask for more.

If May wants to remain in office and deliver a workable Brexit plan, she would be well advised to eat some humble pie. May should accept responsibility for the lack of progress to date, but commit to using her Government's forthcoming White Paper as a fresh start and formally request an extension of at least one year until Brexit comes into force.

The EU can agree a new date for concluding talks and it's to their advantage that a proper deal is in place. A new Brexit deadline of March 2020 would provide more time to individuals and businesses to get ready for withdrawal, as a more serious blueprint develops.

An extension would probably be acceptable to most of May's backbenchers, if begrudgingly so. The hard Brexiters in her midst want certainty that Brexit will happen – and only a minority think it wise to crash out first for the sake of doing so and pick up the broken pieces later.

An extended deadline might also win support from Remainers in Parliament. They have been especially concerned that various risks – such as to manufacturing and the wider economy – have not been properly assessed in developing the current road map. More time could generate greater consensus around better managing these risks.

And what of the public? It's surely relevant that popular opinion is increasingly negative about Brexit. But yet a majority want the Government to get on with it. An extended deadline by only a year is still an exit date and should be acceptable to all but an extreme minority for Brexit at any cost.

Asking for more time to get Brexit right is surely necessary at this stage and would be worth the wait – and would carry support from the EU, most of Parliament and the public. The question is only how much longer May can stay in office while so much crumbles around her.

Only a referendum on May's deal can end the deadlock in Parliament[16]

Now that EU leaders have signed off the Brexit Withdrawal Agreement, Theresa May faces a huge struggle to get Parliament's approval for it. At a time where the country never seemed so divided, the prime minister managed to unite most MPs against her plans. Westminster is at a stand-off. The revolt is growing from all sides the longer it continues, ahead of a vote in mid-December.

If Parliament's Brexit deadlock continues, the public should now decide whether to accept May's deal or remain in the European Union. But a second referendum must be treated with great care. Divisions over Brexit and mutual suspicions are high. Any such decision must command confidence from all sides if only to ensure finality in the result.

As someone who advised the Electoral Commission on the original referendum, which led to a change in the question's wording and options, I knew how to make it fair, neutral and unbiased. A second referendum can, and must, meet that same test.

More than 17m people voted to leave the EU, but without a clear manifesto about what would happen if the UK did. This is in stark contrast to the referendum about Scotland's independence and the then-Scottish Government's *Scotland's Future* white paper which set out the terms for any such win. No similar clarity on policies were available for Brexit. This contributed to different understandings of what an acceptable Brexit should look like – and the ongoing divisions on which plan best captures the public mood.

With no parliamentary majority in sight, May has taken to the airwaves to make her case directly to the public. This is the right

16 'Only a referendum on May's deal can end deadlock in Parliament', *Huffington Post* (27 November 2018).

direction of travel: where MPs remain divided, a final say should be left with voters.

If Parliament does approve May's deal, then it will be the plan for Brexit which will govern what happens after March 29, 2019. But if Parliament cannot accept it – which seems increasingly likely – then May should put her Brexit deal before the public in a new referendum. And the public should be asked to vote on two options: whether they want the only Brexit deal on the table, or whether they want the UK to stay in the EU.

Like the 2016 referendum, a new plebiscite would be legally advisory, meaning Parliament would not be obliged to act on the result; but it would place Parliament under considerable pressure to honour the result. Crucially, a second referendum must not be a re-run of the last one or open a Pandora's Box of continued indecision.

This means a second referendum ballot should not include an option to reopen EU negotiations. Everyone from May to German Chancellor Angela Merkel has made clear that the current deal is the only deal available. Short of a snap election, there is no clear mandate for starting afresh, nor is there time to do so now. If a referendum included an option of reopening negotiations, it would set up a cycle of more future referendums until the Government likes the answer. That would not bring finality or respect democracy.

Some argue that a second referendum would disrespect the 2016 result. But this is untrue. The country voted for Leave, but without a plan for how. Now there is a plan that requires parliamentary support – which it does not appear to have. A second referendum on the terms agreed with the EU would give the public a chance to either reaffirm its choice for Leave and so push Parliament to move forward. Or not.

Nor should an option for a No Deal be on a second referendum ballot. No Deal was never really an option – and politicians on both sides of the aisle have said Parliament will work to prevent a No Deal.

If No Deal was on the ballot, it would split the pro-Brexit vote between May's Brexit and a No Deal Brexit. This would potentially undermine the result because while a majority might again vote in favour of Brexit, their votes would be divided by having two choices, while the Remain vote would be concentrated behind one choice.

I take seriously the need to keep the choice neutral for voters. That's why I successfully advised the original referendum wording should be changed from 'Should the United Kingdom remain a member of the European Union?' – with a 'Yes' or 'No' response – because this phrasing favoured the pro-Remain side. Instead I recommended that remain or leave be added and the Government agreed. The final question was: 'Should the United Kingdom remain a member of the European Union or leave the European Union?', with voters asked to choose whether to 'Remain a member of the European Union' or 'Leave the European Union.'

This neutrality is critically important because a referendum should present voters with a clear choice on fair terms free from bias. This same motivation leads me to back a second referendum for May's deal or Remain.

May has much else to worry about beyond her Brexit deal. Some in her party have threatened a no confidence vote while others – including Labour and other parties – call for a snap election. Neither of these scenarios need block a second referendum – and might even provide a temporary lifeline to May.

Britain is at a fork in the road. The choice – as May herself continues to state – is between her Brexit and remaining in the EU, at least for now. Another referendum can be conducted that respects the 2016 vote while drawing a line under the issue. That's why the public should get a final say if Parliament remains split.

Brexit may have been the making of Boris Johnson – but this is why it will also be his undoing[17]

Prime Minister Boris Johnson spared no time in sacking a record number of ministers to create his No Deal cabinet. He has reformed his Vote Leave campaign band for a reunion tour with co-chair Michael Gove as deputy and strategist Dominic Cummings as chief of staff.

These changes bring the quick win for Johnson's supporters of showing a clear break from the more centrist Tory Governments of the past led by David Cameron and Theresa May. Those who backed Boris will feel he's honouring his promise to make Brexit happen by Halloween. But I'm afraid the real picture is more trick than treat.

Johnson has been in the enviable position of making promises that he never had to keep. As a backbench opponent of fellow Old Etonian Cameron, Johnson had the luxury of having no responsibility for delivering the referendum result he campaigned for.

When later made foreign secretary, Johnson's only contribution to negotiating a deal with the EU was to resign immediately rather than help forge a solution. At every turn, Johnson would rather wound his party's leader to better position his succession than heal the deep divisions across the country he did so much to create.

Now his turn has come – and the time for his reckoning.

The prime minister has promised the public many things, not least an extra £350m per week for the NHS, that were neither honest nor realistic. His supporters have drunk the Kool Aid believing a combination of being more optimistic about Brexit and keeping a No Deal option on the table are enough to bring the EU back to the negotiating table on our terms.

17 'Brexit may have been the making of Boris Johnson – but this is why it will also be his undoing', *The Independent* (1 August 2019).

If wishful thinking was enough, Brexit would have happened by now. May's failure to deliver was not because she didn't want a deal but rather because few others supported the deal she agreed. The devil was very much in the details. May's having a deal wasn't enough. For more extreme Brexiteers, the only deal they wanted was No Deal at all.

Johnson believes a new deal is possible. This is probably fanciful as the EU has already rejected this option, but even if there was flexibility the PM will fail like May over the details.

His alternative vision is surprisingly shallow. A main aim is simply to avoid being locked into the so-called Irish backstop, but without any existing technology or means to do so. Such pigs can't fly – making the possibility of amending May's deal virtually nil.

The more significant difference in Johnson's approach is his commitment to threatening the EU with No Deal if negotiations fail by 31 October. No Deal has become the new priority for Johnson's government. For many Leavers, this is the key to unlocking a better outcome. But how credible is this second bout of wishful thinking?

No Deal is often characterised by its costs – and how the EU's economy will be hit hard too so it should serve as a strong deterrent. But this is only a partial picture that masks why No Deal is not a viable option.

The UK's EU membership has created an interlocking network of agencies and official departments that help maintain the thousands of EU regulations currently in place. Leaving without a deal in ninety-nine days means the UK must recreate this work in about three months so it can hit the ground running. This means hundreds of people recruited, put in post and ready to go.

This is the stuff of unicorns frolicking through fields of wheat while painting red buses made from old wine crates. It's nonsense, and is an indication of how little the new prime minister grasps the enormity of the challenge before him as only someone weak on details could be led to believe.

In assembling a cabinet signed up to a strategy of wishful thinking with an empty threat, Johnson's new look team will likely follow the same old fate of the previous government in failing to deliver Brexit. When I predicted it would not happen, I could not see Boris's rise. Yet the sheer complexity of making the legal and institutional changes required remain such that Brexit will stay out of reach for the foreseeable future.

On his nationwide tour, the promise of a Brexit 'by any means necessary' is already unravelling. Johnson is now saying Britain may stay in the single market for two or more years. This U-turn is a product of watching the pound slip to a new low thanks to Boris's boastful bluster now coming back to haunt him well before his Halloween deadline.

But those who backed Boris never thought he'd blink within days – however nothing speaks more of the UK's declining global influence thanks to Brexit than such policy shape-shifting over Brexit. This wannabe emperor wears no clothes.

As a former classics student, Johnson may delight in tales of tragedy but his is next. It is all too clear from day one that – like Gordon Brown or Theresa May who had the ambition to become Prime Minister but lacked a clear, distinctive vision for their premiership – Johnson's reign will be defined as another opportunity lost where ambition alone isn't enough. Boris shall find that getting fellow Tories to install him in 10 Downing Street is easier than delivering leaving the EU. Brexit has been the making of him – and his undoing.

Boris Johnson's contempt for our constitution is the most dangerous thing to come of Brexit[18]

Depending on who you listen to, Boris Johnson has either enacted a coup this week, or simply conducted some run-of-the-mill politics. The multi-coloured lens of Brexit has a habit of polarising the view.

Leavers like Johnson or his Chancellor Sajid Javid claim the prorogation of Parliament is entirely normal before a new session. After an extraordinarily long two-year period, the time is ripe for a Queen's Speech opening a new, post-Brexit parliamentary session.

Critics, they say, are simply Remoaners looking for any excuse to talk Britain down while crunch talks are held with the EU to avoid the No Deal outcome that anti-Brexit campaigners fear most. Claims by House of Commons Speaker John Bercow that suspending Parliament was 'constitutionally outrageous' are presented as categorically untrue.

The divisive politics of 2019 can make it difficult to see which side is in the right, especially if you have some loyalty to any camp. The truth is that the British constitution is indeed under threat by Johnson, and it will wear the scars. That's exactly how this fragile, flexible beast has always worked.

The warning for Boris is that it always operates best when underpinned by the consent of parliamentarians – and that's precisely what is missing. Let's look deeper.

The claim that proroguing happens is correct. This does happen all the time before new sessions of Parliament. These moments all share a common thread: they last for only a matter of days, not

18 'Boris Johnson's contempt for our fragile constitution is the most dangerous thing to come of Brexit', *The Independent* (31 August 2019).

weeks, and pause Parliament without much, if any, surprise to open a new session.

Everything is different about this time. If the Government simply wanted to start a new session, they could do so by proroguing for one day. Three or more weeks is entirely unnecessary to achieve that goal.

Moreover, suspending Parliament was specifically ruled out only a few weeks ago by the Prime Minister and his chancellor. In June, Javid's campaign team to see him elected Tory leader tweeted (since deleted) that 'you don't deliver democracy by trashing democracy', explicitly rejecting shutting down Parliament to achieve Brexit.

After winning the contest, a triumphant Johnson wrote to Tory members: 'I would like to make it absolutely clear that I am not attracted to arcane procedures such as the prorogation of Parliament. As someone who aspires to be the Prime Minister of a democratic nation, I believe in finding consensus in the House of Commons.'

Within weeks of taking high office, both Johnson and Javid have broken their promises and so, in their own words, have chosen 'trashing' democracy while making it 'absolutely clear' that they wish to preside over a less-than-democratic nation. Rarely have our most senior politicians either wilfully misled or U-turned so spectacularly on an issue of such fundamental constitutional importance.

Under the UK's constitution, the different branches act in light of recognised conventions. One is that the Queen acts on the advice of her ministers, such as in Johnson's request to suspend Parliament. Her role should remain above partisan politics, and she probably had no option but to act on Johnson's advice or risk entering a political dispute whatever her possible legal entitlement to do other than requested.

At present, the courts are hearing cases including one brought by Gina Miller with support from former Prime Minister John Major that seek to find Johnson's request unlawful. Should they succeed, it would pour gasoline on the fire of constitutional outrage that Bercow and others see. This is because it would mean, on the request of her Prime Minister, the suspension of Parliament by the Queen was unlawful and breached the constitution.

Of course, any self-respecting Prime Minister thought to have crossed such a constitutional line would resign in shame. However, shamelessness mixed with a contempt for Parliament lie at the centre of this government.

Johnson's Attorney General, Geoffrey Cox, has the notoriety of ensuring the previous Tory administration was found in contempt of Parliament for refusing to publish his legal advice about Brexit. No government had ever been found in contempt before. Cox was then forced to publish anyway.

Johnson not only kept him in post, but it is on Cox's advice – will it be published? – that Johnson made his request to the Queen.

Johnson's new chief of staff, Dominic Cummings, was found in contempt of Parliament for refusing to answer select committee questions. Yet now he directs the political strategy and surely had some hand in the decision to suspend Parliament.

A government with senior figures at ease with breaking long-held, almost sacred constitutional conventions for the mere sake of securing victory by any means necessary represent a direct attack on our democracy and the cherished freedoms we enjoy as part of this system. The UK's constitution is under threat like never before in our lifetimes for the sake of playing a game of No Deal chicken with the EU that everybody outside 10 Downing Street can see for the farce it is.

The answer though, is not a written constitution which can be inflexible and unable to respond to new problems over time.

Instead, our parliamentarians – in both the Commons and the Lords – have a duty to stand up and defend our constitution, especially when the Government attempts to run roughshod over it. Their moment is next week.

'Take back control' was supposed to be about empowering Parliament, not usurping it. Leavers and Remainers might disagree about Brexit, but they must unite around something more important – our constitution. This is difficult to create and foster, but much easier to decay and destroy.

If we do not act now, the long-term damage will be felt for many years to come and the worst consequence yet of the division made possible by the rush to Brexit before having any clear idea how to achieve it or what it would look like.

I'm the Brexit expert who predicted it wouldn't happen. Now I'm certain I was right[19]

Since the EU Referendum result in 2016, virtually everyone believed that Brexit would happen unless somehow it could be stopped by MPs on the opposition benches or through strong public pressure. Almost nobody thought the Government would fail to deliver on its promise to make the UK leave the European Union collapsing under the weight of the enormity of this task.

That is, except for me. More than three years ago, I became known worldwide as the 'expert' on Brexit who claimed that 'Britain will never leave the EU.'

My view was simple: there were 83,000 or more EU laws. Two years was an impossibly short time frame in which to form

19 'I'm the Brexit expert who predicted it wouldn't happen. Now I'm certain I was right', *The Independent* (29 October 2019).

a definitive view about which of these should be kept, amended or repealed. And such a view would be necessary to form a viable vision for how Brexit would work in practice beyond empty campaign slogans. To 'take back control' there needed to be a concrete perspective about what this means in practice.

And my view has come closest to getting this confusing Brexit saga right.

While many might hope the Government's plans for Brexit might be prevented, my argument was that these plans were simply not up to the complex task of full implementation. For example, how could we increase border controls for the UK overall, potentially diverting from the Common Travel Area, while maintaining no controls at all along the border in Northern Ireland?

This clash should have been obvious a mile away, but it wasn't spotted by a Conservative political elite that routinely forgets about Northern Ireland. (In the current UK citizenship test handbook, for example, immigrants must know how to contact the House of Commons, Welsh Assembly and Scottish Parliament, but not Stormont as it was apparently forgotten and left off the list.)

Solving this border clash is all the more difficult because the Government has said nothing more concrete than it wishes to diverge from EU rules, but fails to say how it wishes to do so. A crucial missing piece in this jigsaw if any way forward is to be worked out.

My position has not been popular – or, at least, it wasn't at first. Most doubted I could be correct given the repeated reassurances May gave the public that she would deliver Brexit. Since she left office, to quote her famous words, we can say 'nothing has changed, nothing has changed' under Boris Johnson either. Like Theresa May, Johnson offers similar promises that can't and won't be kept.

A superficial difference between May and Johnson may be thought to be the latter's sincerity. Certainly, Johnson knows his political legacy rests entirely on the imminent enactment of Brexit in some form – even if his 'new' deal is little different and even worse than May's in weakening our rights and protections. Yes, parliamentary arithmetic was not on Johnson's side. But neither is his Government's true commitment to Brexit. If they were truly so earnest in scaring the EU with a deal or No Deal outcome, then why were virtually all the Brexit preparation funds spent on advertising campaigns instead of actually getting people and new policies in place?

If Brexit by any name is so important to deliver, what explains the failure to compromise by May or Johnson to get something – anything – passed?

Far more time and energy has been spent searching for scapegoats to blame for the Government's failure to deliver Brexit than in getting bogged down in ensuring it did happen. We can only conjecture as to why this is the case from one Prime Minister to the next – and I believe it will remain the case, December general election or none. Perhaps it's in the knowledge that any Brexit will damage the economy and that government would be punished at the polls for it afterwards. Or maybe it's in the hope that either a lost court challenge or, if the EU did not agree an extension, they could be criticised for blocking a referendum result that May and Johnson have little genuine interest in seeing happen.

We might never know their reasons but there are serious questions Leavers should ask themselves about the sincerity of this government in doing what it says. After all, Johnson is not best known for his veracity and there's little evidence that I can see that anything has changed now.

If we take anything away from the last three long years, we shouldn't mistake repeated reassurances that Brexit will happen as evidence that these promises won't be broken.

As long as impossibly short time scales for enacting massive, complex legal changes remain in place, Brexit is no more likely to happen now than when Article 50 was first triggered. There was no plan at the start and little, if any, progress made since.

Not only do I further predict no Brexit before Christmas, but I expect we'll still retain much of what we had as EU members for some time to come at the rate we're going now.

Aftermath

Let me conclude this chapter with some reflections on where we are now.

Brexit was an issue that divided many commentators from the start. There were at least three different groups. The first were pundits who supported leaving the EU. This was a large tent with various perspectives on what Brexit means, as I've noted in my columns. Some thought it was a full break from all EU institutions from the Single Market and Customs Union to other areas like the European Convention on Human Rights. Others thought it was some pick-and-mix of bits they liked minus other parts they didn't. While there were at times intense ideological disagreement about which view was the 'true' view of Brexit supported by the public, it turns out – after several years of spin and counter-spin – that any kind of Brexit will do. Getting Brexit done was a successful strategy – not because it was 'oven-ready' – but because people were sick of talking about it. Brexit had consumed so much energy everything else came to a stand-still and frustrations set in. The public had been promised this would mean something yet nothing happened. At least a headline success story came at last even if the transformative agenda to level-up communities left-behind and let-down remained untouched.

The second group of pundits were Remainers. They were united in opposing Brexit, but differed only in the means to do it.

Should it be through Parliament? Let a General Election decide? Or maybe a second referendum? All agreed Brexit must be avoided and they remained divided over how to do it. This lack of unity did not help this side win the argument. And the tactics were wrong, too. It's one thing to say the leavers weren't straight with the facts to win the vote, but another to claim voters were foolish for holding a different view. Blaming voters for disagreeing doesn't win them back, especially when everyone saying they got it wrong are on the losing side.

The third group were the smallest supporting Cameron's original proposal to 'remain' in a different kind of EU, not yet in place. This argument was hopeless form the start. Claiming to stay in something that would be different, but not different yet, was pinning hopes on a unicorn at the racecourse. It can only be speculated if the result would have been different if the EU adopted the changes proposed at the time *before* the referendum was held.

My views didn't fit in any of these camps. I was never certain what view of Brexit was being pursued by the Government. For example, Brexit was supposed to mean tougher borders but keeping an open border in Northern Ireland. How was that supposed to work if all parts of the UK, including Northern Ireland, were out of the EU in word and deed? Of course, it couldn't and hence a Customs Border was introduced dividing Northern Ireland from the rest of the UK. But we were promised Brexit did not mean this, that an 'oven-ready' deal was on hand and – as soon as it was signed – efforts began to change what this 'ready' deal signed us up to.

I agreed with many of the concerns Remainers had about how the referendum campaign was conducted. I also shared their concerns about the parliamentary stalemate that had frozen all business in its tracks. If MPs could not agree a way forward – and, at the time, they could not – maybe a second referendum confirming a deal on the table or No Deal for now was a way out. I also agreed with the third camp that it was important to show, if we remained a EU member, that we could reshape the EU into something better although I disagreed with the proposals put forward by Cameron and others.

Looking back now, I believe my position revealed a unique place in a heated, polarised debate. While everyone took for granted that Brexit could happen in a two-year period unless stopped, I stood out from the crowd. I never believed the widely held assumption that two years was sufficient time to get a deal – and Brexit – done. My view was simple pragmatism. Brexit of any variety is a major project that could never be achieved quickly or easily. Perhaps I was influenced by a law professor's eye on the thick and thorny set of legal issues that would have to be ironed out first, but I was surprised to be alone. Most pundits focused on the political debate, but overlooked the legal angle. Speeches omitted which laws apply or how institutions work and this requires the details missing for most of the debate.

But like others, not every prediction came true. Some claim the success of 'Get Brexit Done' was the public's support for Brexit. Yet, what I saw from polling didn't support this. In interviews at the time and afterwards, I continue to believe the success of 'Get Brexit Done' lies in getting talk of Brexit done as the public had grown wary of endless talk and little action on this or anything else.

But Brexit is not something that's simply done and dusted. At its best, it is a continuous state of renewal challenging us to create a distinctive British model for prosperity and success. The future prospects for Labour may hinge, in part, in providing a convincing vision for how it might shape this model if back in power. At the very least, Brexit will mean further insecurity about Britain and its uncertain place in the world, as exemplified by the Government's hostile environment. For now I hope for the former and the good this could bring for the future, but, under the current government,

I fear for the latter. It's incumbent on all of us to refocus on where we are now to make the very best of it. History may repeat itself, but never by turning back the clock. Political fortune awaits only those who engage and look forward.

Trump's America

Presidents are not saints, but they were once revered. A popular myth is that George Washington cut down his father's favourite cherry tree when a boy having just received an axe as a boy. When his father came home and saw what had happened, he angrily confronted his son who was claimed to say: 'father, I cannot tell a lie. I cut down the tree.' This never happened, but the myth served the purpose of painting a picture of a leader with high standards of moral virtue. He was someone who should be looked up to by others. The people can trust the President.

There is no clearer evidence that a revolution has come in America than the rise and fall of Donald Trump. He embodies the opposite of seemingly every virtue attributed to founding fathers like Washington, not least the pathological need to say anything but the truth. Or so it seems.

Trump's opponents are horrified by his demeanour and comments. He is accused of holding racist and sexist views – and his frequent tweets seems to almost invite such controversy. But what especially infuriates them is his perceived inability to be honest. And they are aghast that anyone can support him.

But Trump has a loyal following. When challenged about his dishonesty, his defenders say that other politicians tell lies too – but what makes these worse is they hold the wrong views. The key issue is partisanship and what matters is results. Trump supporters feel alienated and left out. Trump's demagoguery addresses them and they respond positively. For those who are struggling, they have little left to lose. Claims that Trump's election won't help the economy fails to convince people who aren't being helped now.

Hillary Clinton was always ahead in the polls, but public opinion does not decide elections. Only votes do that. Like Remain, Clinton was so far ahead in polls for so long that many took her lead for granted. Moreover, also like Remain, support for Clinton was soft. This became more obvious in the last weeks of the campaign where the main pitch was to vote Clinton to keep Trump out – and not because voters should want Clinton voted in. Of course, the negativity was strong both ways.

But Trump's rise is a consequence of a long decline in public trust in politicians, institutions and the media. Trump supporters see all politicians as a part of the same crooked establishment – and they back Trump's call to 'drain the swamp' in Washington, DC. Any unwanted reports are 'fake news.'

They want outsiders, especially with successful business careers, who they hope – and place some trust in – will understand their difficult position and know how to fix it. As wages decline, this fragile trust in outsiders to challenge the establishment is at high risk of fracture as more become disconnected – and there is nothing positive about that. Nothing exemplifies this better than the ensuing insurrection on the US Capitol shortly after the election of Joseph Biden as Trump's successor. Pro-Trump supporters believed they were heralding a new American revolution, that they had every right to storm the legislature and seek to prevent the certification of Biden's lawful victory through brute force. In Trump alone they placed their trust, fearing no consequences from an establishment they had come to see as illegitimate and whose authority had expired long ago. When citizens target officials with abuse for nothing more than counting votes cast for an opponent, trust in the democratic process and in each other has broken down to new lows.

These essays explore the legacy of Barack Obama, the election campaign and its shocking aftermath. Trust – and its lack – again play a key role for understanding where we are and how we can get out of it.

It's less 'yes, we can' and more 'well, we tried' from President Obama and his team [20]

What a long, strange road it has been. It was on a cold day in February 2007 that Barack Obama announced his candidacy to become President of the United States. He had been a senator for only three years and still in his first term – with few thinking his success a realistic possibility.

Obama chose to launch his campaign from the front steps of the Old State Capital building in Springfield, Illinois. Like he has done so well and often, he captured something deeply symbolic: Abraham Lincoln delivered his famous 'House Divided' speech from the same spot in 1858.

He ran against the formidable Hillary Clinton to be nominated as the Democrat candidate. At a dinner, the then Newcastle University Chancellor Chris Patten asked me who I supported in that race. I said that while I supported much of what Obama says and stood for, I was leaning towards Clinton because of her greater political experience. 'Well, Dick Cheney has plenty of experience…' Patten wryly mused. I was surprised to see that Patten, former Hong Kong Governor and Chairman of the Conservative Party, supported Obama. But it became soon clear why.

---

20 'It's less "yes, we can" more "well, we tried" from Obama', *The Journal* (Newcastle) (15 January 2016): 23.

Who the US President is matters. British Prime Ministers choose their Cabinet largely from elected MPs in the House of Commons, but American Presidents can choose anyone they like for their top team – and they are unelected to their positions. This executive team wields significant power – and the President is Commander-in-Chief of the world's biggest arsenal.

The President also nominates new Justices for the US Supreme Court, a body that has become increasingly partisan and controversial in its decision-making, leading many Americans to see the courts as political theatre rather than impartial justice. The fact that some judges are elected in several states and most are active members in political parties does little to help improve this image.

The President has a symbolic importance representing the US at home and abroad. The election of Obama in 2008 was hailed as a watershed moment in American political life. He was the first African-American to become President – and the first born in the state of Hawaii, a place that was a Pacific island kingdom a little more than a century ago.

The expectations on Obama's shoulders were so great that he could never satisfy them all. Looking back now as his final second term as President comes to an end, it becomes clear that his term in office has fallen far short of what his many supporters had hoped.

In his last State of the Union speech earlier this week, Obama highlighted his achievements. Chief among them is the Affordable Care Act commonly referred to as 'Obamacare' that has extended health care to more Americans (over eleven million gained coverage although many remain uninsured).

The national economy has been a particular challenge. Obama said anyone who claimed things were getting worse was 'peddling fiction.' Unemployment has halved during his term in office: *c.*900,000 jobs have been created and the auto industry – at the heart of American manufacturing – had its best year ever. He acknowledged the economy was changing and this will concern people, but tried to show how things are no worse than when he took over from Bush and are in many ways improving.

But Obama could not ignore the fact that many Americans feel 'anxious' about the future. A key issue here is terrorism and organisations like Daesh. Republican opponents are quick to claim that Obama's more welcoming and engaging approach internationally is too weak. Instead of a handshake, they would prefer he waved his fists. To this, Obama said that anyone who doubts America's resolve to tackle terrorist attacks against its citizens should remember what happened to Osama Bin Laden – and that American memories are long.

And there is more to come. Obama spelled out an ambitious final year in office launching initiatives to improve cancer treatment, stricter gun controls and lifting American's Cold War-era embargo against Cuba.

Republican critics countered that Obama's 'soaring' rhetoric simply does not meet the reality. He gives a good speech and can make us feel better about ourselves, but they are nothing more than mere words.

An example is Guantanamo Bay's detention camp called 'Gitmo.' Obama vowed to close Gitmo early in his first term. But eight years later it remains open – and he once again promised he would see it close.

Obama's legacy of much promise under-delivered is not entirely his fault. Republicans in the US Congress have taken a hard line opposing just about anything he says or does just because he says it or does it. They could have seen Gitmo close, but rejected Obama's plans in his first one hundred days and without their assent he cannot get his way.

This is a product of twenty-first century America – a country more polarised than at any point in my lifetime. Studies of American voters have shown the historical importance of identity in supporting one party over the other.

Often voters support parties like they do sports teams. They may not attend every game or vote in every election, but no Red Sox or Newcastle United fan is going to switch sides and support the Yankees or Sunderland. This may not always make sense but sometimes politics doesn't. This is no less true than in the US.

It is nothing new for US Presidents to see themselves as unifying figures and above partisan politics. From Lincoln's Illinois speech that a house divided cannot stand to George W. Bush's claim to be 'a uniter' and not 'a divider', Obama no less sees himself as a bridge builder and open to compromise.

But that is so the old politics. Bridges can only be built when people let you come visit their side – and the Republicans show little sign of any compromise. This is not to say that Democrats are a lot better, but just about every party is. Donald Trump is only the latest ageing Angry White Man that increasingly defines the Republicans' shrinking demographic. More a symptom than a cause.

So long as voters continue to support different parties governing the White House and the Congress, we can expect to see continued gridlock and finger-pointing in Washington. This does little to improve the public's view of politicians or their faith in politics generally.

Last autumn, I spent time as a visiting fellow at Yale University's world leading Yale Law School. Speaking to people about Obama's legacy, it became clear he fell far short of his campaign slogan of 'yes, we can' to something more like 'well, we tried.'

But it is also plain to see that it is difficult to envisage anyone doing much better so long as American politics remains mired in ideological point scoring. It's unlikely this situation will change anytime soon.

If America wants to win over Trump supporters they must be treated like the equal citizens they are [21]

I'm in the United States this week. It is impossible to avoid coverage of the presidential race as the Democrats and Republicans hold primaries to choose their candidates for America's top office.

All attention is focused on 'The Donald': Donald Trump. Many are puzzled at how someone so recklessly offensive can become the likely Republican nominee. This includes many Republican voters who view Trump's rise with alarm.

The key is to look back at the last presidential election in 2012. Democrats ran Barack Obama, who successfully ran for re-election. Obama remains highly popular with the party's grassroots and has some achievements in office under his belt, such as his 'Obamacare' health programme.

But, as I've noted before in my column, Obama's slogan of 'Yes, We Can' was in fact really 'Well, We Tried', as he has struggled to get legislation through a Republican-controlled Congress intent on doing nothing more than oppose whatever Obama does or says just because he does or says it.

Nearly four years later, Hillary Clinton is currently benefiting most from her time working with Obama as the continuity candidate vowing to drive forward many of the reforms Obama has tried to enact unsuccessfully thus far.

Hillary's challenger is Vermont Senator Bernie Sanders, notable for his Democratic Socialism as much as for his surprise victories in key states over Clinton, including Michigan earlier this week.

The 2012 election helps explain the popularity of Sanders. Many who supported Obama's 'Yes, We Can' are attracted to

21 'Trump's success is alarming many Republican voters', *The Journal* (Newcastle) (11 March 2016): 27.

Sanders's determination to go further left. For those frustrated that Obama didn't achieve the impossibly high expectations set for him, Sanders offers a second chance to move America further left – and complete the job Obama started.

But now let's look at the Republicans. In 2012, the party seemed to settle for Massachusetts Governor Mitt Romney. He was too centrist, too moderate, so electable – and tolerated by the evangelical Christian right as someone who could at least secure the White House for that Grand Old Party. And then he lost. Now candidates look to 2012 as an opportunity missed. The leading Republican candidates – Donald Trump and Ted Cruz – present themselves as outsiders and 'true' conservatives. Where Sanders tries to win for the Democrats by moving to the left of Obama, Trump and Cruz aim for a Republican victory by going to the right of Romney.

This is only half the story. Sanders is making things difficult for Clinton, but it seems fairly certain she will be the Democrat's candidate for president. She is damaged by the prolonged contest and has some work to do bringing the party back together. Yet victory is now all but secured.

But what a mess the Republicans are in. Imagine John Major and Michael Howard arguing for fellow Conservatives to not vote for Cameron to become Prime Minister. You can't? Neither can I.

This is what is so extraordinary now with America's Republicans. The last two candidates for president – John McCain and Mitt Romney – have called on fellow conservatives to dump Trump, the front runner in the race. I've never seen anything like it.

There are two key reasons behind this move. The first is the closer Donald Trump gets to winning the Republican nomination, the further away he gets from winning the White House. He is political Marmite – and the problem is more voters dislike him than like him. Winning Republicans is the easy part for him. And the more he woos the right, the more he scares off independents and swing voters.

The second key reason why the GOP top brass are trying to stop Trump becoming the party's candidate is because his deep unpopularity with a growing number of voters is setting off alarm bells in the other races. Senators and members of the House of Representatives will be elected too and Republicans have done well to control the majority. An unpopular presidential candidate can damage this control of Congress – Republican and swing voters may either stay home or vote for the Democrats. So this is more than about winning the presidency – McCain and others are worried about the election prospects of Republicans across the board.

And who can blame them with a front runner like Trump? His few stated policies are that he'd build a wall along the Mexican border, demanding Mexico pay for it, and there would be a ban on all Muslims entering the United States – policies drawn up in some dystopian world that will not come to be.

Watching Trump's recent speech celebrating wins in Mississippi and Michigan was like watching the Home Shopping Network. Instead of looking forward to new election battles, he promoted his Trump hotels, Trump steaks, Trump magazine and all things Trump. As if he was there to make sales, not win votes and lead a country.

His election pitch is just as pathetic: vote for me because I'm more rich than the other candidates (I paraphrase). Trump offers little about what he'd do or who would serve in his cabinet other than – because he's so rich – he knows 'the best people.' We can only trust him – and the many fact checks exposing his fast and loose claims are too long to list.

It is easy to point a finger at Trump voters and sneer at their apparent xenophobia and how they embrace a badly behaving bronzed buffoon – because none of this matters to his supporters.

Many voters are angry at a system that seems out of control and working against them. Living standards aren't rising like they used to and many feel they've been left behind. There is a yearning to set things right, to – in The Donald's slogan – 'Make America Great Again.'

This starts with a deep cynicism about politics and politicians. When Trump calls all politicians liars, the crowd is with him – even as Trump tells his own porkies. It doesn't matter because he is not seen as one of them. The more the establishment tries to tell voters they are stupid, the more these voters are certain they made the right choice all along.

If you want to win over Trump supporters, they must be treated like the equal citizens they are. They must become convinced that making America great won't happen by demonising some Americans at the expense of others.

Voters elect the Governments they deserve. Americans won't find salvation in some political saviour like Trump any more than they could with Obama. There is no quick fix to complex problems that face the country's future.

The real question to ask is what kind of party the Republicans are becoming – and whether they can be a serious governing party again. The signs are not good and this is bad news for American democracy no matter which party one favours. Darker days may lie ahead.

We're not angry when politicians break promises . . . it's what we expect. This must change.[22]

Jeremy Corbyn launched what he called the 'new politics.' This was said to be a more inclusive, kinder way of communicating with each other that might enrich – perhaps enliven – our democracy.

22 'We're not angry when politicians break promises…it's what we expect', *The Journal* (Newcastle) (22 April 2016): 27.

Time will tell if this approach pays dividends for Labour's fortunes in the elections this spring. Corbyn is surely right there's something broken with the way we do politics today in Britain. This is not the first time someone has pointed to flaws in the current system or the urgent need for change. Yet surely there is something new about the way we talk about politics that cries out for different approaches and ideas. Let me explain.

The Tories led a coalition from 2010 and then formed a single-party Government in 2015.

Key planks in their election manifesto were commitments to drive down the national debt and reduce immigration to less than 100,000. These are now broken promises. Public sector debt was just shy of £1,000bn by May last year. No doubt that's a lot of cappuccinos.

But the debt has grown further to over £1,400bn – and the Office for Budget Responsibility predicts it will peak at £1,638bn in two more years. Public sector debt is much worse now than it was in 2010. This is not the only important economic measure for sure. The recovery has been steady, but slow – according to Fraser Nelson, the slowest in our history. Jobs have been created in our region – such as by Hitachi in Newton Aycliffe – although mostly thanks to the efforts of local MPs like Phil Wilson than the Chancellor's policies.

Now consider immigration. The Government has been committed to reducing net migration to the tens of thousands. Despite new legislation, the figures have reached new record highs. Reducing debt and immigration. Two key promises made, but instead of going down, both have gone up.

So where is the public outrage? Has anyone noticed? The explanation is fairly simple, but far from comforting.

It's no surprise to learn that the public greet politicians with some measure of cautious suspicion. Not all politicians have done themselves much favour either. The public's mistrust did not start from nothing.

Nor would I recommend believing everything you hear. Decisions about our shared institutions should be subject to scrutiny not least because of their potential impact on our everyday lives.

We should challenge assumptions made and facts found concerning issues like the economy, education, housing and others out of the need to get things right.

I also don't believe that the facts of a matter should always determine one political solution. Values are important too. We can both agree on the current state of the economy, but reach different conclusions based on values like how we view the role of the state or Britain in a globalised world.

There is no outrage over a government with a track record of broken promises, in part, because this fits with a common frame through which the public understands politics. They distrust the system root and branch. For too many, to engage in political activity is to take part in something mischievous or worse. The mistrust of politicians is transferred to their loyal supporters.

At a time where people and their facts are greeted with hostility or disregard, all there is to rely on is your values and general instincts.

Taking an interest in politics is like supporting a football club with smaller clubs, less interesting T-shirts and where victories are claimed without a goal scored. What counts as good is what appeals to my tribe of whichever party I happen to favour over others.

Let's also not overlook how busy our lives have become, too. As issues become more complex, it's not always easy to understand the relevant problems and solutions on the table. This is no one's fault. But it is yet another source of alienation for many voters.

If this caricature is right, it's hardly surprising so few take much interest in politics. And it matters.

A new election is upon us – and none more important than the EU referendum. *The Journal* published new facts about the benefits from EU membership to the North East. We learned that since 2007 the national average of EU funding in the UK was £82 per person – but £187 per head in our region. This figure comes from European Social Fund grants worth £195.4m and European Development Fund grants of £296.8m between 2007 and 2013.

So shouldn't we all be supporting the Britain Stronger in Europe campaign for Remain? A campaigner for Vote Leave was reported to say the problem with these grants is not that we are net beneficiaries, but that decisions by the EU funding bodies is by 'unelected' persons. This is disagreement about value, not fact.

But the real question is whether anyone is paying attention. As the contest heats up and different numbers are pointed to, these may be heard by most people yet still prove difficult for them to distinguish from gobbledegook. The public's normal anchor of looking to see where parties stand will find the Tories divided and some familiar faces in unfamiliar opposition to each other. A complicated issue can look even more complex.

We need more independent fact-finding from media like *The Journal*, providing the public with information that can be trusted. Such evidence can be crucial points of reference that can improve the quality of our decision-making informed by a combination of shared facts with our personal values.

Finally, we must start to see public service – including service to our national, political discourse – as the worthy enterprise it can be. A few bad apples does not spoil our need for food. Politics is much more than a game – it affects our everyday lives. The more seriously we might take an interest in it, perhaps the more serious our political culture could become.

While there is plenty of talent today in Westminster that are inspiring examples, at least for me, we may require new faces to inspire a greater commitment to public service. The time is ripe for a new politics before it is too late.

Whatever the result of the American election, the United States will become more damaged [23]

Sometimes, elections are important not for their result, but what they reveal. Voters across the country have spoken and many are left scratching their heads about the final tally.

I'm not talking about the UK's elections for local councillors, police and crime commissioners or the London mayor's race. Whether or not they proved a happy ending for any party is probably only being discovered as today's paper went to press.

No, my focus is on the US presidential race. Let's start with the more simple of the two contests. Former Secretary of State Hillary Clinton was the front runner for the Democratic nomination before she threw her proverbial hat – and substantial cash reserves – into the contest. Her pole position was never in much serious doubt, despite a brief scare in the early campaign.

Clinton's opponent is Senator Bernie Sanders, a stalwart of Vermont politics and self-confessed democratic socialist. As a native of Connecticut, I grew up in New England – part of what I call 'the other North East' – in the US, that includes Vermont. No one from my region will have been surprised to see Sanders polling well for so long.

If there is a surprise, it is that Sanders continues to win states from Clinton – like he did in Indiana earlier this week. He may have no chance at beating Hillary to become the Democrat's nominee for president, but Sanders has shown her candidacy is vulnerable.

23 'There are lessons to be learned from across The Pond', *The Journal* (Newcastle) (6 May 2016): 27.

Sanders has undoubtedly moved Clinton more to the political left. However testy at times, this contest has been fairly friendly – or at least in comparison to the other big contest, as we shall see shortly. This bodes well for Democrats coming together in November and taking the fight to Republicans. But the big question remains how much longer Sanders will continue to contest his losing battle – and the longer he stays in, the more damage he may cause Clinton this autumn.

Speaking of damage, there's the Republican Party. The once proud party of Abraham Lincoln that won the Civil War is in the grips of a new civil war threatening to tear itself apart. The election contest looked predictable. An outsider with vast wealth raises spirits, but not votes and exits the stage. Donald Trump's first electoral event – the Iowa Caucus – was no disaster, but he did not win it. All money was on better politically connected and organised politicos such as Ted Cruz, Marco Rubio and someone we used to talk about named Jeb 'Who?' Bush.

We know what happened next. The race became Trump versus the Trampled, as The Donald broke every mould in the book – and without ruffling his goofy nesting patch of a hairdo that would shame a person who cared what anyone else thought. Senator Cruz was 'a liar' and Senator Rubio was routinely belittled – literally – as 'Little Marco.' They say the US president speaks from a soap box called the 'Bully Pulpit.' In Trump's eye, it's all about being a bully.

What began as an acrimonious cage fight seemed to only get worse as Republicans marched straight into a political sewer. It was bad enough to hear Trump's xenophobic hypocrisy daily, until his opponents tried to best him at this game for fools and at their peril. Trump might not have invented the flip-flop, but he has taken flip-flopping to heights no spin doctor has been able to fantasise about yet.

Just you wait for the reminders of his many, many years as a registered Democrat and how – as recently as 2015 – he claimed Bill Clinton the best recent president and, in 2008, said Hillary would make a 'great president.' But don't wait for him to apologise or claim he's done anything less perfect than, well, himself.

Whatever the result, America will become more damaged at home and abroad – hardly 'great again' as Trump dreams. But now let me stick my neck out and offer two more predictions. The first is Hillary is going to win, and win big. Most who turn out to vote are women. Hillary's big trump card – excuse the pun – is more the fact she's not Trump than she is a woman, too.

An astounding seventy per cent of all women voters disapprove of Trump. This fact alone – should it remain steady – is likely to hand the White House keys to the Clintons. The data is little better for Trump looking at voters from ethnic minorities and younger voters.

Trump leads an aging party of mostly very angry white men by being the most enraged at what he sees in the world around him. His ideological tribe is shrinking and not a winning formula in America. God Bless Her for that.

A second prediction is that the Republican Party knows this. Expect to see far more effort taken to retain both houses in Congress than spend limited cash on contesting an unwinnable presidency for a loudmouthed billionaire. It's going to be 'Damage Control Fast, Stupid' at GOP HQ.

Trump's winning the nomination while risking Congress and almost certainly losing his race to Clinton will not go unnoticed when it's crunch time in the capital city.

But let me end on a note of caution. Yes, we in the UK have something to learn from the American campaigns. The first is to reject unlimited campaign funding and prolonged election campaigns – these clearly do little to improve the range or quality of potential candidates and can put many voters off. We've got this right.

Yet the other lesson is that there is a space for authenticity which remains largely untapped. This can take two forms. One is taking a position and sticking with it no matter the changing political winds. This is the stance of Bernie Sanders. A second is seeing authenticity as having unpolished edges and being more candid. Trump represents the latter, but is a poor image.

Being 'real' – and a politician who is not viewed as such, or perhaps viewed as bigger or different from their damaged brand – is becoming a bigger vote winner for the public although this carries huge risks in the forms of embarrassing gaffes. The times they are a-changin'.

The common factor between Trump's victory and the Brexit vote – being intentionally inaccurate [24]

Donald Trump is the new President-elect of the United States. Almost no one saw it coming beyond the planet-sized self-confidence of Trump himself. We all seemed to get it so wrong. Or did we?

The numbers seemed certain right up to the end. Slightly more than half of all US voters are women – and they really did not like Trump. To be fair, he gave plenty of reasons to dislike him including it seems a long litany of inappropriate, if not offensive, comments about women in particular and more generally for months.

A sizeable, growing part of the population are African-Americans and Latinos. These groups disliked Trump even more than women did – and again Trump's controversial statements did little to dent this. Not unlike most other pundits, I saw the longstanding lead

24 'When candidates mislead public to win they cause damage', *The Journal* (18 November 2016): 25.

of Hillary Clinton over Trump in light of significant chunks of the electorate like women and ethnic minorities with disapproval ratings of sixty-five per cent or higher and believed it must be curtains for Trump's campaign. We now know this didn't happen. How could so many political experts get it so badly wrong?

There was certainly no shortage of twists and turns in what was surely the most negative campaign – on both sides – that I have witnessed at any time anywhere. Almost every day led to more eye-rolling revelations of one kind or another from Clinton's health or her emails to Trump's remarks or lack of tax records.

One notable surprise was the decision by FBI Director James Comey to reopen a potentially-criminal investigation into Clinton's use of emails after voting had started. This was as extraordinary as it sounds. Comey had been advised by the Justice Department to do no such thing. Clinton had been exonerated by the FBI only a few months ago. Comey's public foray into the election campaign was so short-lived – he changed his mind exonerating Clinton a second time within days – that it led many to believe it was politically motivated.

Few will be surprised to learn in this most partisan of elections that, yes, Comey was a Republican Party activist until becoming independent before taking over at the FBI. Comey had campaigned for both John McCain and Mitt Romney to become President – some believe his re-opening the email case for a few days was his way of campaigning for a third Republican, Trump, to win but this time it worked. There is little doubt that this will attract close attention into whether it made any difference. The jury is still out on this for now.

In my last column, I called it for Clinton but said while she had the numbers she lacked for inspiration. Her big sell to voters was that she was not Trump. This proved too poor a pitch and seemed to cost her what should have been an easy victory. So I was right, or at least about the real threat to the Clinton campaign that proved her undoing.

Clinton had trouble from the start. In a gruelling primary struggle against Vermont Senator Bernie Sanders, Clinton failed to win over the youth vote or movement politics that Sanders embodies for the American left. Her success came from a better organization – none come more polished and targeted – and more trained boots on the ground.

Clinton likewise won the ground war against Trump with an army many times the size of his across all fifty states. She earned more from fundraising and outspent him on advertising. Yet still she lost because she had what she could buy, but too little what she had to earn – inspiration.

When the dust settles, I would be unsurprised if it turned out the pollsters did not do that badly. They saw a close race with Clinton ahead, but in a margin of error meaning that Trump was in with a chance – however much few wanted to believe it would happen. It is true that there are 'shy' Trump supporters who probably told pollsters they supported a different candidate or were undecided because they wanted to hide their endorsement of this most unconventional of American presidential candidates. But I doubt it was statistically significant.

What lost it for Clinton, and Remain during the Brexit vote, was the failure to motivate their side to vote. In a democracy, it's not the majority that rules but the largest group that turns out to vote under the rules. If Clinton and Remain supporters are more numerous, but Trump and Brexit backers turn out in greater numbers at the polls then the latter win every time. The mystery is solved. Trump surprised the world because his supporters were more keen to see him win than Clinton's team was to see him lose.

There have been many parallels drawn to Brexit, but let me identify the one I think most accurate: being intentionally inaccurate. The Brexit campaign made three key pledges. First there would be £350m per week to the NHS. Now we know there will actually be cuts. Second there would be a points-based immigration system. Now we know that won't happen. Third we were told Parliament would take back control. But now we see the Government trying to silence and bypass Parliament to trigger Brexit as it likes and when it wants clearly flouting the UK's constitutional arrangements so rightly pointed out by the High Court. Brexit was won on promises that won't be delivered.

Likewise, enter Trump. He claimed he 'has a plan' and 'it's foolproof' to defeat Isis in his first term. When asked for what it is, he said he could not tell anyone because then the enemy would find out. Trump said he'll make the economy double and make Mexico build a wall on America's southern border while he restricts any Muslim from travelling to America. Don't hold your breath for any of this to happen – it won't.

The big problem with all of this is much more than any single election. When candidates for public office knowingly and avoidably mislead the public in order to win, they reduce a contest about the public good to a mere political game demeaning our common endeavour.

They damage the institutions they seek to represent and shape by providing false hopes that breed further mistrust in our public officials. I'm not half as disappointed with the immediate election results as I am with the damage the election conduct has done for results to follow.

Politics is about something bigger and greater than any one person's ego or career plans. It must be more than about just wanting to teach a lesson, but to provide for a common future with prosperity. Those that see the trees but not the forest are not our heroes but pose a risk to all that we've built together for the wrong reasons.

The shock and awe we felt about Donald Trump is now seeping through the United States [25]

Donald Trump has been US President for a hundred days. While it feels much longer already, for others his win is still painfully setting in. This was the outsider with no chance that won anyway.

Like many, I wrongly thought Hillary Clinton would win after leading in national polls for so long. But I also wrote for this paper before the election that Clinton's supporters seemed more motivated to keep Trump out of the White House rather than put Hillary in. Giving people something to vote for counts more than asking for their support to stop the other side. There's a lesson here for our general election this spring, too.

Trump promised the world during his election campaign. That he was a deal-maker who gets things done – and he promised big changes in his first one hundred days.

Judged by his own campaign promises, Trump's start has been a complete failure. Pure and simple. He has achieved not one significant policy change promised during the election.

When it came time to vote on whether to end Obamacare, Trump choked and played chicken not even going through with a show of hands in Congress. His first sure thing wasn't even tried.

Trump criticised Obama for spending too much time on holiday – only to surpass all presidents by the sheer number and cost of his frequent trips usually to his own Florida resort – where he conveniently raised the cost of membership for those wealthy enough to pay who in turn can dine alongside the US President and foreign leaders. This is no free lunch – and Trump is raking it in.

25 'The shock and awe we felt about Donald Trump is now seeping through the United States', *The Journal* (29 April 2017).

Trump was also highly critical of the quality of Obama's team. Americans were told that Trump would bring in 'the best.' Take his word for it. But then we saw why he didn't offer many names – he didn't have many in mind. Key posts in his administration remain unfilled. The real movers and shakers appear to be his daughter and her husband. The nepotism is nauseating.

And then there is what he's done. Trump has issued one executive order after another. Presidents can do this – although Trump is already outdoing all those before him.

These orders are subject to rules – namely, they must be within the law. This is one of Trump's weaker points. For all his daring others to take cases to court, Trump seems to be losing every case he wades into.

So why do executive orders? They are a way to get legal change without going through Congress – strongly suggesting either Trump's team don't know how to get legislation through or don't have much confidence of success despite having a Republican-controlled Congress.

So what do Americans think of this? I enjoyed a wonderful two weeks travelling across the country. I was honoured with a Distinguished Alumni Award from Arizona State University giving a public lecture and talks there as well as giving talks at the City University of New York's Graduate Center and an extended interview on Connecticut's famous news anchor Ann Nyberg's flagship programme. In other words, I was visiting states right and left – red and blue – West and East – and one thing constantly came up. Everyone wanted to know what we in the UK thought of Trump.

And so I told them the obvious. That a lot of us were gobsmacked that Trump won because he seemed so genuinely unfit for office – and some of us were downright frightened that the world could become a bit more dangerous with someone like him in charge of the world's most deadly military.

But then I found what many Americans think about Trump. I struggled to find anyone who supported him with any enthusiasm. The shock and awe we felt is now seeping through the US political system right and left.

Yes, it was easy to find people who had real concerns about Clinton. But for all the inappropriate, rude and simply offensive behaviour of Trump, voters believed his promises. No holidays all the time. An end to Obamacare. A new wall with Mexico.

What they got is something very different. Trump's on holiday about every week. Obamacare continues untouched. No wall with anybody.

This has been enormously damaging for him. He claimed he was not like 'politicians' and that only he could 'drain the swamp' of Washington, DC and bring real change swiftly. Instead, he's turning out to be even worse than politicians: wholly impotent in getting legislation passed – saying one thing, but delivering something very different.

And I've said nothing about Russia. The alleged links between the Kremlin and Trump's election aren't going away – if anything, they are becoming more serious. I found no one who thought that Trump's team was innocent.

I was pleasantly surprised to see that just about everyone I met agreed with me that the real reason Trump shot missiles into Syria was to help deflect attention from his Russia-related problems – and manufacture a 'crisis' with Russia to make it look like the two were at odds. Everyone is seeing through this sad charade.

I suppose one of the defining lessons we can take away from Trump is don't promise what you can't deliver – especially when your appeal is wrapped up in being able to deliver big.

And the more that Trump fails to do anything but produce hot air, the more he looks like an especially incompetent politician – the reality is turning out to be the opposite of his empty rhetoric.

This isn't to say everyone regrets they cannot change their votes to Hillary. That isn't true. They just want somebody else. Almost anyone else – as Trump's election shows, the public is eager for something different.

An old friend of mine put it to me: 'Is this really the best we have? Does nobody want to be President any more?' She's right.

So during the coming general election please, reader, think long and hard. Contributing to the public good is such an important service our MPs and prospective parliamentary candidates offer us. I have enormous respect for many of our elected politicians – and encourage everyone to get involved in the process. We should have the best in our politics – and avoid the worst which we can see emerging in Trump's White House.

Theresa May will only regret Trump's state visit[26]

Donald Trump's three-day state visit from 3 June is a bigger mistake than most probably realise. Of all Theresa May's blunders, this could well stand among her greatest hits.

May was the first foreign leader to visit Trump at the White House rushing out to widely photographed awkward hand-holding through the White House colonnade. Trump is hardly the first US president to receive such an invitation from the Queen, but he has succeeded in doing what Ronald Reagan and Barack Obama never achieved in getting his now without needing to win a second term.

The only explanation given repeatedly for cosying up to the Donald is a hope that a state visit with Her Majesty is a price worth paying for Trump to agree some new trade deal and bring a bonanza home to Britain. Cue reminders only heard on this side

26 'Theresa May will only regret Trump's state visit', *Huffington Post* (26 April 2019).

of the Atlantic about the special relationship between the US and UK with the hope this old alliance could provide May the long-awaited lifeline she needs before her government is officially on life support.

May's supporters will be nervous about the expected size and scale of record protests. This could see the return parade of the baby Trump balloon through London streets aimed at denting Trump's ego as much as evening news headlines.

Rescinding a state visit is virtually unheard of. Leaders with controversial relations to the rule of law and human rights have been entertained before and will be afterwards. American presidents invite different treatment to some degree based on their own sense of uniqueness as self-proclaimed 'leader of the free world.' It is only right that those who claim to uphold the highest standards are criticised when they don't rise to meet them, even if they are not much better than dictators elsewhere around the world.

This is especially true for Trump and the long, dark shadow of the Mueller report hanging over his presidency. Its damage to Trump, his reputation and those closely associated to him is far from over.

But May's mistake in wanting a state visit for Trump is not simply because state visits should not be used to buy a new trade deal with another country or because Trump's values seem so at odds with ours. Her error is in thinking that rolling out the royal red carpet for Trump could lead to a Brexit bonanza.

We can be so absorbed by our own Brexit crisis in Britain that it can be easy to only think about how Trump might bail May's leadership out with a deal instead of remembering what Trump promised his voters about the deals he would make. He campaigned to 'Make America Great Again.' A key part of this pledge was to end America's trade deficits with foreign countries. This was to be reversed and keep more dollars at home than sent abroad.

Trump might be wrong that he's the greatest dealmaker in history. America's trade deficit is now at a ten-year high and Trump has vowed to end it. After many years of running a deficit, the US runs a small surplus with the UK. Unless the man who wrote 'The Art of the Deal' can be fooled into a deal that breaks his campaign pledge to cut trade deficits, Trump won't knowingly sign up to any such deal. This is especially so given he has vowed to fight for his re-election after bruising mid-election results that saw his Republican Party lose the House of Representatives and nearly lose the Senate.

In short, May's offer of a state visit to win a more lucrative trade deal with Trump is the making of a deal for the wrong US president at the wrong time politically. As we've seen before when he last met with May, Trump's loyalty is mostly to those he was close to before his election – and he has fired many of them, too. Perhaps May's plan would work with a different leader in a different time. Trump's visit shows no sign of leading to success and will only lower Britain's standing in the world as our over eagerness to make any post-Brexit deal looks as desperate as it is.

Biden's America

A new dawn is breaking in America. This is not the same land of my birth, even if the same country in name. The US is a country of two sides: left and right, Democrat and Republican, plaintiff and defendant, guilty or not guilty, the home team or away. There is nothing new with a polarised public, but what is new is the further erosion of anything resembling a middle ground. Once upon a time only a few decades ago, moderates were mostly in control of both political parties. Now they're an endangered species with no one left to put them on a protected list.

After a poisonous campaign, Joseph Biden has brought much needed relief for the global community keen to see America back playing a key role on the world's stage. The early signs are his campaign will be a continuation of projects started under Barack Obama's administration, but with Vice President Kamala Harris taking a visible lead in high profile areas arguably designed to prepare her for a White House run in the next election.

Yet, the America now governed by Biden and Harris is a different place. Obama's presidency was marked by a sense of hope for the future, that deep wounds were healing. However, large parts of the country saw a very different picture. They were increasingly insecure about America's future and their place in it – and their sense of alienation mixed with desperation led many to look to unconventional saviours like Trump to put the brakes on economic and social changes that had left these communities falling behind.

Whatever the merits of globalization, its champions too often address fellow believers who share in its benefits and not those further disadvantaged. It was inevitable this split would create two camps – the first highly skilled and mobile able to thrive from globalization and the second more working-class and closely tied to their communities for whom global interconnection has meant stagnating wages, job insecurity and declining opportunities. It's no wonder people in this situation have grown frustrated with politics as normal and backed someone like Trump, claiming to support backing rust belt industries and protectionism. They put their trust in his promises, and he failed to deliver. When those you trust in desperation fail, placing what trust you've got left in someone else gets harder. For this reason, broken political promises damage all parties and, in so doing, our democracy.

Biden must pick up the broken pieces left by Trump, whose legacy is a more bitterly divided country than ever. American politics isn't merely polarised, it has become poisoned. It will not be good enough to simply please Biden's supporters given the deep distrust and hostility faced by opponents. Biden must bring hope for the future beyond anything Obama's election offered to create a bridge of common, shared purpose across ideological divides. He cannot aspire to make everyone support him, but he must endeavour to ensure all support democratic institutions and the processes that underpin them. Insurrections born of sour grapes fermented by online conspiracy theories cannot be tolerated as just another protest. It is a crossroads with the future health of American democracy at stake. Whichever partisan side we back, we can all rally behind this cause. And, for the sake of my native country, I hope many will.

UK Politics: between Hope and Despair

There is no specific tipping point for our current political crisis. Widespread public concerns about the evidence used to justify the invasion of Iraq – in addition to doubts about its legality – cast a very long political shadow damaging the public's trust in its politicians more generally, as all became scarred by the debacle. So, too, the financial crash in 2008 where we woke up to discover financial institutions were on the brink of collapse with significant, longstanding consequences for tens of millions of people – none of whom had any responsibility for what had gone badly wrong. Factors like these events have only fuelled a long poisonous drip of public distrust in its politicians and public institutions that has grown over several years.

Much of the problem's sources are, of course, the politicians and public institutions themselves. Making promises to win votes, but breaking them shortly afterwards is an all too common stereotype – with plenty of illustrations giving rise to it. The public craves someone – or some group – that spoke to their concerns and did as they said.

For example, the Liberal Democrats tried desperately to tap into this *Zeitgeist*. In 2010, they ran an election ad featuring leader Nick Clegg claiming no more broken promises. They said other parties make promises only to break them after winning votes, so the public should turn to an alternative and change the balance of power in Westminster.

When the votes were counted, Clegg and the Liberal Democrats become kingmakers and soon were confirmed coalition partners with David Cameron's Conservatives forming a new government. So far, so good for them. But then came the inevitable compromises, including the decision to increase the fees for students going to university.

Normally, such compromises are a normal part of politics. However, the Liberal Democrats had promised to be uncompromising in their adherence to their principles – and every single candidate for Parliament signed a pledge against raising fees. So when the party of principle and no broken promises then broke the only election pledge that every candidate had plastered across social media, the effects were devastating – and the party has not recovered years later from the political fall-out. Voters stopped looking to them for an alternative.

During the five years of that Coalition Government, the problems of public distrust only grew. One issue was the referendum on Scotland's independence. This debate became increasingly divisive, acrimonious and led to serious questions for the first time in a generation about the future of the United Kingdom in its present composition. Some of this is charted in the essays below. A second was a national referendum on changing from a 'first past the post' system to alternative vote, which lost heavily. This event saw the Government sanctioning a referendum on a change that most in the Cabinet bitterly opposed. This was only a dress rehearsal for what happened with the EU referendum to follow.

We then saw other changes. The launch of Police and Crime Commissioners meant to help increase democracy, but yet consistently attracting only a relative trickle of voter participation.

There were then mayors and regional powers for some, but not all. The country was being sold mixed messages and promises that were too often untrue.

The lack of trust created several changes, each revolutionary. In distrusting the spin and Iraq invasion of the Blair years, Labour went away from the centre-ground to Jeremy Corbyn in a clear break – only to shift yet again a few years later to Keir Starmer. The Tories have moved from Theresa May, who was seen as a steadier pair of hands with an attention to detail, to the overly confident Boris Johnson whose grasp on facts can be far more elusive. The public began to view some press reports as 'fake news' echoing this phrase from America's Trump who directed it at any critic no matter what they said.

These events show an impatience the public has for politics as usual. There is a willingness to consider and vote for new options. This is partly a product of hoping for a better future, but also perhaps born out of despair – if things could not get much worse, what risk is there in taking a punt on finding different answers? There is a hunger for change waiting to be tapped.

While only a few were driving the Government's agenda, this legacy of increasing distrust was shared with the political class as a whole. All were – unfairly – painted with the same brush. This polarisation was not only bad for those in political office who can face horrific levels of abuse, especially online, but it has surely persuaded a great many to see the sacrifice needed to become an effective public servant as a vocation for somebody else, reducing the talent pool.

It is easy to view many of the tumultuous events that followed the financial crash – most especially the further erosion of trust – with despair. Our country needs the brightest and best amongst us more than ever. Yet, never has this work had lower public confidence and respect is far removed from what should be deserved.

There is realistic optimism to be found that in these times a new beginning can be born. As our current crisis evolved over several years, it will not be changed overnight. If we are troubled by the situation, we cannot wait for others to get around to changing minds. This task becomes our collective responsibility as citizens both publicly and privately. We don't have to accept the status quo as inevitable. These essays explore these issues – and how we need to have greater trust in our leaders, institutions and each other if we are to break out of the current crisis towards a time of optimism and hope.

Tories forget how the Internet works: 'delete-gate' reminds them[27]

The 1996 election campaign that brought Bill Clinton to the White House fundamentally changed the way campaigns are run in more ways than one. Clinton's success owed much to the genius of James Carville, the lead strategist behind his successful election campaign and creator of 'the war room.' This was a political command centre where strategists and their media officers worked together to counter-attack opponents with unprecedented speed.

Their lightning-fast responses were made possible thanks to a database that collected all the available information about opponents so that it could be used against them. Old speeches were trawled for past proclamations and long-forgotten incidents raked up to cause fresh embarrassment. All this information could be sent out to journalists at the drop of a hat, as soon as the opportune moment presented itself.

27 'Tories forget how the Internet works: delete-gate reminds them', The Conversation (15 November 2013).

Carville's war room revolutionised the way election campaigns are conducted in a model exported to Canada, the UK and beyond. Much of its success was its adaptability for running a campaign in the twenty-four-hour news age. Campaigns could respond almost instantly to just about anything with little advance notice when the war room's database was well organised.

The Conservative Party recently hired Lynton Crosby, an Australian strategist who assisted London mayor Boris Johnson's re-election campaign. He has been credited with 'sharpening up' the party's nascent campaign ahead of the expected 2015 general election and already has his war room up and running. But his war room reveals something new about their uses and limits.

It is sometimes said the best offence is a good defence. In an election campaign, the less troublesome information there is in the hands of your opponents' war machines, the less they will be able to launch attacks on you. If the Tories could restrict the available information about themselves to opponents, then they could enjoy a strategic advantage when it comes to disseminating rapid press releases countering claims on the campaign trail.

And that's exactly what the Conservatives did. Or at least thought they did.

Despite earlier promises that government should be made more transparent so politicians could be held to account, the Tories have tried – literally – to erase their recent online history. In an act of brazen Machiavellian chutzpah mixed with untold naïvety, the party has tried to erase records of speeches and press releases published between 2000 and its coming to power in May 2010.

This was not just about removing content from the Conservative Party website, but also about removing all such records from the internet. The Tories launched a bot blocker that barred pages for public consumption – one aim appears to be to make it nearly impossible to conduct online searches for embarrassing pre-Coalition speeches. Or at least that's what they thought they did.

However, there was a significant flaw in the plan. The personnel in Crosby's war room clearly don't understand the internet. Removing online content post-publication can be easier said than done, especially where the content is by a party in government.

'Deletegate' has been made all the more ridiculous by the relative ease with which the missing content has been retrieved. It's readily clear why Crosby's war room thought it would be a good idea to try to brush some past pronouncements under the carpet once you see what was removed.

For example, among the pre-2010 proclamations made by PM David Cameron that were removed from the Conservative Party website were promises to offer no major structural change to the NHS, a commitment to increasing state spending, a pledge to permit voters to remove individual MPs halfway through a Parliament and support for the transparency in politics that the internet brings and we should welcome.

The error of Deletegate is in thinking the internet is like paper and not fluid. Newspapers or books can be seized and burned. They can, with enough effort, be permanently deleted. The internet is more like a stream that can be managed and shaped, but where deletion might be impossible to achieve.

Labour has now been exposed 'managing' the content of its website to delete old content but it doesn't appear to have brazenly attempted to wipe the internet clean of the content, perhaps realising that this would be a near impossible task.

The war room is a modern approach to running an election campaign designed for our media age. The aim of winning elections may remain the same, but the means by which elections are contested has been fundamentally transformed. Thanks to Crosby, so too has the adage of the best offence is a good defence. Deletegate indicates that the information war may be best won through information management rather than delete bots. Sometimes what appears to be a good defence is a better offence for opponents. I'm sure Carville would agree.

If Holyrood gets more powers, English views on regional assemblies might change[28]

One of the key themes of the referendum campaign will soon be aired when the three unionist parties in Scotland make a joint declaration about plans for more powers for Holyrood in the event of a no vote.

It is not difficult to discern why they see this as necessary. Each party has put forward different views on what more powers for Scotland within the union should look like; and the nationalists have repeatedly questioned whether they can really be trusted to deliver more powers as promised. Most recently, one of Quebec's leading political academics was quoted in the Scottish press warning that more powers will be off the agenda if the Scots stay put.

One dimension to this discussion that has not received much attention is the tension between what the Scots seem to want – more devolution – and what the English think about it. Given that most of the UK electorate is based in England, their views could potentially influence what happens north of the border if there is a no vote.

Last week's NatCen British Social Attitudes survey sheds some light on this subject. First, it confirmed that attitudes in England about Scotland's independence have taken a new turn, with growing support for Scotland remaining a part of the UK. While new

28 'If Holyrood gets more powers, English views on Regional Parliaments may change', The Conversation (16 June 2014).

opinion polls showed the Scots heading closer to being evenly split on leaving the UK, opinion in England is hardening in favour of the current political union.

Only twenty-one per cent of people living in England – about one in five – think Scotland should become independent. This is a fall from twenty-six per cent in 2011. People in England are expressing an ever clearer view that Scotland remain part of the UK.

Point two is that even fewer people (sixteen per cent) believe it is in England's interest for the UK to become dissolved and this figure is unchanged from 2007. It seems that English opposition to Scotland's independence is based on the view they are 'better together' than apart. People in England see a United Kingdom with Scotland as in their best interests.

It is not that the English oppose independence because they fear the loss of Scotland would lead to some crisis of identity, but rather a view of shared interests. While some may question the UK's place in Europe, the English largely do not question England's place in a United Kingdom.

That doesn't seem to mean the Scots are welcome on any terms. Slightly less than half (forty-eight per cent) of people in England surveyed responded that they favoured Scotland having a devolved Parliament.

NatCen did not ask specifically if the English were in favour of more devolution for Scotland, but it did find that support for an English Parliament had plunged from twenty-nine per cent in 2009 to nineteen per cent today. More than half (fifty-six per cent) are content with England's laws being made through the UK's House of Commons. This is the same figure found in 2002 despite the fact that many non-English MPs can vote on laws that effect England alone.

One possible interpretation is that English reservations about devolution explain their wariness about Scottish devolution.

But equally, these findings would indicate that the English are not keen on more power for Scotland.

The context is that there are questions about the extra benefits that Scotland is said to enjoy over others south of its border. There is also continuing debate over whether MPs from outside England should vote on matters that affect only England.

Put together, there may be a tension between what Scotland wants and what the majority of UK voters would like them to have. Could this affect what the Scots are offered if they stay in the union?

I think it is unlikely. The Scottish Parliament has been a success and the unionist parties have made ever-louder noises about handing over more tax and spend powers. To anyone questioning this handover in England, Westminster politicians would have an obvious reply: would you like more powers yourselves?

Paradoxically, the present answer is 'no' of course. Would this view begin to change if more power was seen heading over the northern border? It would not be surprising if it did.

And even if this didn't happen purely out of logic, the risks of it being triggered are likely to increase. Suppose a major policy decision affecting only England won parliamentary approval thanks to non-England MPs, for example. In short, the days of scepticism about English devolution may be numbered.

Customs at Gretna Green? Neither side is telling the whole truth on this[29]

One question that keeps raising its head in the Scottish independence debate is about border controls and what would happen

29 'Customs at Gretna Green? Neither Side is telling the whole truth on this one', The Conversation (10 July 2014).

between Scotland and the rest of the UK at border towns like Gretna Green – a particularly pertinent subject in a holiday month where people are more prone to crossing borders.

The answer depends on who you ask. On the unionist side, Shadow Chancellor Ed Balls has been leading the charge. He claims that border controls are inevitable because immigration rules for both sides of the border would not be the same.

The nationalists don't dispute that. They support a different immigration policy. Alex Salmond, Scotland's First Minister, has stated plans to increase net migration into Scotland by ten per cent to about 24,000 in total each year after independence. This is aimed at expanding the workforce to finance the state pension. Salmond has accused his critics of using immigration to scaremonger voters, pointing out that his proposed increase in net migration is only about 2,000 above the average figure for Scotland between 2001 and 2011.

But Salmond has argued that such differences should not preclude an independent Scotland becoming part of the common travel area between the UK, Ireland and the outlying British islands, where internal border controls are unnecessary. Since the UK and the Republic of Ireland have made the travel area workable despite different immigration policies, he argues, there is an existing framework that would facilitate open travel across the UK-Scotland border.

So which side is right? To start with, it should be said that the common travel area is not a free travel area as such. It is true that individuals who have lawfully entered Ireland or the UK do not normally require leave to cross into the other – although Irish-bound flights from the UK do pass through passport control, even though this often doesn't happen in the other direction.

But the UK's immigration rules are clear that some people are still subject to controls, such as those entering Ireland unlawfully;

persons who have overstayed their leave; or individuals that would normally require a visa to travel to the UK.

While many people cross the UK-Irish border for work or family outings, temporary entry within the common travel area is not a permanent entitlement to indefinite movement for all, irrespective of their particular citizenship. This may not have consequences in practice at the border, but it does mean that immigrants to Ireland can't simply use that country's different immigration policies to get a legal right to come into the UK.

This means that Scotland's inclusion within the common travel area would not mandate the absence of any border controls – contrary to what the SNP have claimed in their independence white paper, 'Scotland's Future.'

As well as planning to increase immigration figures, Scotland is also planning a more relaxed approach to citizenship than the UK. In the UK at present, any non-EU citizen wishing to obtain permanent residency must pass the 'life in the United Kingdom' citizenship test. Despite the fact that the test has serious problems, for which I have previously recommended solutions, all major parties remain committed to it, and we will likely see a new fourth version after the 2015 general election.

The SNP is on record claiming there will be no such citizenship test for residency or naturalisation in an independent Scotland. Instead, the SNP's white paper proposes a points-based immigration system that would also 'lower the current financial maintenance thresholds and minimum salary levels for entry' to 'open up greater opportunities' for new migrants to Scotland.

In a similar vein, another major issue for British immigration policy is English language proficiency requirements, since the Government introduced new rules requiring applicants to provide additional evidence of satisfactory English. No such rules for naturalisation, either for requiring proficiency in English or Scots

Gaelic, are included in Scotland's Future. This suggests they will be either scrapped or no decision has been made yet. In short, there are numerous things about Scotland's immigration plans that are not yet clear. It is currently more aspirational slogans than a fleshed out system of rules.

Nonetheless, the direction of travel is obviously to be more liberal than current UK policy. This runs the risk of Scotland becoming an easy target for migrants who gain entry to take up work but who always intended to cross the border shortly afterwards. If this started happening in practice, you can be sure it would not go down well with the rest of the UK, nor possibly Ireland, which has itself tightened up on immigration in recent years.

Would this see Scotland excluded from the common travel area? It seems highly unlikely, since it surely wouldn't be in either side's interests to impose border controls. The costs of setting up and maintaining such a system would be high and there would be consequences for economic activity, too.

What might be more likely is that Scotland's application to the common travel area would trigger a review of the whole system. This was on the table late in Tony Blair's administration before it petered out. With immigration concerns running high, especially in England, it is not hard to see this prospect returning. If so, the UK would be in a position where it could use the prospect of denying Scotland access to the common travel area as a means of checking Scottish immigration policy's liberal tendencies. The question would then be to what extent Edinburgh would risk calling London's bluff. If we ever end up in that situation, the power politics will be fascinating.

Will UKIP be a one-hit wonder?[30]

UKIP. The party everyone is talking about. But will they be celebrating big wins in the North East next year? No.

Earlier this month, *the Journal* published a map of what our region would look like if UKIP made the same gains against Labour as found in the Heywood and Middleton by-election. The results look significant: UKIP would win eleven constituencies from Labour in the North East. This could make for uncomfortable reading for the Labour Party, which has a massive presence in our region – and its Labour Central is based in Newcastle.

However, by-elections are poor indicators of party success in national elections. Plus, Heywood and Middleton is not Hartlepool or Middlesbrough: local issues matter and so too the particular candidates.

You don't need to speak about public policy with as many potential voters as I have to know the public seem frustrated by Westminster politics. Part of the reason is probably because a Tory-led government shrinking the size of the public sector was likely to be unpopular in the North East anyway. It might also be explained by an economy that has recovered for some, but not others.

But we shouldn't underestimate the importance of organisation for an election campaign. UKIP punches above its weight in getting noticed in headlines. It has a long, long way to go before it can mobilise a serious threat to the major parties. This requires not only greater financial support, but also members on the ground to help get out the vote. It's no good leaving favourable voters at home on election day – UKIP needs to ensure a strong turnout of its supporters and this requires an organisational capacity they still lack.

30 'Will UKIP be a one-hit wonder?' *The Journal* (Newcastle) (27 October 2014): 17.

A further issue is scrutiny. Publicity is highly useful, but be careful what you wish for. Close scrutiny has not always turned out well for UKIP as its candidates have been found to depart from the party's platform – even UKIP leader Nigel Farage described the party's 2010 General Election manifesto as 'drivel' (an extraordinary remark for a party leader to make – is that what UKIP thinks of its own recent policies?). It's one thing in low turn-out elections to be carried by protest votes and support for a party leader, but the focus can change to the candidates in general elections and UKIP has not won a seat in Parliament in those circumstances. Perhaps they can retain Clacton-on-Sea in the South East, but they won't win in Saltburn-by-the Sea in the North East.

The big question is then not if UKIP expects big wins in 2015, but whether the seeds will be sown for breakthrough success in years to come. I'm no fortune teller, but predict that if UKIP does not adapt as a party it will die.

Politics is a lot like Darwinism: standing still is usually a safe path to electoral extinction. Labour underwent change to win big under Sedgefield MP Tony Blair. PM David Cameron won his party's leadership over David Davis in his attempt to modernise the Conservative Party.

UKIP is like a one-hit wonder lacking a number one hit. And it's a record they play again and again. But when your party is linked to one person like Farage and one policy that leaving the EU will solve more problems than it creates, the worry for its supporters is that politicians don't hold power forever and popular policies will attach to other parties.

This requires parties to have more than one big name and not put all eggs in a single policy basket. The good news for Labour, the Liberal Democrats and especially the Conservatives is that UKIP isn't listening.

The biggest worry in the North East is the cuts that are coming next[31]

George Osborne's final Autumn Statement for this Parliament was drafted clearly with a crucial general election this spring in mind. There was expected investment in roadworks, including the creation of a dual carriage way for a thirteen-mile stretch of the A1 between Newcastle and Ellingham. Osborne also announced a continuing freeze on fuel duty and abolishing Air Passenger Duty for children under twelve from the first of May – only a few days before the general election takes place.

News such as investment in the A1 is good news for our region, but many argue it should go further – literally – by making the A1 a dual carriageway through to Edinburgh. Likewise, the Government's support for the 'Northern Powerhouse' is welcome rhetoric – although much of the investment appears headed for Greater Manchester.

It remains crucial that the North East is recognised in word and deed as part of this investment so that we do not lose out to other regions in the North of England or to Scotland as greater powers are devolved to it.

The main headline from Osborne's budget statement is the planned change to stamp duty on homes costing more than £125,000.

This may have a limited impact on the North East as many of the homes in our region are on average below this threshold and so not subject to stamp duty anyway. For example, average house prices are £120,545 in Newcastle and £85,438 in Sunderland. Families purchasing properties worth the average cost of a London home – about £510,000 – stand to save £4,900.

31 'The biggest worry is the cuts that are still to be revealed', *The Journal* (Newcastle) (12 December 2014): 17.

Serious economic concerns remain. While unemployment is less, the problem is that many of the new jobs are low wage and part-time. Those in work have continued to endure pay freezes or no meaningful pay rise. These factors contributed to a shortfall in the Government's budget of about £21bn – about half of it in income tax. The Government's relief for businesses taking on apprentices under twenty-five years old is welcome news, but much more remains needed to support reforming relevant funding mechanisms to make it more effective.

The biggest concern for our region is the cuts we can expect next. The Office for Budget Responsibility predicts that if the Tories deliver on their pledge to protect spending on schools and hospitals we should expect significant cuts to public services of about fifty-seven per cent less than in 2009/10.

There have already been substantial cuts to local councils and public services in our region which have caused difficult and sometimes painful decisions.

However, the majority of the Government's cuts do not kick in until after the May election. But worse still the full scale of cuts needed remains unclear. This is likely to put even greater pressure on our local councils which have struggled already under existing cuts – and these are not of the scale many predict we will face soon.

So while there is some welcome news that will benefit our region, it coincides with heavy costs conveniently timed for after the 2015 general election. We can hardly blame the Chancellor for drawing up a budget aimed to win votes this May. But we must ensure the North East is firmly rooted in the Government's plans to develop the 'Northern Powerhouse.'

The Government should also be as clear about the cuts we can expect as they are about the investment they promise. Otherwise, voters may come to see this budget as a cynical attempt to win votes by trumpeting a few goodies to distract the public's attention from deep funding cuts on the horizon.

Waiting for a credible message of realistic optimism[32]

Welcome readers to my first monthly column for *The Journal.*

They say that a week is a long time in politics. The bad news is that waiting a few months for the start of the general election will feel like an eternity. And that's before the Prime Minister finally agrees to listen to the public and to take part in televised debates.

The Coalition Government's slow march to formally launching the next general election has exposed some of the top issues we'll hear even more about during the weeks ahead. It's interesting to note what is said and left unsaid.

For the Tories, gone is any echo of New Labour's claim that things can only get better. No, the Conservative election tune is more like country roads take me home. Their election poster features a bumpy street that asks voters to please stick with the status quo. Imagine motivating voters with slogans like: What do we want? More of the same. And when do we want it? We already have it. Not the most inspirational message.

The Liberal Democrats can hardly be blamed for not wanting to mention all the things they became known for in 2010, such as promises to end tuition fees and their promise of no more broken promises. Instead, they present themselves as a kind of brake pad with a guilty conscience. Lib Dems seem to talk more about how the Government might have been without them. It's an odd way of

32 'Waiting for a credible message of realistic optimism', *The Journal* (Newcastle) (30 January 2015): 18.

being positive to say things are bad, but at least we kept them from getting much worse. Or so they promise.

Then there is Labour's Ed Miliband. The Leader of the Opposition really is the most difficult job in politics. The Tory-led government has repeated the mantra so often that Labour was somehow to blame for a global financial crisis that many people have actually come to believe it. But which of us genuinely believes things would have been better if the Tories were in power instead?

The biggest challenge for the Labour Party is its greatest opportunity. Too much of what passes for serious 'criticism' is better understood as playing the man and not the ball. Labour's opponents seem to think weaponizing attacks with half-truths and gossip might see off voters. It's almost as if the Tories thrive on feeling sad.

Labour's opportunity is connecting its future vision to its past achievements. Let this be an election about a government's record in office. Cameron's efforts simply don't compare to Labour's achievements on health, education, jobs and public services pre-crash. Not by a country mile, or even a bumpy country road.

Cameron's Government is happy to follow Labour's lead, but then makes things much worse. One example is Labour's introduction of the Migration Impacts Fund in 2009. Its funds were drawn from increasing application fees for visas and related documents and used to reduce strain on public service providers. The current government announced it would stop the programme within two months of entering office, but retain the fees.

This is a problem the Government is only beginning to recognise in parts of the country, such as Middlesbrough which has received a disproportionate share of asylum seekers from the for-profit organisations that now help manage this system. The election may hold some surprises, but not where most are looking. Watching UKIP is almost like viewing The Titanic. Both are about faulty ships, but only one is a tragedy.

The problem with protest votes is that they can add up to voting in an electoral mistake that's really worth protesting about. No one can be blamed for wanting change and something to believe in. It can be tempting to send out a message of 'none of the above' when feeling dissatisfied or disillusioned.

A credible message of realistic optimism could be exactly what voters want. Realism is central. There will be serious constraints on what can be achieved in the near future and this must be acknowledged. But likewise we shouldn't settle for the politics of let's grin and bear it the next few years. We need a vision of a Britain worth building together.

This is a part of the realistic optimism that, if made credible, could be transformational and help tip the balance in May. It might also strengthen our shared political lives, too.

John F. Kennedy was right. Ask not what your country can do for you... [33]

The General Election is over and we know what happened next. The large number of non-voters was perhaps more surprising than the result: over thirty per cent of eligible voters stayed away from the polls. That's one in every three despite intense media interest and uncertainty about the expected outcome. We will never know what the result might have been if things were different.

The biggest surprise of all might be that so many did vote. While the main parties won the most seats between them, the public shows a growing appetite for supporting parties representing none of the usual suspects to send a message to the Westminster establishment.

33 'John F. Kennedy was right. Ask not what your country can do for you...', *The Journal* (Newcastle) (29 May 2015): 18.

I don't know which is worse: politics reduced to empty slogans endlessly repeated or a politics of protest without fresh ideas. It is little wonder the public are increasingly turned off from voting when they see politicians selling brands without a product, or those who can only talk about the flaws of others without any policies to promote.

But it's not that there are no differences between the parties. There are plenty. What's lacking is an inspiring vision worth voting for.

This characterisation is only partially true. The election campaign saw some fabulous candidates across the political spectrum working their socks off on the doorstep and engaging voters in new ways. They deserve more credit than they often get.

I am inspired by the hard work and dedication that so many of our MPs and parliamentary candidates put into their campaigns for the honour of representing local people. A privilege entrusted only to a small few.

It's much easier to criticise others than lead by example. Far more people talk about how they'd put the world to rights if only they were an MP or councillor, but then avoid standing for election themselves or helping support those that do. Few of us may have the time and perhaps fewer the interest.

This is a problem for our democracy and, in particular, our political system. Party membership is at historic lows for many of them. Less than one per cent of UK voters is a member of the Labour, Conservative or Liberal Democrat parties today. This is about a seventy-five per cent drop since 1983. People don't see the value in joining like they used to.

Why is this a problem? For two reasons. The first is that low party membership means political parties have smaller talent pools they can use to select candidates. They are simply fewer people to choose from. I'm not talking about candidates for Parliament alone, but for all offices national and local. This could be solved if there were more independent candidates, but the parties continue to dominate election results.

The second reason this is a problem is because fewer people have a say over a party's leadership and future direction. The people who might please party members may be very different from those who might win elections. Low party membership does the parties and our democracy few favours.

The parties have themselves to blame for the most part. They need to motivate people to join them and take an active part in reinvigorating our national politics. The parties need to reconnect with voters beyond election day alone. This may involve making the case for their relevance for their supporters beyond election day, too.

But let's not avoid closely looking at ourselves. Parties don't run themselves, but through their individual memberships. Many people I speak to are passionate about politics. But they don't become involved because they think it won't make a difference. This defeatism is a major hurdle our democracy must cross and there are no quick solutions to change it overnight.

Citizenship matters. But it's easy to take for granted. I moved from the United States to the UK in 2001 and I've lived in the North East for most of this time. I passed the UK citizenship test in Newcastle and became a British citizen soon afterwards. Few immigration policy and law experts immigrated themselves and this direct knowledge has helped give me an edge over other commentators on migration that has benefited me professionally as a political and legal adviser and scholar.

But we all benefit from actively engaged citizenship. You don't have to be a naturalised British citizen to see its value and importance for our shared political life.

A commitment to public service and the public good helps sustain and reinvigorate our political community. This is not merely good for any one group, but for us all. There are many challenges to be faced and the future of our political parties is only one, and perhaps not even the most important by a long shot.

The lack of available candidates to choose from is almost as bad as the lack of interest in voting for any one of them. It can be tempting to think this is a problem for our political parties to sort out and not you or I.

But it's a problem for all of us that we must confront. My fear is things might get much worse before they improve. John F. Kennedy told Americans to ask not what their country can do for them, but what they can do for their country. These words continue to resonate today more than ever and give us all something to consider seriously.

Labour must keep its eyes on the prize: winning[34]

A party deeply divided. This is how the media portrays Labour and it plays directly into the hands of Cameron and Osborne, providing a welcome distraction from internal Tory battles over Europe.

This image is the product of three things. First, an unexpected general election result. While few predicted a Tory majority, there remains a real disappointment about what might have been. I know many are still coming to terms with a victory that was not to be. We can't rewrite the past, but we risk more problems in future if we don't dust ourselves off and rebuild fast.

Secondly, the leadership election. The decision to hold a longer contest was so lessons could be learned from our election defeat.

34 'Abstaining on the welfare bill was sensible—Labour must keep its eyes on the prize: winning', *LabourList* (21 July 2015).

Instead, far more energy has gone into propping up a favoured candidate to defend Labour in future than holding to account the first one hundred per cent Tory government since Blair's landslide election about eighteen years ago. It's little wonder that the biggest successes thus far in this Parliament have come from the House of Lords led by the formidable Lady Angela Smith of Basildon.

Finally, the Welfare Bill. Harriet Harman's decision was sensible: abstain on the Bill's Second Reading so we can focus attention on crucial amendments ahead of future votes. Not everything in the Bill is objectionable and some it, like creating more apprenticeships, was a part of our election campaign manifesto. Instead of hamstringing the next Labour leader, better to leave options open and pursue meticulous line-by-line scrutiny in committee. Abstaining on the Bill now does not mean letting it pass. Nonetheless, more than twenty per cent of Labour MPs broke the whip voting against the Bill anyway.

These three things have led to deep disagreements about why the election was lost, which candidate is most likely to lose the next election and flaring tempers over the Welfare Bill vote (and a vote we'll soon forget by next month).

Debate is healthy and it can help revive a party in search of self-confidence and fresh ideas but only where this is conducted in a spirit of shared commitment, with Labour's best interests as our focus.

Perhaps our biggest problem is that in an election campaign characterised by a surprising degree of welcome solidarity, too many seem keen to air dirty laundry in public. I don't believe our party is as divided as the Tories and right wing press will tell us, but we must look to ourselves to better control our narrative.

In the 1960s, Ronald Reagan called on his fellow Republicans to honour the 11th Commandment: 'Thou shalt not speak ill of any Republican.' This principle didn't stop Reagan or anyone else from disagreeing with his fellow party members. But it did help keep their eyes on the prize—for whatever their differences, each shared a commitment to winning the next election.

I'm not one to favourably quote Reagan, but Labour can learn lessons from this. We should begin by recognising our own rule: 'Thou shalt not speak ill of any Labour Party candidate.' We should spend far more time airing our disagreements with the Tories than each other. And colleagues should keep in mind that what we say openly about party members can and will be used against us in future elections.

So let's not do the Tories any favours. Our party will only be as divided as we want it to be. Let's keep our eyes on the prize: winning the next election. Please.

Now is time for the real campaign – and time to come together[35]

Jeremy Corbyn is the new Leader of the Labour Party. There should be nothing surprising about it. He has held a commanding lead for much of the leadership campaign that showed no signs of letting up. Yvette Cooper enjoyed a clear surge towards the end, but perhaps too little and too late. Corbyn's victory was never in doubt from the time his campaign well and truly took off – and Stephen Bush deserves credit for seeing this take shape first.

And yet everything is so different. Corbyn was the almost candidate that nearly didn't make it to the leadership ballot scraping through at the last pip. Literally. Whatever he lacks in designer clothing and smooth talking, Corbyn clearly makes up for in his passion and commitment to Labour's democratic socialist roots.

35 'Now time for the real campaign—and time to come together', *LabourList* (14 September 2015).

Corbyn will now face a challenge in moving from backbench rebel since 1983 to frontline politics for the first time. This transition is all the more difficult given he's not only at the top table, but calling the tunes. The principled rebel may find life as Leader of Her Majesty's Most Loyal Opposition difficult given past disloyalties.

During the campaign, I speculated that the real winner of the contest would be neither Corbyn, Cooper, Andy Burnham nor Liz Kendall, but David Cameron. The Tories have increased their lead over Labour since the general election to fourteen points and growing with UKIP starting to fade away on eight per cent and shrinking.

We've heard much speculation about the causes and largely from those who had warned against a Corbyn victory. But I think the biggest danger to Labour's electoral future is not its leader, but its internal struggles. The Tories are divided about issues like the UK's membership in the EU. My biggest concern is that Labour's division can run much deeper than that, if not nipped in the bud fast.

Corbyn can help heal this rift quickly – and he shows every sign that he's ready to do so. Party leadership campaigns can be healthy as different views are aired and challenged. But the battle for leader should end once the votes have been cast and counted. There will be another contest in the future, but it is time all of us came together: whatever our disagreements, they are surely dwarfed by our shared overriding commitment to see Labour win the next general election.

A Corbyn shadow cabinet of a wide range of talent from all sides of the party would help put this principle into practice. This is something I've advised before to make clear overtures to segments of the party that supported other candidates to help end whatever rifts exist. If we don't end our differences, then the Tories will happily expose them and we'll be no better off no matter who you supported during the campaign.

While there were some concerns about women in the shadow cabinet, I think Corbyn has done well to ensure that a majority of posts did not go to men. He is clearly setting out his own vision of leadership with a different view about what constitutes a 'top' role in the Cabinet and he's right that jobs like Shadow Education and Shadow Health are not minor posts. This is all welcome news.

He's also put his own stamp by introducing a new role in Shadow Minister for Mental Health, held by Luciana Berger, and Gloria de Piero is Shadow Minister for Young People and Voter Registration. These are important positions filled by excellent MPs and a delight to see.

Inevitably, the media will exploit any detected rifts however it can. We learned much more about what might go wrong and who won't serve in Corbyn's cabinet than what might go right and who was likely to fill key jobs. Undoubtedly, Corbyn may struggle to keep his fellow MPs onside given his track record of going his own way.

But he's won a commanding victory that cannot be ignored. And we should remember that MPs might have preferred David Miliband, but when the party chose his brother Ed the PLP came around immediately showing impressive solidarity and support for the new leader. Corbyn may surprise again by enjoying a similar reception. The Whips Office under Rosie Winterton does a superb job and her remaining in post is a more significant boost than many may realise.

Jeremy Corbyn wasn't my first preference. But he is the leader of the only political party for me. And so he can count on my support and I hope others will rally around him now, too. Winning back 10 Downing Street is an enormous challenge no matter who is Leader of the Opposition, widely recognised as the most difficult job in politics. That's true for anyone in that position and yes that includes Tony Blair.

Let's not make the job more difficult for Corbyn than it already is. We can each play our part in making the most of the positive energy and clear mandate he has to lead the Labour Party. The leadership campaign was just a warm-up act for the real fight ahead. And we'll need every supporter we can find if we're to have a chance. I'm in. Are you?

Don't let the Northern Powerhouse go the way of the Big Society[36]

No political party wins an election by default. The Conservatives deserve credit for their May victory. Their majority comes with a mandate to spearhead significant changes outlined in their election manifesto. But already the rails are coming off just months after returning to power.

The Big Society is based on a big idea: more voluntary charitable activities can help revitalise local communities. The world need not be divided up into either the public or private sectors. There is a crucial place for the so-called 'third sector' of voluntary and non-profit organisations that can play an important role in society. One Labour MP told me at the time: 'I wish we thought of it first.' Social capital should be promoted – so what's not to like?

But we know what happened next. The Big Society became the Big Flop. You could say the Government made a pig's ear of it, but this may be misinterpreted.

David Cameron claimed the Big Society was about supporting the voluntary sector because it could be more effective at delivering

---

36 'Don't let the Northern Powerhouse go the way of the Big Society', *The Journal* (Newcastle) (25 September 2015).

desperately sought after help to those most in need. Instead, it was really about a hope that someone – anyone – would magically fill the large gaping holes left by government cuts.

The result was unsurprising. Four or more relaunches and still the Big Society is nowhere in sight. Many services have remained curtailed or cut with nothing to take their place. The Prime Minister expected that removing the state's reach would create a space others would rush out to fill. Some have, including faith-based organisations who all deserve our continued thanks for the brilliant work they do making life that much better for the many who need a helping hand.

But things have never taken off how the Government expected. A potentially big idea left to wither on the vine. Perhaps the only surprise is not that it has flopped, but that it has not yet been officially dropped.

It's worth reflecting briefly on why it failed. Yes, there was something mischievous with a government willing to gamble on pulling funding for public services in the hope that unknown others would do the same work for free.

Yet this is also a government that has praised individualism over community solidarity. Claims of 'we're all in this together' rang hollow as the new economy sees the same winners and losers in a market that never learns its lessons. People increasingly look out for themselves and their personal material well-being first. We ask 'what's in it for me?' and not 'what's best for us all?' They are not to blame. As community solidarity recedes, self-interest is all that remains unless something is done to reverse the continuing decline.

I'm worried that another of the Government's big ideas – creating a Northern Powerhouse – might go the same way as the Big Society and for the same reasons.

Devolving power from Westminster to regions. Greater prosperity for the North of England linked with greater investment. What's not to like?

Something not a world away was thought up by Labour first. Plans for a local regional assembly were also soundly defeated as everyone in the North East knows. The people were consulted and they did not approve of what they saw.

The deadline for North East Combined Authority to put forward their plans for devolved powers and how they'd be used passed earlier this month. Devolution brings with it powers to raise and spend resources with greater power over areas like transport, homes, planning and health. The idea is this will help different authorities prosper by developing competition between them. The waiting game is now on to see who's in and who's left out.

When it comes to regional devolution, we're not all in this together. Greater Manchester got the green light first. A region already at a competitive advantage was given booster rockets. And the news gets worse: in his first budget George Osborne listed areas such as Sheffield, Liverpool, Leeds, West Yorkshire and even Cornwall which will be lined up for devolution powers. Basically everybody but us. The North East looked more like it was in a Northern Doghouse than powerhouse.

A sticking point for regions like ours is the Government's insistence each has an elected mayor. I've voiced my concerns before. If devolution deals are agreed with plans for an elected mayor, there would be an unelected mayor imposed first – if Manchester is a sign of things to come – to serve for months if not years as we wait for a change in the law bringing in elected mayors. To accept elected mayors is not to get them, or at least not yet.

These elected mayors are supposed to become little Boris Johnsons throughout the land, as if this is what is needed. They would replace the Police and Crime Commissioners. This could mean as yet unelected mayors replacing elected PCCs.

After stinging criticisms of their plans for PCCs and the low turnout nationally for their election, this looks like a clear admission by the Government they should never have done it – even though some like Northumbria's Vera Baird and Durham's Ron Hogg have done brilliantly.

Some liken the introduction of regional mayors to the American 'model.' But that would break the mould. The better analogy is to Governors. Mayors are for cities like London and Middlesbrough, not vast regions like the whole of the North East of England.

But this is a Government that isn't very good at learning from the US where it can. Americans have been practicing devolution since its founding. A federal republic, its fifty states are empowered to raise money and manage programmes in all the areas the Government has in mind for regions and much more.

A crucial difference is that states like California and Connecticut may have very different sizes, but each plays by the same rules. The one has no more powers than the other to manage transport or housing policy under their authority. This equal playing field allows each to compete on fairer terms.

The big risk to devolution's success – and that of the Northern Powerhouse – is some regions will receive bespoke deals and at different intervals. There will be no fair playing field and some have started while others must wait. This gives an advantage to those in front like Manchester while everyone else plays catch up.

The Government should give more care to getting right the launch of this important programme rather than rushing in – only to regret it later like it has done with the Big Society flop and one-term PCCs. The early indications aren't promising.

The friends that Jeremy Corbyn never knew he had[37]

Jeremy Corbyn has given us all something to talk about. There can be no denying his victory in the Labour leadership contest was not foreseen by anybody – including his most vocal supporters. No one expected the sheer scale of the vote he achieved and this is a credit to his campaign and message to the people who mattered – Labour activists.

It is also clear politics will continue to be interesting for some time yet. Since the last general election, the Labour Party has doubled in size: more people joined the party since May than are in the Conservative Party. The growth in members and supporters is surely a good thing, although it will be crucial to turn them into a powerful electoral asset – and overturn the bruising defeats of 2010 and 2015.

The shock factor of Corbyn's rise to become Leader of the Opposition has led to much discussion about how this might all become undone and fall away like a bright flash in a pan. All attention has been directed towards his opponents within the party and beyond.

While no one can be criticised for not seeing this election result coming, these predictions of imminent doom can sometimes sound not like predictions but rather hope that things might go sour fast – and so pundits might say they weren't too off if a more expected face were to take over.

But there's no sign of this coming, and that's a good thing. As leader, Corbyn should have an opportunity to set out his stall. The now much-expanded party membership did overwhelmingly

37 'Valuable friends Labour leader did not know he had', *The Journal* (Newcastle) (6 November 2015): 23.

support Corbyn's message and they are unlikely to fall under the spell of a different tune anytime soon.

I think we have spent too much time over-analysing the opponents of the Opposition leader – and too little time reflecting on his friends. And I'm not talking out of context about who Corbyn has or has not called a friend in the several decades he has served as a Member of Parliament.

Corbyn faces many challenges, now all well-rehearsed, in improving Labour's electoral position in Scotland, working effectively with Labour MPs who mostly supported other candidates and taking on what is genuinely the single most difficult job in politics – serving as Leader of the Opposition.

Not unlike any politician there is much that can go wrong – but there is also much that can go right. The great philosopher of statecraft Niccolò Machiavelli argued that expertise alone won't make a great statesman – it also takes winning the favour of lady luck. And that brings me to a house of ladies and lords.

Perhaps the biggest surprise – yes even larger than his meteoric rise – is Corbyn's secret weapon: his outstanding team on the Labour front bench in the House of Lords. Led by the formidable Baroness Angela Smith, the Labour Lords have been able to achieve what the Labour MPs might only wish for – victory after victory halting the rushed, ill-thought-out passing of new Bills that have sent Cameron and Osborne back to the drawing board time and time again. The Government has suffered twenty defeats since May alone. And Baroness Smith and her team have achieved this more by hard graft than the graces of Lady Luck.

The most impressive is their forcing the Government to shelve – at least for now – a proposed £4.4bn in cuts to tax credits that support the working poor. Needless to say, the Government acted furiously. How dare the unelected Peers tell elected MPs what to do? And shouldn't they have abstained on a money matter?

The truth is such arguments stink like a large pile of festering manure on a hot steaming day. The House of Lords has only decided that the Government should consider their proposals more closely. The Commons may be like a House of Cards, but the Lords is more a House of Scrutiny. They bring experience and expertise – often from their time serving governments, major public or commercial bodies and include a healthy number of distinguished academics from leading universities – that enriches law-making.

When governments attack the integrity and distinctive function of the House of Lords they likewise undermine their own. It is our elected leaders that give support to the growing number of Lords, not least the record-breaking high number created under Cameron's Governments. They have an authority that comes from Cameron and others helping to put them in their place.

And the thought that anything money-related must be rubber stamped by the Lords goes far beyond the present convention applied to budget bills – for if granted, the Lords could vote on nothing at all that came with a price tag. That's not how Parliament can and should work.

The Labour Lords have been impressively effective in getting the party's views across – that is proving invaluable to Team Corbyn as the victories begin to stack up with more and more accomplishments achieved.

The Labour Lords are the friends that Corbyn perhaps never knew he had – or could begin to rely on to deliver. After all Corbyn is a well-known opponent of an unelected chamber. Nor is he alone: the Labour Party's 2015 General Election manifesto committed it to supporting the creation of an elected senate to replace the House of Lords.

But the politics we have is not always our ideal. Few might conjure up an unelected legislative body these days, but it is what we have – and it is a surprisingly effective and welcome chamber.

I doubt Corbyn (or I) will change our views about the need for parliamentary reforms, but I also have little doubt that he may come to see the Labour Lords as a powerful ally in Parliament. This is no unhappy union or marriage of convenience, but political reality. And so often it can yield surprising results – like this.

A house divided cannot stand. Can all these new groups help Labour win?[38]

Over one hundred days has passed since Jeremy Corbyn became leader of the Labour Party. There are some real achievements to show for it already – not least Labour's victory on tax credit cuts for working families. This was a welcome holiday treat and not least for everyone that benefited.

But being Her Majesty's Most Loyal Opposition is no fairy tale. It's often more, well, 'Grimm', where the only happy ending is to form a government – and the pathway to power can often become a road to oblivion. No party has the right to govern if it merely waits its turn in the queue. Any such opportunity must be won – and there are costs.

We will soon see some significant, long-term consequences decided by this Parliament that we need to be ready for. While both the UK's population and Cameron's appointments to the House of Lords continues to rise and rise, the Government is committed to cutting 50 of 650 MPs from the House of Commons. That's a reduction of roughly nine per cent. All in the name of making constituencies more 'fair' by their catchment areas becoming more equitable in population sizes.

38 'A house divided cannot stand. Can all these new groups help Labour win?' *LabourList* (30 December 2015).

But this isn't only about redrawing constituency boundaries, but rewriting the political map altogether – and in a way that will favour Tory election victories. The upshot is that Labour will need to up its game should these changes go through. Only can Tories confuse 'fairness' with an election system designed to make Labour Governments less likely.

The Labour Party's team in Parliament has done well – perhaps surprisingly well – given its being an Opposition and not in power. A key success story has been Labour's especially effective front bench team in the House of Lords led by Baroness Angela Smith.

Factionalism has been a problem for the Left for some time. And the media loves to exploit any divisions it can conjure up. First it was the Blairites versus the Brownites. Then attention turned to the Miliband brothers. Now all eyes are on Corbyn's supporters and their critics.

And now there are the new groups. We have Momentum and most recently Open Labour joining Blue Labour, Labour First, Labour Together and Progress. (These groups only seem to grow in number – and there may well be more at this rate by 2020.) That's a lot of emails and voices clamouring to be heard.

We hear things about what Labour is really supposed to be about 'in its DNA' and so forth that undoubtedly contribute to a healthy debate, but many party members may well get confused about what Labour's position is on policies versus what any of these other groups endorse. And the more members and the public become confused, the more difficult success at the ballot box may become over time.

The early poll numbers are in and they need to improve – although we should all now be wary about what they really tell us. But the signs thus far strongly suggest adopting a clearer message – especially on some issues like the economy.

A house divided cannot stand, as Abraham Lincoln once

warned. Nor can a fractured political party take on the Herculean task of moving from opposition to 10 Downing Street. It's about more than simply winning votes, but public confidence – it is much easier to say than do.

So let me come out in favour of a different group – the Labour Party. There is much of value in our new and existing groups for reinvigorating our party that makes for a healthy democracy. I think it's great for people to come together to help plan how we can build a progressive future – it will take all the people power we can muster because the Tories aren't going to hand over the keys to 10 Downing Street on a plate.

But it is also easy to lose sight of the main prize. I'm not a party member to see a faction or two score well. I'm in this to see a Labour government. If I wanted to only protest but not contribute to governing, then perhaps never joining a party is the way to go. But I'm not willing to stand by and let the Tories make Britain less great when so many today need Labour in power.

If our growing number of pro-Labour groups helps us achieve a Labour government, then that's brilliant. I'm a member of most of these groups and don't discourage others from doing likewise. We're all on the same side however sometimes this can be overlooked. But the end game is not the promotion of one group to the detriment of the party – the Labour Party must come first and not only some ideologically pure vision of when it is or is not 'Labour', whatever that happens to mean.

This Christmas all I want is to build a foundation for a future Labour victory. Not by taking Labour 'back' or backwards, but by moving us all forward together. The challenges we face today are different and will continue to evolve. Our strength is in our shared determination to build Labour and our growing membership. It's time to start planning to create the best government that Britain needs to have.

This isn't something Old Saint Nick could have left in any stocking last week, but sometimes the best gifts are the ones we forge by our own hands. Rebuilding a Labour Party that can reclaim government is no easy task and we need to keep the debate about how we can collectively achieve this goal without collapsing into a thousand factions.

Why the arguments for scrapping Trident don't add up[39]

Theresa May's first major success in Parliament was winning a vote to renew Trident – and continuing Britain's nuclear weapons programme.

Trident is understandably controversial. Nothing highlights that fact more than when the Prime Minister said she would use it, if required. No one wants such a weapon to be deployed, but should it be retained to collect dust?

Most striking to me is the case against Trident. Arguments for its rejection are weak at best and far from conclusive.

Last month, Ronnie Campbell MP told *The Journal* that Trident had become irrelevant for two reasons. The first is, as Campbell says, 'the supposed threat from the Soviet Union is now gone.'

It is unclear why this threat is thought to have been 'supposed' and not actual. There is precious little doubt among military historians that the Soviet Union did have nuclear weapons aimed at several Western targets, including the UK. The Soviet Union did pose a threat at least insofar as it had our country in the scope of its most deadly weapon.

39 'Why the arguments for scrapping Trident just didn't add up', *The Journal* (Newcastle) (12 August 2016).

Today, it is clear that, while the USSR may have come to a political end, there remains a renewed Russia. Putin has been actively reclaiming the geopolitical place of the USSR in today's world, but under a Russian flag.

Yet even if Putin's Russia is not seen as a threat, the argument that we should scrap a permanent weapons system in response to a perceived temporary lull in hostilities risks reckless short-termism that no defence policy should accept. Nor is any one country the sole possible source of any future threat. Doing otherwise puts all the eggs in one basket.

A second reason why Campbell opposes Trident is because it 'is useless against the real and present danger from terrorism.' But it is unclear from what evidence this comment comes from. If it is not evidenced from the latest national security briefings, then this is a significant gap. It is also unclear whether there is only one 'danger' at any one time.

While suicide attacks by lone individuals or working in small groups have made recent headlines, they do not exhaust the threats that Britain faces. Anyone who thinks that conventional military tactics with boots on the ground can't be found in conflict zones today neglects Russia's annexation of Crimea in Ukraine for a start.

This aggressive action by Russia in Ukraine is notable because Ukraine unilaterally disarmed its nuclear weapons system – a disastrous move that Trident opponents wish for Britain. While it is highly unlikely this weapons system would ever have been used to prevent Russia marching into Crimea, it is at least as unlikely that Russia would never have crossed the border had Ukraine retained its full defence system.

This is a case of 'what if?' – and the problem with such a gamble is sometimes you get it wrong. Like what happened in Ukraine.

Another concern is that the weapon system is not fully independent. Opponents claim its use requires cooperation from others, like the United States.

But when was it ever a good thing for any state to act alone free from any constraint or discussion with others? States should always act in accordance with international law – and so not fully independently anyway. Besides, to say Trident is not independently triggered is no argument against using it at all. International law exists because there is agreement across states about how they should interact. This does not so much constrain the use of law than it does provide its normative and symbolic significance. When the world speaks, we should listen.

Others say that Trident is useless against smaller, dispersed aggressors so it should stop. However, global threats exist as larger, conventional aggressors too. If you design a defensive system for only one, you miss the other – at potentially horrific cost. Advocates for renewing Trident do not want it maintained forever as a good thing – most want to see an orchestrated multilateral end to nuclear weapons. I'm more certain that I want to live in a nuclear weapons-free world than my wish to see Trident continually renewed. My support is not set in stone and I am open to changing my mind.

But the arguments from critics can be disappointing. A final example about costs makes this point clear.

Critics highlight the fact that since Trident does not get used it must be a waste of money. The billions spent on maintaining the system can and should be spent on something else.

This misses a key point: that the cost is justified not by the failure to be used, but its success in not having to be used. Britain will not become less of a target without Trident.

Ending Trident does not mean an easy cash flow into other public services or tax cuts. Not every penny is spent on nuclear material or hardware. Many of the pounds invested in Trident are earned by the hardworking men and women who have built and maintained Trident. Ending it means cutting jobs – and thousands of them.

I have not set out a positive case for Trident. Instead, I have considered the case for getting shot of it. None of it seems conclusive.

This is not to say that Trident should be renewed repeatedly far into the future.

But those that want it stopped need to think again.

It's easy to protest what you don't like. However, the public deserves better – and, hopefully, leading to a world without weapons of mass destruction.

Why our lack of trust in politicians and public figures is damaging us all[40]

Trust is political gold dust. Hard to acquire and easy to squander. Once it's gone, it becomes even more difficult to build up. And don't our politicians know it?

Many decisions are made on trust. Leaders who win our confidence also receive our votes. At the last general election, voters had more trust in the Tories to lead the country – fuelled by negative campaigning about how their opponents did not deserve trust.

For all the promises that 'Remain' offered of a brighter future, a general mistrust of 'the Establishment', from seasoned politicians to CEOs of Britain's most successful companies, contributed to a Brexit vote. Pro-EU voices were not trusted to put Britain's interests first.

40 'Why losing trust in political leaders damages all of us', *The Journal* (Newcastle) (26 August 2016): 27.

Trust colours how we perceive politicians, too. Liberal Democrats were almost fatally damaged, not by their decision to join a governing coalition with the Tories but for reneging on their promises about tuition fees. When they agreed that university fees for students should be kept – and be trebled to £9,000 per year – this damaged public trust in the party.

Anyone looking back on their 2015 election campaign remembers two things. First is that every candidate held large signs with promises on tuition fees that were soon broken. Second is the famous television advert with Nick Clegg claiming 'no more broken promises' – only to go on and do so on tuition fees.

Notably, the trust that was lost is not only among those who voted for the party – it was amongst the public at large. Trust is something both friends and opponents can share even if they disagree on much else.

The recent #traingate curiosity is an illuminating case study. Labour leader Jeremy Corbyn has built an enormous store of trust among his many supporters for his opposition to the Iraq War and the continuation of Trident. Whatever else his critics might charge, he has been trusted to act in principled ways.

This is why the disputed incident on his train journey to Newcastle for a leadership debate against challenger Owen Smith MP is so potentially damaging. It is because it has the potential to weaken his greatest strength: the trust friends and foes have in the positions he supports. Decades of dedicated service can be brought into question from a brief clip.

And as usual it was not what took place that has done the most damage, but how it has been handled. While this one event does not appear to have moved the goalposts for either Corbyn or Owen, the first signs are that trust and public confidence in the leadership has not been enhanced. Winning over much-needed voters is made more difficult by a one-off media storm that challenges trust.

This feeds into something deeper. Our lives are built on trust. No child can survive without the support of someone else. While we may become more independent over time, we also become interdependent. Our reliance on others does not end with growing out of infancy. Trust does not become less important over time.

Jeremy Corbyn is right to say we're heading for a new kind of politics – even if it is not kinder or gentler. Ours is a cynical time of mistrust of each other. This breeds antagonism and division. The terrible online trolling and abuse seen in recent years is a predictable result.

So what to do for a public that mistrusts elites? We place our hopes and dreams in their opponents.

Donald Trump's greatest asset for Republicans is that he's not a Republican politician. Likewise, Corbyn's best attribute for his many Labour supporters is that no Labour MP has voted against his party more often. In becoming the anti-Republican or anti-Labour they somehow rise above them to become a purer or at least better brand than all the rest – who are tarred for being more of the same.

If this outcome looks bleak, it's because for many people that is how the future looks – bleak. Parents don't expect their children to do better than they did. Young adults get on the housing ladder later and later – and through no fault of their own. A land of plenty looks more and more like a land of plenty for someone else. And I've said nothing of financial insecurity or immigration.

Politicians and the media have much to answer for in how we got to where we are. Daily attacks and cheap stunts may score political points today, but they damage the wider institution over time benefiting few of us.

Yet we the People have the Government we deserve. If left as a political class, we can all continue to mistrust their every move – or we can do something constructive about it.

John F. Kennedy was right that we should ask more about what we can do for our community instead of what can others do for us. I don't mean to downplay the importance of a social safety net or ignore the common values and ideals that make us a community.

But the most damaging thing of all arising from the increasing lack of trust in public officials is that fewer of us are inspired to work in the public interest for the betterment of our community and our great country. We can have public figures to believe in again – but they will come from you and me, not from nowhere.

And I have hope. The incredible achievements of Team GB at the Rio Olympics was inspirational. We don't need medals to fix our political system. But we do need more citizens with a willingness to do so.

To the winners of the big votes go the spoils – but now we have to grapple with the consequences[41]

The year 2016 proved to be one of surprises from start to finish. There were triumphs ranging from the fabulous success of Britain's outstanding Olympians and Paralympians in Brazil – winning a record number of medals – to London electing Sadiq Khan as its first Muslim Mayor.

The past year has also brought much sad news of celebrity deaths. From David Bowie and Prince to Glenn Frey and Merle Haggard in the music world, and from Muhammad Ali to Elie Wiesel in the world beyond music – it's as if we're all entering a new, strange world marked more by what is missing than what is there.

41 'A year in which folk suffered shock after shock', *The Journal* (30 December 2016): 21.

Somewhere in between the triumphs and sadness lie two great surprises: Brexit and Trump. For some readers one or both will be seen as a kind of triumph, yet others find only grief. A remarkable range of emotions for capturing something that hasn't happened, or at least not yet.

Theresa May can say 'Brexit means Brexit' all she likes. Britain is still as much a part of the EU today as it was on June 23. The only things that have changed is just about everyone who wanted Britain to Vote Leave ran for the hills as soon as the verdict was announced. This was not about 'taking back control,' but leaving one giant mess for somebody else to clean up.

First gone was Nigel Farage who quit as UKIP leader. From his Twitter account, it appears he cares much more for living in Trump's America than Britain post-Brexit. This really should give his game away. Then Boris Johnson decided against standing for leader of the Tories. Next Michael Gove quit running to lead the Tories within days of launching his bid. It makes you wonder – seriously wonder – why they fought for Brexit in the first place. None seem to have much, if any, interest in actually making it happen.

Some argue that the shock wins of Brexit and Trump have one thing in common – the public have had enough of elites and are instead looking to upset the apple cart. Both campaigns had something of an insurgency about them in taking on an establishment and aiming their fire at a political elite – whether in Brussels or Washington, DC – that was untrustworthy.

Of course, there is more than a grain of truth in this. Politicians are held in lower esteem than journalists – perhaps even columnists who write about politicians. When one MP gets embroiled in a problem, this can tarnish all MPs. This is not unique to Parliament – an unhelpful waiter can damage the reputation of the finest restaurant.

An age of deference to politicians and the media's less scrupulous eyes once upon a time is now an age of bitter cynicism amid a wide range of news sources in print and online. If we are uncomfortable with what is reported in one source, we can go to something less scrupulous until we reach an alternative reality providing a comfort zone.

Yet this cynicism has become a kind of postmodernism gone very bad. It is one thing to challenge arguments and demand evidence, but it is another to do so without any respect for argumentation or genuine evidence.

When Brexit said leaving the EU would mean restricting immigration, this was not strictly speaking true and they should have known it. We can leave the EU but still be part of the EU free movement rules that come with membership of the European Economic Area (EEA) – each is part of a different legal arrangement. Norway is an example of one such non-EU country with EU free movement. The referendum paper mentioned the EU, but not the EEA.

Similarly, when Trump said he had a foolproof plan for defeating Isis, but then couldn't say anything about it – beyond that it would be 'great' – because then the enemy would know it is simply breathtaking.

So while I agree that supporters of Brexit and Trump sent a message about rejecting the status quo, I don't accept the pollsters did all that bad a job. The real common thread connecting these two shock victories was the certainty that neither would happen. We were all so sure the UK would stay in the EU and that Hillary Clinton would enter the White House that too many of those who were so sure stayed home. If everyone who was for Remain had turned out, Britain would not be scratching its collective head wondering a full six months on precisely what, if anything, Brexit means. It's just gobbledygook so far. And if voter turnout was higher in the US, we'd be talking about Clinton instead of Trump.

In short, the big political surprises of 2016 were a result of some not taking the outcome for granted. The winner of every election is not who wins over the most voters, but who gets the most votes. Voters and votes are different things. The side that wanted victory most got it and there is a kind of natural justice about it.

But Brexit and Trump have more in common than this. They also represent the risks of taking a punt. Did you hear what Theresa May's government was up to recently? Probably not, because they are still sitting around a white board trying to figure out what Brexit means. Their best idea thus far is to propose a 'Great Repeal Bill' that will neither be great or repeal. It will freeze EU law in time so we can literally spend years repealing or amending legislation one by one. While Europe will have moved on in ten years' time, we might still find ourselves bound by outdated European rules because our government today simply doesn't know what else to do next. This is anything but control.

During Trump's first visit to the White House, he found out – for the first time – that he had to fill jobs not only in his Cabinet, but throughout the whole of the West Wing. Until a few weeks ago, he didn't know this. Next month he becomes Commander-in-Chief of the world's most deadly military power. This is not a good omen he is genuinely prepared for the office he is to take up.

None of the above are reasons against supporting either lest I be accused of having sour grapes. To the winner goes the spoils. But I hope that readers of whatever political inclination will agree with me that in 2017 let's view public service as the public good it is – and treat it with the sober seriousness it deserves. Our democracy is worth it.

The three reasons why June might still turn out to be the end of May[42]

This has been a difficult few days for our Labour Party. With significant gains in local elections, Theresa May might feel confident calling for a general election this June nearly one year after the EU referendum. The Conservative Party enjoys a double-digit lead in the polls over Labour and what remained of public support for UKIP is now facing collapse, to the extent that they bizarrely fled their own press conference. Thankfully, our losses were not as great as some had predicted. No one should underestimate the hard work and determination of Labour councillors past and present with our supporters to take on the Tories – and not least ourselves.

We have three more reasons to be cheerful that June could become the end of May:

Economy

The Tories score best on the economy by promising voters that their money is in safe hands. This issue is a cornerstone of their support – and to lose public trust could be a game changer.

Since 2010, the Tories have vowed to reduce the national debt and deficit, for which they blamed Labour but, more than six years later, the national debt has actually grown to more than eighty per cent of GDP – higher than at any time under New Labour. As chancellor, George Osborne borrowed more in his half decade than Gordon Brown did over ten years.

Our economic recovery remains fragile and lower unemployment figures has been managed in part through a surge in low-skilled – and often low paid – work and zero hour contracts

42 'The three reasons why June might still turn out to be the end of May', *LabourList* (10 May 2017).

since the Tories took power. We in Labour need to grasp that the Tories are vulnerable on the economy given their record – and they cannot assume voters will give them a free pass. Labour needs to hammer home the message that May's rhetoric isn't Britain's reality.

Immigration

David Cameron promised to reduce net migration to the tens of thousands – and May renewed this pledge on Monday. Voters supported the Tories over other parties as best positioned to control the country's borders.

But, again, their record does not support the rhetoric. Since 2010, net migration has hit record highs – and has been much higher than at any point under New Labour. This is a straightforward point: that Tories talk about less migration, but the reality is the opposite. As my research revealed, the only drop in the latest migration statistics may be down to more British citizens leaving and not coming back. Net migration counts everyone coming in or out of the UK the same way – a thousand professional workers are treated no differently than a thousand students. This is poor management.

But net migration also includes British citizens and we should say this: any Government's immigration strategy that can be met by encouraging more UK citizens to leave is not worth having. We need to let this fact get in the way of Tory rhetoric. Four out of five voters don't believe the Tories will do what they say on immigration. We need to remind them again and again, letting the Tory record speak for itself.

And we need two more things. First, we should prioritise reducing impacts of migration through a migration impacts reduction fund. Tories confuse having fewer migrants with having less impact from migration. They are wrong. Fewer migrants in A&E is more likely to mean fewer doctors than patients – increasing waiting times still higher. We need to get this message heard and loudly.

Secondly, we need to be engaged with the public. Let's promise to launch a new advisory group on citizenship that can get people talking what being a British citizen means for them. We've been there before in 2004 leading to a citizenship test sat over two million times, but without a single consultation or focus group to see whether it really has helped support integration.

My research has shown it hasn't and may even be having the opposite effect. Let's bring the public in to rethink the chaotic, complex and divisive immigration rules made in their name that have done little to win confidence and caused much damage and distrust. We can do better. Let's relaunch an impacts reduction fund that the Tories cut and a national conversation on citizenship that the Tories seem afraid to have.

The Ghost of 2015

The Tories are also haunted by a ghost of 2015 – in the form of possible prosecutions of thirty or more Conservative MPs and election agents. If only one investigation of a sitting Tory MP proceeded to a conviction then this could be highly damaging.

It surely does not help to have the shadow of possible prosecutions hanging over Tory candidates during a national election campaign. We need to remind voters that May's snap election is a knee-jerk response to possible prosecutions of her party's members for breaking election rules to win seats. This should not be rewarded by voters. Especially when wrongdoing is being denied.

In short, May's big lead rests on shaky foundations of a questionable record across key voter concerns like the economy, immigration and possible Tory Party charges relating to the last general election. Labour is already quickly closing the gap. A Brexit divorce bill of €100 billion won't help the Tories either. May's party is more vulnerable than many think – even on their key issues of the economy and immigration.

Getting the message out won't win an election by itself. But failing to exploit gaping holes in the Tory's policy armour won't make victory any easier.

If the public really does lose all faith in its politicians, where do we go then?[43]

Donald Trump didn't happen by accident. Politicians are not held in the high esteem they once were. In ancient times, those believed best able to rule were either born or held special knowledge for it. Plato argued individuals were born of different characters like metals ranging from gold and silver to bronze. Only those of a 'gold' character had the right stuff, but they also required special insight – they we kings who should be philosophers.

Few believe most politicians are made of gold or philosophically rich – and what was once a status of great esteem is held by many today somewhere around tabloid journalism. Or lower.

The political classes share much blame for this. The few that have been found out in scandals or questionable use of taxpayers' money create a large dark stain on the many that do no such things. Politicians contest for more than our votes, but also our trust. This trust is more easily lost than gained.

It gets worse. Ours is an adversarial system. The courts of law and political opinion are plays where what is true is whatever survives being challenged. Each advocates for their side against the other. The result for our politics in Britain is a culture of taking sides – mine against yours, one against others and so on. It's not always easy to see what they are taking sides about as our globalised world becomes increasingly complex.

43 'If the public really does lose all faith in its politicians, where do we go then?' *The Journal* (27 May 2017): 53.

At a recent public lecture, I was asked by someone in the audience about why should the Government allow in any migrant without a job. My answer was simply that some of the migrants might be the spouses and children of working migrants. 'Yes, of course' was the reply from the crowd, but it shows that some big issues aren't always so simple.

These delicate nuances don't go very far in winning debates in an adversarial system. You will only hear about overall migration numbers, but rarely the detail of how this might be managed through a system of different tiered visas because, well, such minutiae can require travelling with care. Few have much time for that, unfortunately.

And so we have political classes offering ideas big on vision and little on specifics about our society's most lofty vision for the future where each side claims the other is not only making a mistake, but possibly entering into wickedness.

Little wonder there is traction for change. Something or someone different that rises above this. Offering bold visions with authority that can win our trust.

For many decades, a growing number of American politicians have claimed if the public wants virtuous leaders it should turn its back on 'career' politicians and choose captains of industry found in the business world. This is because they get things done rather than talk about getting things done that don't happen or go to plan. Or so they say.

Donald Trump is the logical conclusion of this alternative to politics as usual in all its gory mess. His supporters trusted him to help make America great again and show how deals can really be done – after all, he claimed to be the world's greatest deal-maker as a property tycoon.

But oh how different the worlds of business and government really are. In Trump's corporate bubble, he is not only a king but a dictator. Like he did on reality television, he was an executive who made decisions on hiring and firing, consulting only when he wanted to with only those he wanted to consult with. He was the boss on top.

Now he's in government and struggling. He's still an executive and has decisions to make, but he cannot exercise the control he has in his business empire. Trump might be at the top of a hierarchy, but the President is head of only one of the three branches of government. He cannot get his way on everything just because he wants to. As Trump has learned, the courts and Congress have a say – and a veto. This is a new world he needs to get used to fast and isn't doing so.

These checks on power are there for a reason. One is that it helps prevent abuses as one branch provides oversight on another. A second is that – unlike some of Trump's failed business dealings – successful governments cannot go bankrupt. Trump's firms have gone bust multiple times, but American government must go on. The kinds of risks acceptable – even dissolution – for one are unacceptable for the other, or at least if you think it is unacceptable for a country to want to collapse into political mush.

Furthermore, America is a democracy even if it's not operating in the way many would expect a democracy to function. The people have a say and their opinions matter – and this works much differently than in most firms.

Trump has struggled with this. He and his supporters have commented about wanting to sack anyone in the civil service that doesn't like his policies as something worse than unpatriotic.

But when you can't just hire whoever you want for every role based on ideological purity, there will be give and take between those elected and their support teams that can highlight the problems located in the missing details somewhere within bold vision statements. This is not insubordination but a reality check.

The Russia affair is another example of where Trump struggles. As with Watergate, serious allegations about the conduct of the winning side of a Presidential election have emerged, including an independent special prosecutor being fired by the winning candidate. If you're a CEO, then stopping unwanted committees by snooping on colleagues might be acceptable. But if you're President, you only make it worse.

Trump is quickly becoming the poster boy for why putting a businessman hellbent on operating a business-like model for government doesn't work.

Yet the lessons here are not that the business world has nothing to offer running government, but rather it is not a case of either/or. Governments can't go bust and must be more risk averse. Their shareholders are effectively all of us. But they can operate more efficiently and be more responsive to shifting economic and political landscapes.

However, the biggest risk is that if the public loses faith in its politicians and then, through Trump, its business leaders where else might it turn?

For my last regular column at *The Journal*, let me offer two final thoughts. The first is that we will get the politicians we deserve. If we don't like what we see, we should take more responsibility for that – and this includes taking up public service.

The second thought is that it's right to call out opponents as wrong, but important to recognise all are committed to a common good. It can be easily lost in our adversarial system that we're all in this together, but in terms of our democracy we really are.

It's easy to find excuses for inaction or pointing fingers at others, but in a democracy we are empowered to be the change we want for our communities.

The noble gift of public service should be celebrated much more than it is for campaigners this election – I hope more are inspired to become involved.

Boris and Gove's treatment of British mum in Iran shows how they betray our citizens[44]

Does anyone need convincing that Boris Johnson and Michael Gove care more for their own careers than the national interest?

First we have the 'gaffe.' Nazanin Zaghari-Ratcliffe has been in an Iranian prison since April 2016. Held in solitary confinement, she was imprisoned for five years after a closed trial for allegedly attempting to overthrow the Government, which she strenuously denies. Nazanin has been subjected to lengthy interrogations and denied regular access to her young daughter.

Johnson, the foreign secretary, made a bad situation much worse telling MPs that she was 'teaching people journalism' – her family claim she was on holiday. Nazanin was dragged back to court a few days later where she was told she may face new criminal charges extending her prison sentence for an additional sixteen years.

Any competent minister would realise the gravity of the mistake, withdraw these comments and issue a correction with full apology. Not so with Boris. He takes no responsibility for his words or their effects. Instead, Boris blames others for taking his remarks 'taken out of context' and leaving them 'misconstrued' rather than admit he got it wrong.

Understandably, Zaghari-Ratcliffe is reported by her husband to be 'angry at the original comments, angry at the footage of

44 'Boris and Gove's treatment of British mum in Iran shows they betray our citizens', *LabourList* (13 November 2017).

avoiding the question' not least because it could treble her time in prison for crimes she denies.

In normal times, no Prime Minister could leave such a grievous deed unpunished and would proceed to an immediate sacking. But these are not normal times and Theresa May is fast becoming the weakest PM in living memory. Virtually silent and hapless like the victim in her own horror show, a government run by zombies on autopilot.

And who should be the only man in Britain to come to Boris's defence? None other than his backstabber-in-chief Michael Gove! When asked about Nazanin's case and why she was in Iran, Gove said 'I don't know,' thereby pouring more fuel on the fire for the Iranian authorities who appear ready to use these remarks in increasing a terrible miscarriage of justice against a British citizen. The carelessness, the lack of compassion and failure to stand up for British citizens is breathtaking and beyond contempt.

So what brings Boris and Gove together to defend the indefensible? The answer is they both realise they share a common fate and that these irresponsible comments about Nazanin are, for them, a mere sideshow. Boris and Gove are two rats on a sinking ship sticking closely together with eyes on becoming its captain at almost any cost.

A 1,500 word memo penned by the duo during the summer recess and delivered to Gavin Barwell, May's chief of staff has been leaked. In their memo, Boris and Gove issue instructions to May on how Brexit should be run issuing several demands – effectively, Cabinet ministers holding the prime minister to ransom.

One way to describe this outrageous political stunt was how the *Daily Mail* put it – Boris and Gove were putting the country ahead of personal ambitions creating 'an invincible double-act' in any future Tory leadership contest. Anyone who thinks there's anything invincible about Boris or Gove forgets everything that happened in the Tory's last leadership election – and everything about politics where nothing can be taken for granted.

There is an alternative explanation for why Boris and Gove are coming together despite their very public falling out. It's got nothing to do with putting Britain first, but everything to do with 'taking back control' for themselves at the expense of everyone or everything else. Brexit talks aren't going well at all. Instead of trade deals being the 'easiest in history' to make, talks between the UK and EU haven't moved past the first post with eighteen months left and counting. Thus far, none of the promises made by Vote Leave have been delivered as the EU and UK businesses begin to prepare for a No Deal – and no win – scenario.

As cabinet ministers, Boris and Gove can wish to have done things differently but share in collective responsibility for what their government does – or does not – deliver. At the moment, this is somewhere between nothing and diddly squat.

If May is unable to deliver the deal they promised voters in the referendum, she will take a large share of the blame – but the reputations of Boris and Gove may be left in tatters as the guys who promised everything and did nothing. It's this that concerns them more than anything else and brings them together despite all that's happened between the two men since the referendum vote was won.

May is left in a Catch-22 situation. She requires every vote she can get with a minority government. Brexit has split the Tories on Europe like never before and to sack both risks creating rebellious backbenchers with nothing more to lose. Yet failing to sack disloyal ministers from your cabinet – or even being perceived as unable to do so – is every bit as damaging.

This is a government in name only for all to see – and never at a worse time with so much at stake over Brexit. In single-mindedly looking after the interests of their personal careers, Boris and Gove not only weaken any hopes for the Brexit they campaigned for, creating a better deal and stronger ties outside the EU, but seem ready to run rough shod over supporting British citizens around the world.

How Meghan's royal baby could become an American – and secure the special relationship for good[45]

The news that Prince Harry and Meghan Markle will have their first child this year was greeted warmly by the world's media. The couple give the monarchy a new face and fresh approach, and the royal birth an opportunity to improve the 'special relationship.'

The newest member of the House of Windsor can claim dual nationality from both the UK and USA when born in a royal first. While he or she would be British through Prince Harry, the child could become an American citizen through his or her mother. This is where things can get interesting.

The royal baby would be able to obtain two passports, but his or her parents can only use their current one. Prince Harry does not qualify for American citizenship and Meghan will need to live in the UK for at least five years before she is able to apply to become British despite being Prince Harry's spouse. So the baby could have more passports than either parent. This might also be a royal first.

As a royal, the baby would be required to refrain from voting in British elections when eighteen years old out of convention. But no such restriction appears to be in place to stop him or her voting

45 'How Meghan's royal baby could become an American – and secure the special relationship for good', *The Independent* (28 April 2019).

in US elections. It would be possible for the Queen's grandchild to run for political office in the US or support other candidates. That would certainly get attention on both sides of the Atlantic.

There are downsides to being a dual citizen of the UK and the US however, which I know personally. One is that Americans must file annual tax returns and potentially pay taxes to the US – an issue that might affect the royal household. This is true even if someone has never lived in the US, earned any income in the US or left the UK. While America might not be the world's police, the US authorities have a reach over their citizens around the world as a global tax man – and this reach would potentially extend to Prince Harry and Meghan's children.

The only way to break free was to do what former foreign secretary Boris Johnson, a dual national of the UK and USA since birth, did and pay a large fee to the US government in return for ending forever his citizenship.

This should be avoidable and unnecessary. Citizenship is about a connection, not a backhanded way to get bank records and tax receipts from people paying full tax elsewhere. Prince Harry and Meghan Markle's child could make a new start in redrawing this imperialistic worldview, allowing the part American royal in Britain to pay his or her taxes to the UK only – and perhaps in return help create a new bond with the US at a time when post-Brexit Britain needs it most. The royal baby's Americanness can be far more important to the special relationship over time than President Donald Trump's controversial state visit this June.

We should all welcome the Duke and Duchess of Sussex's good news for this special year ahead – and the new opportunities this modern royal family can help make possible to develop a more special relationship across the Atlantic.

Nigel Farage claims Leavers are the true democrats – this is why he's wrong[46]

Parliament's inability to agree a withdrawal deal meant the UK did not leave the EU on 29 March. Theresa May's government confirmed a new target date of 31 October with Brussels. This gives fresh hope to those wanting Brexit softened, if not cancelled, as progress remains stalled.

This is more of a trick than a treat for Leavers. Delaying Brexit is seen as a denial of democracy. The problem is no longer reasserting Britain's sovereignty, but defending our democratic politics. To oppose Brexit is linked to being against democracy itself.

This link is the rocket fuel propelling Nigel Farage's Brexit Party into pole position ahead of European elections within weeks of being formed. Clearly, this single issue campaign has resonated with many potential voters at the expense of other parties. The difference isn't divided support among Remainers – as Leave voters have multiple options too – but the Brexit Party's single-minded push to make supporting Brexit a vote for democracy, thus appealing to something deeper in our British values.

Appealing to democracy is a strong, Trump-like card, but it is also the Brexit Party's Achilles' heel. Democracy matters in making political decisions legitimate. Democratic legitimacy goes hand in hand with the rule of law. One side wins over others in receiving the most votes, but not by any means. Each side must abide by the same standards to ensure the process is fair. Stuffing ballot boxes with fake voting cards is no more fair or acceptable than breaking campaign finance rules. When

46 'Nigel Farage claims Leavers are the true democrats – this is why he's wrong', *The Independent* (18 May 2019).

rules are broken in an election, defending the result regardless of what went wrong isn't defending democracy but subverting it.

It matters crucially that the democratic process was put in danger during the referendum campaign. When one side cheats to win, it doesn't deserve the trophy without a rematch. This isn't about politicians misusing statistics on a bus – although Boris Johnson could be in court over his repeated £350m claim shortly. No, this is about breaking the rules to win.

Arguing a vote won unlawfully should be defended in the name of democracy makes a mockery of not only our democratic system, but other British values like fair play and the rule of law. That does not mean Brexit cannot or should not happen, only that the referendum result doesn't have the democratic legitimacy the Brexit Party claims.

Pro-Brexit voices are quick to remind voters that the main parties promised to honour the referendum outcome. They did. But this does not mean a Leave victory means any kind of Leave will do. Brexit campaigners promised options ranging from a Norway model to full single market access and beyond – sometimes saying both. This explains the confusion over what people really did want. Saying 'Brexit means Brexit' was probably the only outcome different Leavers agreed upon.

Many might say politics trumps prosperity given the growing support for No Deal. This might speak to voter intentions now, but it's easy to neglect the fact these supporters think economic warnings about Brexit are fake news. But while there is nothing illegitimate about voters choosing an option widely seen as against their self-interest and detrimental to their current living standards, whether or not people are wrong to think Brexit is best for Britain is not the point.

Our democracy is under threat from the Brexit result. The legitimacy of the result is undermined by the unlawful means used to reach it. Maybe voters will want Brexit in greater numbers, but they should be asked in a second referendum. But it must be clear that its point is not to give the public a second chance to fix its mistake, but to give the winning campaign side another opportunity to win by the rules rather than by breaking them.

The sooner both sides in the Brexit debate see that a second vote is in their interests whether pro-Leave or pro-Remain, we have our best hope for breaking the current gridlock in Parliament – and we stand up for the democracy we hold so dear. Failing to back a second vote is to say democracy only matters when you like the result and that would betray our British values altogether.

Why Theresa May's political career is stained[47]

Since serving as David Cameron's Home Secretary, Prime Minister Theresa May has supported the Conservative Party's policy of reducing net migration to the tens of thousands.

Her bungled handling of immigration is a useful analogy for better understanding her poorly managed handling of Brexit and how it has all gone badly wrong.

May's announcement that she will step down conveniently came at the same time the latest net migration statistics were revealed.

Originally earmarked for release the previous day, the new figures show little has changed with net migration at over two and a half times the Government's target.

A good day for her Government to bury unwanted news.

May's staunchly ideological commitment to cutting immigration has overseen the largest net migration in recent UK history, far outstripping anything that occurred under Labour.

47 'Why Theresa May's career is stained', *The Northern Echo* (30 May 2019): 14.

The more she promised to reduce numbers, the less this target was in sight.

And why?

A belief that those concerned about migration halted would be satisfied with tens of thousands instead of none. This was never true, never going to happen under the immigration system she was overseeing and not addressing the main issues driving concerns about immigration.

People rightly worry about longer A&E queues but fewer migrants don't make that better since migrants are most likely to be in A&E as a doctor or nurse than as a patient. But May never let such facts get in the way of an ideological commitment to deliver on promises that would not address the main concerns.

This was not due to a lack of trying. May introduced a hostile environment that brought in tighter checks on opening bank accounts or renting private accommodation. These checks led to the Windrush scandal with lawful residents and citizens threatening with deportation because they did not have the correct identity papers. Not only did these new checks ensnare the wrong individuals, these measures have not actually uncovered a single person previously unknown to the Home Office. Not one. Tough sounding rhetoric, but lacking substance and driven more by partisan politics than practical reality.

May's migration clampdown extended to students which she refused to remove from her net migration target. There had long been concerns about making sure foreign students had sufficient English ability. Sure enough, some problems were certainly found. Yet again May's Home Office overreacted, leading to legitimate students being removed from their courses and their visas through no fault of their own in a scandal that is only now coming to light.

All these wrongs from Windrush to students and beyond were as heartbreaking as they are predictable. Theresa May's immigration problems – promising numbers will go down while driving them up, sticking with ineffective policies that were often counterproductive – are all set against a politician that rarely compromised and put partisanship above the public good. Facts were never allowed to get in the way of an ideological commitment.

All of these vices resurface with a vengeance when we consider Brexit.

Promising to deliver a Brexit that her critics seek is in name only. Or making the recommendation to Brussels that it should agree an Irish backstop to keep an open border in Northern Ireland that becomes her Brexit deal's biggest stumbling block.

At each stage, May's key contribution was her biggest undoing.

This is especially true with her insistence that No Deal is better than a Bad Deal.

Whatever the merits of keeping No Deal as an option, it is difficult to imagine a more damaging outcome of Brexit than No Deal which is precisely why so many MPs who support leaving the EU have blocked the damage No Deal would do to their constituencies. May was happy to keep No Deal as an option that she refused to utilise – and it's a phrase that has haunted her since she first said it. Planning each part of her Brexit deal without any discussion with senior Cabinet ministers and disrupting negotiations at a crucial early stage so she could call a snap election (seeking to increase her majority which spectacularly backfired) May will surely be most remembered for failing to deliver Brexit.

But her failure to deliver in other key responsibilities like immigration leading to the Windrush scandal and more are a part of the same narrative that will stain what should have been a distinguished career in politics, as Britain's second woman Prime Minister.

How Labour's next leader should approach House of Lords reform[48]

Everyone running to replace Jeremy Corbyn as leader of the Labour Party is committed to fundamental change of Parliament's upper chamber – the House of Lords – and want it reformed or abolished. This is not new for Labour leaders, who have traditionally called for a change of this kind. It is only the detail of the new arrangement on which Rebecca Long-Bailey, Lisa Nandy and Keir Starmer could disagree. How many members of the reformed chamber should there be? How would they be selected? And what different powers, if any, might they have? These questions go straight to the heart of the future of our parliamentary democracy.

The first point worth making is that a second chamber is worth having. To have only a House of Commons would be to create a parliamentary dictatorship: the majority will get whatever they want, whenever they want it. There would be no more substantive scrutiny than the Government wanted to entertain. A great means for enacting manifesto commitments quickly, but no way to govern well.

So long as the body continues to exist, Labour should continue making appointments to the House of Lords. The alternative is to let this body slowly wither on the vine, or at least slowly extinguish Labour's place in it. Until the Lords is changed, Labour would be choosing to make holding the Government to account more difficult. Labour must do the best it can with the powers currently at its disposal.

A second chamber can, and does, play an invaluable role. The House of Lords is a chamber of scrutiny where detailed analysis of

48 'How Labour's next leader should approach House of Lords reform', *LabourList* (4 March 2020).

legislation happens by a body of members with a wealth of experience and expertise. A distinctive feature of our Parliament is that we have world-leading experts in medicine and science as well as the arts, humanities and social sciences able to introduce bills and help scrutinise legislation, as well as serve on parliamentary committees.

But this leads directly to the main concern that very many will rightly have with the House of Lords: its undemocratic foundations. Members are unelected, with a small number of seats either inherited or given to the Church of England hierarchy. Perhaps they bring valued experience and expertise, but the selection process raises many issues and many more questions.

Until the institution is changed, the next leader should adopt Corbyn's idea of nominating only those committed to the democratic transformation of the Lords. And what then? Reform is a thornier issue than it might seem at first glance. Making the Lords democratic will have consequences, as a democratic mandate could justify more powers. This would fundamentally change the relationship between the Commons and the Lords.

The gridlock we see in the US Congress between its elected representatives and senators could arrive in Westminster. While the Lords must be democratised, it should aim to enhance, rather than disrupt, the delicate balance between the two chambers.

The by-elections of hereditary peers must end. This was previously proposed by Lord Grocott, and gained strong cross-party support. Their membership has no place in twenty-first century Britain. Numbers also matter. The second chamber should not be larger than the first, nor anything like the size it is today. There is a model for how to achieve a cutback in a report by Lord Burns, although this has been blocked by the Government. These plans should not be shelved so that the Government can pile up patronage.

Some argue that the Lords should be elected through a proportional system. In other words, winning forty per cent of the popular vote does not mean forty per cent of MPs, but it should earn that share in the Lords. Individual Lords would not contest elections, but the appropriate number would take their seats based on the election results. This would help create a democratic mandate for a similar profile of peers today, in terms of experience and expertise, but a potentially ineffective scrutiny chamber if its majority always mirrors the same party's majority in the Commons.

Alternatively, the Lords should become senators running for election like MPs with their own mandate. The appeal is to have a chamber of similar democratic legitimacy to the other. But, again, the potential cost is significant in terms of constitutional balance. If a senate had its own democratic mandate, this would create an environment for gridlock with neither side having any need to give ground to the other as noted above. This raises the question of constituencies. If elected peers or senators are not MPs, then on what basis might they be selected? The same population electing MPs? Apportioned by regions and, if so, which ones?

One particularly interesting idea is to introduce a model of federalism, as raised during the leadership contest by Keir Starmer. This is a powerful, structural way to bring about a radical devolution of power – and his ideas go far beyond Westminster, to local communities as well. If the Lords is to become a different kind of body, it must have a different kind of mandate. This presents a great opportunity to rethink its size, shape and popular legitimacy that extends far beyond numbers. We must challenge the system of patronage, as it is often perceived, in the eyes of the public.

With all Labour leadership candidates calling for radical reform of the House of Lords, one point on which they can all agree is the need for a Royal Commission on its future. This would be an advisory public consultation about a fundamental part of our democracy's future, such as part of a broader constitutional convention. This is not a new idea. A Labour Government held a Royal Commission, led by Lord Wakeham, about twenty years ago. It recommended cutting the Lords to 550 members, having an independent body make most appointments (in order to tackle peerages as patronage), creating regional membership for a minority through proportional representation, that ministers should become accountable to both Houses an removing hereditary peers.

Two decades later, it is time for Labour to run a new Royal Commission on similar terms as before, but also reflecting on a new federal structure. Perhaps it will come to similar conclusions as Wakeham. However, the public must be widely consulted and various options explored. It is critically important that we get the size, selection and structure right to improve public confidence. Working these plans into a broader constitutional convention would help join things up well.

Labour has transformed so much for the better, from schools to the NHS and beyond. And we have begun the work on reforming the House of Lords for the better. Much work remains to be done. We must be resolute in our ambition to democratise the second chamber – and address the constitutional issues, as well as the issues of how it is constituted. It is a pledge that any of the Labour leadership candidates can make: to finish what Labour started.

Labour's Pathway to Power: The Next Steps

The Labour Party has lost four General Elections in a row. The last in 2019 handed the Conservatives their largest governing majority since Margaret Thatcher was Prime Minister in the late 1980s. Any pathway back to power faces an enormous uphill battle. If this was easy to overturn, it might have happened by now. This daunting reality must be in frame when reflecting on how Labour's fortunes can and should be improved.

We are not in normal times either and obviously so. Leadership contests tend to end in a public celebration of supporters with live crowds on live television. Yet as the contest was ending, the pandemic and a national lockdown the likes of which none of us have ever seen before ushered in. I remember the time well as my last trip outside the North East was to meet with Keir Starmer at his Vauxhall HQ during his campaign. I hope he's among the first I see when restrictions are lifted. But the point is his journey to becoming leader was not ordinary. Gone were the cheering supporters and images of happy faces standing behind a new team and making a fresh start.

Since the last General Election, there have been a wide range of views about what steps Labour must take to win back power. Much of this rests on overly simplistic claims about which one thing will make all the difference. This debate will be familiar to anyone following it.

One view is that the problem can be solved by new faces, a few going as far as wanting another leadership contest. There have been changes afoot with a reshuffle in Starmer's top team, most notably on comms and political strategy. (I'm especially pleased to see my first student, Luke Sullivan, named political director. He's the best I've taught and an outstanding appointment.)

But simply rearranging the deckchairs won't magically prove a game changer by itself. Others say it's not so much the people, but the policies, and a more radical set usually echoing what was already put before voters without success in 2019. Yet this neglects concerns about how Labour policymaking can pack a better punch

– less can be more – and more of the same won't produce the large swing in support needed. Finally, another view is Labour should turn up on the volume and be more vocal about its opposing the Government.

But the public is generally turned off by shouting matches and what wins over is not simply disagreement, but a positive vision. It's not so much opposing as proposing that is key. Kim Leadbeater's success in Batley & Spen for Labour is one example.

These suggestions share a common thread about the need for Labour's sharpening its distinctiveness and the message of change we offer. I want to raise a few next steps on how this might be achieved taking as a starting point that mimicking our past may only ensure continuing defeats:

New look

David Cameron did not become Prime Minister because he changed his party's logo, but the new look set a clear, discernible marker that he was offering a refreshed party. The rebranding helped to send that message. It was a symbol that the Tories were under new management. While many criticised the move from Thatcher's freedom torch to his crayon-coloured oak tree, Conservatives have won four elections in a row under this banner.

In contrast, it has been decades since Labour underwent any similar exercise. It's time to rethink our image to help highlight our moving forward. If we look different, voters may look differently at us and this would be a welcome first step in transforming our party and its electoral prospects. It might be considered whether a new image coloured a familiar dominant red, but laced with white and blue more visibly communicates the 'stronger together' vision for Britain. No doubt this would begin to get more talking about the forward direction Labour is moving in which can only help.

New message

The next step is to follow this new look with a cross-cutting new message in line with calls for tighter message discipline. I'd push for 'competence with compassion' – which we're already seeing in Labour's statements on immigration matters – permeating every sentence in every interview or press release. It should be repeated so often it creates a kind of political hypnosis making people say it in their sleep.

These are two clear divides that can define our success sharply distinguishing the Conservatives from Labour. Incompetence runs deep through this government like a festering rot. We need to remain laser-like in exposing the ever-increasing litany of dithering, delays and failures from this government, but be more attentive to communicating clearly how we would be decisive and create better outcomes. Nobody will think we're ready for government if we only show them that the Tories aren't fit for office. We need to earn the public's trust in our greater competence. Again, it's not just about what we oppose, but what we propose in its place.

The second clear divide is compassion. Every soundbite and message from across our party must be clearer that we are on the public's side and we can understand their hopes and fears. It's no good saying we're with the many if most vote for others. We need more empathetic engagement, and there's lots of evidence from the front bench – on issues like violence against women and girls or Windrush among many other examples – that this connects with our fundamental Labour values, represents a clear divide between the Tories and us, and is gaining cut-through.

Renewal

But a new look and message only address more surface-level steps in Labour's pathway back to power. At its heart is our vision and the policies that are part of it. So those who say policies matters enormously are right, but I'd argue we should focus more on improving the process of policymaking and promotion of policy outcomes.

Hopefully, we'll all be back together again for our annual conference. This is a hugely important event for members coming together and for our policy discussions, but we must build on this. We might improve how this is managed, but a substantive message of change must go deeper and convincingly so.

People want to come together and share ideas, but they also want to feel included. While many may wish to do so in-person, technology has made it possible for hybrid meetings to become more commonplace, too, which should be exploited to make events more accessible.

One early commitment should be setting a timetable for regional conferences across every part of the country. (I'm happy to volunteer playing host in the North East to help get this started.) This will help re-energise our membership, revitalise CLPs and their working together, and create more welcome opportunities for all to contribute – and feel more included.

Labour benefits from the expertise of a wide range of academic experts, such as in the Labour Academic Network that I lead, and experiences of many more from work. The party should include in its policy-forming committees additional seats at the table for these voices. This will support a more thorough vetting of ideas. We have a wealth of talent that has too few opportunities to engage. Leafleting and phone banks are not nearly enough. We can and should make more use of the talents of our membership – and expand beyond anything like what we've done before. Better utilising our expertise and experience in policy development alongside a more active regionally-informed consultation would help bring out the best in our party.

Rally

There is no quick fix to returning Labour to power. The steps above are only the first part of a longer journey. But, finally, we must recognise that we're all in this together. When Labour wins, we all win – and when we lose, we all lose. It does not help our future prospects in any positive direction if we are not working together as a team.

And we have an extraordinary asset in our leader, Keir Starmer. When the worst smear the right wing press can come up with is that he's been knighted for his outstanding public service as Director of Public Prosecutions or that he gets everything right but only in hindsight, things can only get better from here. His competence and compassion throughout his career is personal testament to the virtues of competence and compassion that run through our party – and a further reason why they should be a mantra through to the next General Election.

Our party is a broad tent and this is a strength. Our members are passionate which is why so many feel so strongly about how we can best secure a future government – this is also a strength. All parts of our party must rally behind it. A wider, regionally-informed approach to policymaking that makes better use of our members' insights and experiences is something all parts of our party can stand firmly behind.

We must also look the part of a government in waiting rather than a perpetual opposition. A new look and message are crucial for making this change in tone and style visible, backed up by the credible substance of a more thorough and engaged policy forming process. Our work is only beginning – and we've a mountain to climb – but under Starmer and with our membership another future is possible if we're willing to fight for it.

Starmer's team is playing to win, rebuilding strategically and knowing Rome wasn't built in a day. Whatever the next by-election outcome, a new look and message alongside a more visible and engaged platform are next vital steps towards returning Labour to power.

In Search of 'British' Values

There has been increasing attention to the fostering and promotion of 'British values' over the last two decades. It is said that these values are the glue that helps keep society healthy. Everyone shares in some wider vision of who 'we' are. But it's worth pausing to consider the origins and evidence.

The focus on British values became a priority in 2001. The cause was not the Iraq invasion, but the riots in Oldham. The concern was that there were communities deemed to be living separately from the mainstream. These separate communities were identified as being in predominantly Muslim working-class areas. 9/11 only expedited what was already in the pipeline, including a new citizenship test for anyone wanting to become a permanent resident. Part of the test's purpose was to check that new immigrants knew and accepted 'British' values making the UK their new home.

The list of British values – democracy, the rule of law, individual liberty, mutual respect and tolerance of those of different faiths and beliefs – are, of course, not unique to Britain. While we might not want to cut any of these from this list, we may wonder why these – and only these – values count.

These values are not the product of a public consultation, but a government decree. Politicians made and promulgate their list of 'our' values.

This is a problem on several levels. First, those who disagree with the list can view it as an imposition. Secondly, the Government too often directs its concerns about adopting British values to immigrants as if no one British has engaged in criminality or intolerance. When directed at specific communities, this can only heighten their sense of alienation.

And what difference has this made? There seems precious little evidence that we will make better active citizens of immigrants if enforcing an arbitrary, abstract list of values to be accepted. Instead, it can appear a bit like a Don Quixote chasing the wrong target for the wrong reasons.

I believe there are British values and that they matter. But I also believe this is something for the British public to decide for themselves. A public conversation about what these values are would go a very long way to building a better, collective understanding of how they should be understood, their relevance in contemporary society and more of a buy-in for their continued support. Such things are meaningless if they are merely words on a page to be memorised for a test either at school or for citizenship. Values live in individuals' interaction with others in a community. We must go to the public to uncover a clearer sense of this normative glue that holds us together – and to maintain it for the future.

The Government's strategy for tackling extremism is more Little Britain than Big Society[49]

This week the Prime Minister David Cameron announced his 'comprehensive strategy' for tackling extremism. Cameron said

49 'The Government's strategy for tackling extremism is more Little Britain than Big Society', *The Journal* (Newcastle) (22 October 2015).

that 'we need to build a more cohesive society' underpinned by important British values like liberty, democracy and the rule of law.

It did not take long at all for the Muslim Council of Britain to make clear they found this strategy unhelpful. It is easy to see why.

The strategy is more concerned about radical Islam than Islamophobia. This is one of many areas where the Government has the balance wrong. Both are of concern, but clearly Cameron is really only worried about one and not the other.

For all his concerns about hate crimes it is surprising not more is done about them. One welcome first step would be the creation of a Hate Crime Register – that might function like the Sex Offenders Register. This could help send a signal that such behaviour is a serious wrong to victims and our community.

It is curious that only Sharia councils are singled out for not always following legal rules. All demonised with brief short comments. Clearly, our PM is either beginning to have a moral panic – or someone advised him to look like he is having one.

In short, the strategy is one-sided. It is the view that extremists are to be singled out and punished. Our schools and universities, local authorities, charities and more are all to be policed from within to root out the enemies in our midst.

It can be difficult for some to accept that most extremists are native-born, they were raised in our country and educated in our schools. To argue that we need more education almost misses the point given how many came through the system.

But there is something fundamentally overlooked. It is not just that there are extremist ideologies to confront – there is also alienation. So often a propensity to extremism and violence emerges from people who feel excluded. The left out. The overlooked.

Alienation has the potential to make people look to society like an other, a club run by others and for themselves. To be alienated is to look at society and fail to see yourself as having any meaningful stake or say in it.

If people were less alienated, they would better acknowledge the value of their contributions. But this is not something a few classes on why you shouldn't hate will instil in confused minds.

The Government will only find the key to unlock the many dangers lurking behind alienation when it grasps that it must not only win over minds, but hearts as well – and the latter might make all the difference in the world.

It's no surprise the shortest section of the 'comprehensive plan' is about building partnerships. This is because this is where the Government have got this fundamentally wrong.

Cameron understands tackling extremism in much the same way someone might want to launch an offensive against a foreign enemy. Those who hold extremist views should stop. They should be identified and re-educated. And repeat. This is based around the idea that integration is something others do to join with us. The hard work is to be done by them – they are to change.

But there is another model. This does not deny the importance of integration, but seeks to promote it better. This is the view that integration is not only something that others do to us but something we do to them. Effort is not only for one side.

This perspective is helpful because it draws our attention to the idea of the community as a kind of achievement – which it is. And one worth maintaining.

But this requires a more genuinely 'one nation' kind of thinking. Unfortunately, this is very much in short supply with the current government. When partnership is described as nothing more than loosely linking unknown others to some kind of support network, things are not looking promising one bit.

This shows the one-sided thinking at the heart of this plan. More a strategy to win over backbench Tories than take the fight to extremists.

If Cameron's government was serious about countering extremism, they would adopt several positions – in addition to launching a hate crime register. Instead of an amorphous network of vague interaction, there should be less of a top-down police-styled response – and more understanding extremism from the bottom up. Central to this is grasping the damaging psychological self-understanding that sees itself as alienated without a stake in the wider society.

The ability to communicate well in English is regularly identified as a crucial factor in how well people can integrate and make their contributions to society.

This should spur the Government to launch a war – not on any faith, but on ending adult illiteracy. While the Government recognises it is a problem, they make no solid plans for what it might do next.

Cameron's counter-terrorism strategy seems more geared towards Little Britain than the Big Society. Perhaps the latter is still an idea whose time might come one day.

We need less top-down thinking, a greater effort to tackle illiteracy, more recognition of the wrongs of hate crimes and that despite working with people to gain their trust it should not be expected by shoving our ideas down their throats.

We must convince and persuade. Bring the argument to counter extremist propaganda for sure, but also realise that our efforts may be more fruitful if we listen more effectively so we can realise how best to make our case for our values.

It won't be easy, but there are ways we can fight this barbarity[50]

The terrorist attacks across Paris have alarmed us all. No one who values human life can look at these actions as anything but murderous violence that have no justification. Killing and seriously injuring hundreds makes nothing right – and it should be rightly condemned.

Freedom is a precious gift. It is hard fought for and easily sacrificed; it is a product centuries in the making – and yet it is what these terrorists seek to destroy.

This may seem unintelligible. Why would anyone seek to limit the freedom of all – would that not lead to less freedom for them too?

Such a view gets much wrong. This is not about freedom for all and certainly not about religion. No, this is about power – political power.

The clue is in the name – the so-called 'Islamic State.' They have a political cause – to impose their rule over lands in Iraq and Syria. Make no mistake about it. This an earthly movement with a worldly aim.

There are two ways to get noticed in global politics. The first is to be a global power. And that's hard – otherwise, every state would be one.

The second way is to get noticed alongside a global power. This is much easier. Any organisation can claim to be the alternative to the status quo or dominant groups. The more difficult task is getting people to talk about your group when talking about others.

And that's what Islamic State is doing in its international propaganda activities. Why? The more it can show it is more than a

50 'It won't be easy, but there are ways we can fight this barbarity', *The Journal* (Newcastle) (19 November 2015): 21.

club, but a state-like force on a global stage then the more it hopes it can build some source of legitimacy at home and abroad for itself in future.

It's easy to mistake the horrors that the Islamic State visits on its citizens as some kind of twisted revenge for the invasion of Iraq. There are reports that some Iraqi military elites who became alienated after Saddam Hussein's downfall have had a hand in building the Islamic State in Iraq.

But the Iraq invasion does not answer why these terrorists targeted a Russian passenger jet and French citizens in Paris – neither Russia nor France supported the Iraq invasion. Yes the power vacuum post-invasion is a continuing problem, but it is more an opportunity than a cause for the Islamic State's twisted brand of the new politics.

We are now faced with a choice – and it's easy to have some sympathy with each side of the debate. There will be some that say some form of military action is justified – people cannot be killed in the numbers we've seen without some robust response. There will be others urging caution: we must have a plan to build a peace – not merely start a war with Iraq – coupled with a clear example of what might go wrong. We must be effective without making a bad situation much worse.

Prime Minister David Cameron has not asked me for advice. But if he did, I'd recommend the following course of action:

The first act should be to follow the money – and turn off the tap. The Islamic State is able to function as an organisation because it has resources. Its economic waters must run dry. Shut off its funding and it can no longer stay afloat.

A large share of its funding comes from the oil fields along Syria's eastern borders. They need not be seized, but there should be a much greater effort at ensuring this oil does not enter the marketplace. A coordinated effort with Russia and Middle Eastern partners should be forged – it is in no one's interest that Islamic State continues to finance its destabilising programme of barbarity.

The second act should be to turn off the tap of the Islamic State's propaganda machine. Yes their messages should be countered and corrected, but much more can be done to shut down their recruitment websites and social media platforms. This is not about closing free speech, but rather hate speech. Groups hell-bent on murder have no right to recruit new members and on their terms. Make their online presence begin to disappear and you begin to extinguish a major source of their publicity. This would also require a coordinated effort, but again one where overlapping interests exist with a common purpose.

The third act is especially difficult – sow the seeds for security and hope. The people of Syria and Iraq need to construct their political futures for themselves. They will need time and space for this to unfold. Western governments may not always like what they will see. But there is a massive difference between a sustainable, stable political system and what these countries have now. We should keep focused on what should be avoided and leave to these people what should happen – in a new future, their future, without terrorists holding them to ransom.

The so-called Islamic State must realise that their murderous actions will yield consequences with a price that is too high to bear. Their choices are not free and without penalties.

There are more ways to do this than just military action. The risks of military action are that they play into the Islamic State's view of crusaders versus jihadists. These risks also include the lives and well-being of innocent civilians and our troops.

There is more than one way to fight barbarity. We can do more to choke off its funding and its ability to recruit through online, hateful propaganda. An organisation starved of resources and publicity becomes a poor unknown. Its projected sense of strength and power is reduced. It is much easier to win support when there is something to offer in return – but should the oil run dry or become unsellable it pulls the rug from under its business plan and the firm could go bust.

Islamic State has shown that the only thing more frightening than the political vacuum in parts of Syria and Iraq that existed is what they are doing to fill these spaces. Ending the Islamic State's stranglehold on power does not make everything OK. I have yet to hear anything convincing about what a post-ISIS Syria should look like.

So I have no recommendation for the Prime Minister on this beyond that the peoples of Syria and Iraq should be able to get on and choose their own futures. They want ISIS no more than anyone else.

But whatever happens next it is crucial that no one can say with a shred of credibility that the crusades have restarted somehow or that virtuous believers should take one side and murder the other. This is utter bunk that stinks to the high heavens.

The world has never had a single government and it is large enough to accommodate a diverse political space. We can all enjoy a prosperous future together. Let's not let the self-appointed preachers of hate tell us – or anyone else – otherwise.

The trolling and the tweeting are becoming a crisis[51]

Politics has rarely lacked passion. Few of us may be political party activists, but most of us are actively engaged in some way with what our elected representatives in Parliament are doing. We may not all

51 'The trolling and the tweeting is becoming a crisis', *The Journal* (Newcastle) (4 December 2015): 23.

have the time to study the full details of every policy proposed by government, but many of us are aware and take some interest in Westminster life.

It's often remarked that Parliament is not held in high regard. Some will say that politics is a dirty business and the constant drip of a few MPs or Lords exposed for some perceived wrongdoing does little to improve the public's image of them all. As in so many walks of life, the misdeeds of the few reflect badly on all.

But I believe there is something else to consider. Our world is changing – and becoming increasingly busier and complex.

Technology has transformed the ways in which we work and communicate. Twenty years ago many people used typewriters and did not own a mobile phone – or know anyone who did. Today we find emails, social media and text messages have done more than simply replace handwritten or typed letters. We can now communicate more quickly and more immediately to more people than ever before.

It's become easier to send or receive messages and this is a great gift. But it also comes with costs. The ease and simplicity of getting in touch with others means we can get overwhelmed. Have I responded to that last text or email? I didn't have an email address until about 1995 – and now I can get well over a hundred emails per day. There is so much everyone is saying that it can be difficult to know what to think of it.

This impacts on how we engage in politics. Much of what passes for political knowledge is the soundbite or headline.

This is a problem for two reasons. The first is few people can find the necessary time to examine further the details of what is happening in Westminster and world politics.

But it does mean snippets selected as snapshot summaries of views can often distort – and distort quite radically – what these views actually are.

The second reason this is a problem is that despite the greater ease of communicating with each other this does not always foster open minds and widening discourses. On the contrary, the World Wide Web has increasingly become not an interconnected web, but a collection of various echo chambers.

Research by leading academics like Cass R. Sunstein at Harvard University found – should it surprise us? – that we tend to engage with other like-minded people. This was discovered to encourage 'group polarisation': groups of people sharing similar views tend to become more polarised and more extreme as members understand – and overemphasise – some value or shared commonality.

To put that in English: if you bring together people who share a similar view about politics, we can expect to see they will become more polarised in their political views from the mainstream over time. The internet may not be a liberator, but can reveal a deeply misleading view of political realities.

This problem is creeping into a public crisis. For many people, most of their communications with others will be done remotely and not face-to-face. And so much of this will be in text message length tweets and sound clips – at least when it comes to what so often passes for communication about politics.

The tendency for like-minded groupthink to evolve into something more extreme can be found readily. People who hold opposing political views are not merely wrong or endorsing the wrong principles. They now become 'scum.' Our fellow citizens and political equals become stripped of their equal dignity. They become something less than human and so deserving of contempt and disregard.

Recent events provide another illustrative case in point. On Wednesday, MPs voted in favour of airstrikes in Syria. There was a clear majority bringing together Parliamentarians from several political parties around the chamber.

Reasonable people disagree sharply on this issue. And this was acknowledged by one MP after the next. Each weighed the arguments for and against carefully. As each should.

Prime Minister David Cameron did his side of the argument a disservice in allegedly branding opponents 'terrorist sympathisers' and he should apologise if he said those words.

But then take a clear view of what was said by the other side. As an expert and commentator on immigration policy, I've been subjected to some nasty trolling online over the years. But this has usually been by a handful and short-lived. I find it more depressing than threatening.

I support Jeremy Corbyn's view of what the 'new politics' should be about: we should encourage debate, discussion and democracy in a climate of respect treating each other with dignity. I've spoken with Jeremy and know he opposes in the strongest terms the online abuse of others. I also know his view is shared by people I'd consider the true so-called Corbynistas who supported his campaign from its start. They want to open politics up and make it more inclusive, not divisive and abusive.

But in reality the 'new politics' in Britain has become an ever more deeply polarised place for a minority, but one that has become increasingly vocal and nasty. All in the name of abusing and dehumanising opponents through misleading, overly simplistic and sometimes downright false beliefs.

Consider again the Syria debate. The Rt. Hon. Hilary Benn, Shadow Foreign Secretary, helped close the debate with what many neutral observers found to be the single best Westminster speech in years. It happened to also be in favour of airstrikes in Syria.

Benn argued that the so-called Islamic State were fascists that believe 'they are superior to every single one of us in this chamber tonight, and all of the people that we represent. They hold us in contempt. They hold our values in contempt.'

And for this the trolling army of ideological purists proceeded to subject him and many others – not to dialogue or to press arguments – but to abuse and worse, showing that they held them in their contempt with a smugness betraying a clear self-belief in ideological purity.

I believe part of the reason that Corbyn's frequent interventions to stop such online bile have not been very effective is because many of the trolls aren't Labour members or supporters. They are merely the product of politics in a complex world where we're swamped by communications with too little time to do much more than shout at each other. It's easier to be a purist than grapple with life's complexities.

This is the 'new politics.' Neither kind or even very informed. People's dignity prosecuted and judged in soundbites with a click of the mouse or a tap on an iPhone. The good news this is still background, a minority. The bad news is that it's starting to take root. We need a new politics. But I'll take Corbyn's professed vision of respectful disagreement any day over online trolls who betray it daily.

I swore an oath to Queen and Country. Why must public officials be the only ones to do the same?[52]

All public office holders should swear an oath of allegiance to British values, according to Communities secretary Sajid Javid. He claims that public officials must accept basic values like democracy, equality and the rule of law. The new oath will also apply to all new migrants in plans expected to be unveiled this spring.

52 'I swore an oath to Queen and Country. Why must public officials be the only ones to do the same?' *Daily Telegraph* (20 December 2016).

Only migrants becoming British citizens must make this show of loyalty today. I should know – I did it in 2011 at my citizenship ceremony. If Javid wants his fellow ministers to 'lead by example', he's already years behind migrants like me that have met this new yardstick already.

New citizens are required to pledge loyalty to British values and this is meant to help us integrate. We swear to respect the rights and freedoms of the UK, observe its laws faithfully and 'uphold its democratic values' as British citizens. Such words have been said at UK citizenship ceremonies now for over a decade and nothing new with versions in English and Welsh.

Javid's plan is to implement Dame Louise Casey's recommendation in her recent report into integration that there should be similar oaths of allegiance for public officials.

However, the Government has never conducted any review into whether policies aimed at improving integration for new migrants actually work. Requiring migrants to sit a citizenship test that arguably few British citizens could pass deserves to be mocked as 'like a bad pub quiz.'

I'm happy to support the promotion of British values, but where's the evidence saying an oath does combat extremism or leads to a more harmonious society? Something so important for all should not be required from only a few – anything less is a betrayal of British values like equality and fair play.

Javid neglects to mention that migrants becoming new citizens do more than only pledge their loyalty to freedom and democracy, but must also make an oath of allegiance to the Queen, her heirs and successors – is not our monarchy a part of Britain too? This is an omission that no migrant would make for the simple fact that we had to do it.

In her report, Dame Louise spoke of some communities living in isolation that did not share in British values like toleration, singling out Muslim neighbourhoods. A lack fluency in speaking English is a key contributor to their separateness. Dame Louise recommends more support for English in harder to reach communities – and this would be welcome to counter real-term cuts in provision by the Coalition Government.

A shared language is an important bond that brings communities together. Poor English is not unique to migrant communities and it is estimated that as many as five million adults in England are functionally illiterate. Improving English may go much further to bringing together citizens old and new than repeating an oath in under one minute. It would also be more than a cheap gimmick which may explain why the Government is choosing to prioritise one plan over the other.

Finally, British values are not for ministers alone to dictate. These values are our values. We should not be content to let the Government decide what should be included and promoted in our collective name.

Let the public be consulted and the people contribute to what we should all uphold. Anything less would be contrary to the British values that Javid wants to defend, not least our democracy.

Is turning our back on British values the price we must pay for a deal with Trump? [53]

Earlier this week I was invited to speak in the Houses of Parliament about the continuing migration crisis and what Britain can do about it. The meeting was organised in the grand-looking Gladstone committee room by the All-Party Parliamentary Group on

53 'Is turning our back on British values the price we must pay for a deal with Trump?' *The Journal* (10 February 2017): 25.

Refugees, a cross party and so non-partisan group of MPs, Peers and supporters galvanised around policies affecting refugees.

The audience was a wide-ranging assembly of political opinion including Tories, Labour, SNP, Liberal Democrats and cross-benchers – even Lord Tebbit sat in for most of our discussions. My fellow panellists were distinguished members of organisations like Amnesty International, the Refugee Council and UNICEF and chaired by the tireless and charismatic Lib Dem Peer the Lord Revd Roberts of Llandudno, one of Britain's greatest champions for the rights of refugees.

Our focus was to discuss the Government's to be proposed safeguarding policy for unaccompanied child refugees. We have all seen the harrowing images of migrants fleeing war torn parts of the world – many of which are areas where the British military is engaged actively trying to help bring peace and stability. I'm sure we all hope that the violence soon ends and community rebuilding starts swiftly, but we can neither expect all who live in harm's way to simply persevere and cling on until that hoped-for happy ending becomes a reality.

War and desperation have led many to leave their homes perhaps forever in search of safety as refugees. Not all who begin this difficult journey live to complete it. For those of us who have never had any comparable experience, it is almost impossible to fully understand the hardships so many face that the rest of 'us' – who live and work in our region – do not.

Some of the migrants seeking refuge are children travelling with family, but others have lost their families during a conflict in their home country or parents have become separated or died while on a journey to a brighter future.

The Labour Peer the Lord Dubs, who was himself a Holocaust survivor and an unaccompanied child receiving refuge in Britain, called for what was is known as the Dubs Amendment – where

Britain would accept up to 3,000 lone children from Syria who satisfy the requirements for receiving asylum.

So there was much to discuss at our meeting to inform government policy. How should it manage effectively the processing of claims, the introduction to this country and their integration into British life?

Less than an hour before our meeting started, Lord Roberts got wind the Government had decided to scrap the Dubs Amendment. Despite promising hundreds and a few thousand, they now said no more than 350 in total. A little more than ten per cent of what was planned. And this was released on the day of the Brexit Bill vote in the House of Commons – a time where the Government thought it wise to knowingly, foreseeably and avoidably bury this bad news at a time and place few news outlets would report it.

Theresa May's government sends out a loud signal about what Brexit means for Britain by this action. If Brexit means Britain will once again be free standing on its own feet and able to become the country we want to embody, we're now a country so ready for global leadership that we immediately slam our collective door tightly shut on the world's most vulnerable people. A country cannot be great that turns its back so readily to those who are so small.

We also see May's government offering not a compassionate conservativism, but a moderate Trump-ism. Trumpology is the new faith in 10 Downing Street. While Trump wants to shut the door on all refugees, Britain's elevated role is to only shut out the most vulnerable refugees. What motivates the Prime Minister to mimic a widely condemned – at least in Britain – policy by the increasingly unstable and irritable President Trump is anyone's guess. If being mean and turning our back on British values is the price to pay for a deal with Trump, it is perhaps a Faustian bargain we should avoid.

Moreover, it is alarmingly perverse to target and U-turn on children. Let's get some things straight. Yes the general public has concerns about immigration and tends to inflate how many are asylum seekers. Now in our seventh year of Tory-led Governments, the facts remain that net migration has never been higher than under Tory-led Governments. The more they promise to bring it down, the higher it goes than we ever saw under Labour. If the public wants less net migration in fact – rather than empty promises – they had less under Labour even at the height of Eastern European migration.

About sixteen per cent of all immigrants claim asylum and sixty per cent have their applications refused. This means asylum seekers who can stay are only about a small handful – and British citizens coming back from gap years or work abroad count for more net migration into Britain than refugees. Lone child refugees are the smallest number of the lot – and yet it is they the Government wants to prevent. If it's about compassion, they're wrong. If it's about reducing net migration, they've lost the plot.

In my remarks to the parliamentary group, I highlighted four concerns. First, the Government should get clear on its existing duties before committing itself to new obligations. The Home Office waited until bulldozers came to demolish the Calais Jungle, yet our duties to migrant children were already in place long before.

Secondly, the Government should address inconsistencies like the postcode lottery of guardianship that supports lone child refugees in Scotland and Northern Ireland, but not in England or Wales.

Thirdly, all efforts seem concentrated on how to keep people out with little attention to what to do with supporting those who have come in. We need to act much more on integration recognising it is a two-way street where individuals and communities have roles to play.

Finally, we need a champion for the cause. If the Government supports taking any asylum seekers, as it does, then it needs to act like it. We all know where Trump stands even if we disagree with him. The Government must either show some leadership or find someone independent of government who can show it for them.

Tackling a global pandemic

The world changed when the coronavirus Covid-19 became known at the end of 2019. Within a matter of weeks, thousands died and hundreds of thousands became ill. Lockdowns were enacted across the world as governments scrambled to protect their citizens from the biggest global pandemic in a century.

The situation is unfolding at present. We have much to learn about this dreadful disease and how to defeat it. While each claimed to follow the best scientific advice, those that acted swiftly to test frequently, trace and isolate saw the best results. And countries like the UK and USA that were relatively more reluctant to lockdown have seen the more deaths.

The finger pointing blame game is already in full swing. Scapegoats are being called out domestically and, increasingly, internationally.

There will be a time for closely examining the strategies taken by different countries to recognise mistakes and identify the lessons to be learned. Until this work is completed, any finger pointing is premature – and diverts crucial time and focus away from protecting public health as best as possible.

These essays offer some reflections on the current state of the global pandemic as it unfolded in the first half of 2020. It is clear that whether or not countries get this wrong – or if perceived to get this wrong – will significantly impact public trust. Getting the public to lockdown and follow heavy restrictions on the way that they work, travel and keep in touch with friends and families is a big ask to make. We all want governments to get this right. But if failing to put enough of a priority on saving lives becomes a growing concern, it will have consequences for many years to come.

In a time of national crisis, Brexit can wait – but woe betide the Remainers who gloat about it[54]

Over the next weeks, and probably months, the UK will be battling the coronavirus pandemic. Covid-19 has thus far claimed 16,000 lives worldwide. Boris Johnson likens the UK's approach to fighting a war, and so he should. There are more than 6,500 confirmed cases in the UK and that number is rising rapidly.

After avoiding public appearances for several days as the outbreak began to take off, Johnson has rightly agreed to daily briefings so the public can be informed on progress. Days after his first Budget speech, the chancellor, Rishi Sunak, announced a £350bn package of measures to support businesses and the wider economy.

This wartime-like approach is needed given the rising death toll, especially in Italy, and the very real fears of the British people that we might be next. This battle against Covid-19 is a war the Government must win, so it must prioritise the health and safety of all citizens, directing all its efforts to their protection. It is increasingly clear the pandemic will be with us for several months, and its after-effects for far longer.

54 'In a time of national crisis, Brexit can wait – but woe betide the Remainers who gloat about it', *The Independent* (24 March 2020).

Given the gravity of the situation, the Government must immediately request an extension to the current Brexit transition period for at least six months — and avoid fighting a war on two fronts.

Many EU countries are in lockdown. Brexit trade talks are on ice. An eleven-month time frame for agreeing a complex, comprehensive trade deal was already thought by many experts to be inconceivable. The onset of this coronavirus has now made it absolutely impossible. There will be no progress of any kind.

Politics is about priorities; forging new trade deals is not top of the list for any country at the present time – including our own.

The government has repeatedly said that it wants a comprehensive trade deal rather than a No Deal Brexit. If that is true, postponing talks and prolonging the transition period is the most sensible way to achieve the Government's ultimate goal at a time of national emergency. Choosing to stick to an arbitrary date for ending the transition in December on principle makes no sense given the fast-moving circumstances.

This is not the time to choose to split the focus of all government departments into tackling two major issues at once when we simply do not need to do so. Postponing an end to transitioning out of the EU would allow a total focus on the biggest threat to public health in a century. This should not in any way be undermined by other political aims.

And in doing the right thing and asking for an extension, Brexit's opponents should not gloat but welcome such a decision in the national interest. This is a time where we most need to rally together.

Stopping the 'get Brexit done' talks is what any wartime-like government should do. To leave hanging our full exit from the EU without taking any account of the current crisis's profound effects is irresponsible.

The sooner the Government makes clear its desire to let Brexit matters wait until after ensuring the public's health and safety is protected to the fullest extent, the better. Anything less gets both the Government's priorities and its principles wrong.

Boris Johnson shows us how *not* to tackle a global pandemic

Only a few months ago, the big issue being grappled with by 10 Downing Street was whether or not to push hard for church bells to ring across the UK marking Britain's exit from the European Union. The church congratulating the achievements of the state. To be done at 11pm UK time (and midnight in Paris and Berlin). They were simpler times.

Prime Minister Boris Johnson is consumed by politics. What matters is power – and patronage. Those who could or would not support him to 'Get Brexit Done' might as well be Labour MPs. Rebels expelled, only partisan loyalty rewarded.

The Covid-19 outbreak changed everything in virtually every way. The Johnson administration seemed so distracted by how best to celebrate its winning power and championing its legislative agenda that it was relatively slow off the mark to begin a lockdown to protect public health and save lives. As the rising death toll in Italy and Spain began to raise significant fears something similar might happen in the UK, the Prime Minister seemed overly desperate to do only as much – and as little – as he had to. Johnson doesn't like tough decisions and too regularly confuses being charismatic at parties with having leadership at a time of crisis.

We now know this strategy fell very short of its goals. As the first – and, hopefully, only – wave comes to an end, the UK has the highest death rate in the world and the most deaths of any country in Europe. This is not success; it is a significant tragedy with surely an independent review to understand failures to follow in the short term.

At first, Johnson used scientists as his human shields. He reassured the public that the Government was simply following the best science. Of course, why not act more quickly and deeply as had happened elsewhere with lower death rates? Did the Germans have different science? Surely not. The only difference was that different political decisions were made in Britain than elsewhere. The results were far more deaths.

The messaging could hardly be blamed. 'Stay at home' was the official advice once a lockdown was finally agreed. This led to real hardships as people could not be with loved ones in their final moments nor visit with family as they had before the crisis. Everyone was to stay home, stop the spread of the virus, save the NHS by not overwhelming it and helping the country move forward.

But the messengers were different. Johnson's chief advisor, Dominic Cummings, helped draft the official guidelines justifying police action and penalties for breaking the lockdown. Only after being positively identified over 240 miles north of his home in London at his parents' estate in Durham did it become increasingly clear that Cummings may have flouted the very guidelines he helped to write and which millions faced hardships in following. Families were separated. Loved ones died alone. But, for the PM's right hand man, exceptions were permitted – or so most of the public believed.

And it got worse. After 10 Downing Street claimed Cummings had only gone to Durham and locked down, his car was positively identified near a beauty spot in Barnard Castle on a day that also happened to be his wife's birthday. Cummings denies breaking the lockdown rules – and said he drove sixty miles round trip from

Durham to this beauty spot with his family in the car to check whether his eyesight was good enough for a drive home to London. Or so we found out from a press conference – delivered in the rose garden behind 10 Downing Street, a space normally used only by the Prime Minister. The message was clear: Johnson, Cummings, what's the difference? If you have one, you get other. Like the Sith, they come as a pair.

Of course, the sheer hypocrisy – or at least the strong appearance of it – infuriated the public on a scale not seen in many, many years. And, of course, it brought out howls of outrage from political opponents.

But the biggest problem at the heart of this shambles is the loss of trust at an especially critical time. The UK is facing the most significant pandemic in a century. There have been approximately sixty thousand extra deaths over the previous year. People have sacrificed their freedoms enormously in a collective effort to stop the spread of the virus. Sick relatives died alone in hospital. Parents and grandparents could not embrace their children. Most accepted the need to stay at home, even if they had no garden or outdoor spaces to enjoy.

Not so for the PM's top advisor. For him, travelling to see family far away seemed like a good idea – while everyone else sat at home as per his own recommended guidelines. And then spending a couple of hours in the car and walking around a local beauty spot on what happened to be his wife's birthday.

I've yet to meet a lawyer who thinks Cummings did not break either the letter or spirit (and probably both) of his own lockdown guidelines at some point in this affair. But even if this was not so, it cut through and led to deep popular anger. The reason is clear: the public was asked to accept, on trust, significant restrictions when it appeared those in charge were acting in a more relaxed way. One rule for the PM and his chums with impunity, but another for the people. It's a curious form of populism where popular views are treated with such contempt.

Within days, police were reporting that citizens were using Cummings's behaviour as an excuse to do activities that the police thought to be breaches of the lockdown. This is much more than a public order issue, but public health – the more interaction there is, the more likely the virus will spread and lead to additional, avoidable deaths.

The continuing erosion of trust isn't just a threat to democracy. It's threatening the lives of the public. With the Prime Minister choosing to stand with Cummings (whose behaviour has been criticised by government scientific advisors), he has put partisan politics before public health and safety. Making a pandemic an issue of partisan loyalty will almost certainly be punished by voters. The first rule of politics should always be to protect the well-being of their people. When this is secondary to personal ambition it is a sacrifice the public should not – and will not – tolerate.

A Higher Education

My day job is Dean of Durham University's Law School, where I am the UK's only Professor of Law and Government. While I was a graduate student in the United States and Republic of Ireland before moving to the United Kingdom, my academic career has been mostly spent here. From PhD student to Law School Dean, there have been several issues of real concern that I have written about over the last twenty years. A sample of these essays are included below.

One topic is the issue of multidisciplinarity and joint appointments. The current and future focus of academic research draws heavily on working across different disciplines. Yet, at least in the UK, joint appointments of academics to two or more departments is almost unheard of. This is an anomaly that undercuts the full potential for such work – and undermines Britain's competitive advantage. (Coincidentally, the piece also led to a prompt offer to create a joint appointment although I did not pursue that opportunity further.)

A second topic was the politicisation of research funding. There is nothing novel about governments wanting to invest in academic research about key issues, such as Brexit or Covid-19. What is novel is seeking to fund projects that explore a campaign slogan. One such example was the Arts and Humanities Research Council including the Tory slogan of the 'Big Society' as part of its funding priorities. I led an unprecedented protest leading to dozens of fellow peer college reviewers resigning *en masse* and several petitions calling on them to drop it. This made Transparency International's corruption report on education. Understandably, this had a profound impact on trust in funders to support the best research based on academic quality and not simply trying to find favour with the political leaders of the day, or some have said.

A third topic is the political and policy benefits of academic research. During my career, the UK has revised the way it assesses an academic department's research quality by incorporating some assessment of its wider impact. While I was originally sceptical, I have become an ardent supporter. A key reason is it incentivised universities to support their academics in working with politicians and policymakers. However, the full potential has not yet been realised. For many years, I have advocated that academics can and should play a greater role in developing policymaking within and outside political parties.

A fourth topic is academic freedom. This also taps into a very specific form of trust, namely, the trust that academics have to pursue research findings wherever they might lead without fear of reprisal. This case involves a junior government whip who requested names, teaching materials and, more ominously, lecture recordings from Vice-Chancellors about Brexit – presumably to expose any individuals or comments that said or did anything unfavourably, or so many speculated. The universities minister at the time, Jo Johnson (and brother of the current Prime Minister), claimed this was all part of a book – one that remains unpublished.

A fifth topic concerns trust that graduating students have qualifications that are fit for purpose. I explore this through a couple of essays exploring recent attempts at reforming legal education, specifically, for qualifying solicitors. Their proposed 'super-exam' has nothing super about it – beyond being a fantastic mistake.

Together, these essays showcase the manipulation of higher education from forces outside that lack a focus on the public good – and the lack of engagement from policymakers where the public good might be best served. They also draw out how these errors might be overcome and rebuild trust both within higher education and beyond the academy.

Better together[55]

The days of mono-disciplinarity are swiftly fading. Academics from across the UK are under increasing pressure to engage in interdisciplinary and multidisciplinary research. Research funding bodies regularly favour project proposals that bring together two or more academic disciplines, or that involve 'bridging' teams from different disciplines collaborating to stimulate new lines of research enquiry.

Meanwhile, universities are restructuring, merging departments to form new schools that bring together several disciplinary subjects. Local funding for projects and seminar series remains widely available at many institutions, but this funding is often contingent on the work bringing benefits to at least two diverse subjects.

The merits of these developments may be debated. But there is no disputing that the universities, research funding bodies and the Government are all committed to this process, actively encouraging greater collaboration between academic disciplines. Why then are joint appointments virtually absent from the UK sector?

The current system works against such appointments. A prized academic working in two different disciplinary departments would count for less in each than someone working in only one.

55 'Better Together', *Times Higher Education* (10 February 2011): 26.

For example, such an academic may count as no more than 0.5 staff in each area, which reduces the impact of their work in research assessments. It is far more valuable for a department to keep its professors all to itself than to share them with others.

But if it is beneficial for academics to work in more than a single subject, then it is surely wise to appoint scholars to more than one discipline, where appropriate. The move would help expose them to new ideas and research programmes to which they could contribute.

Joint appointments would also demonstrate the value added in teaching and research across more than one discipline. In that sense, such appointments could be considered an indicator of 'impact.'

In any case, many academic staff already teach and research in more than one discipline. Joint appointments would recognise the actual contributions that staff are already making.

This could further encourage others to engage more often in interdisciplinary and multidisciplinary work, helping to advance the clearly stated commitments of their universities, research councils and government.

Joint appointments would clearly embody the disciplinary ethos within higher education today.

This method of working has been a great success elsewhere, for example in Canada and the US, in a variety of fields. Professors who have joint appointments are highly prized and their status is often a clear acknowledgement of the breadth of their influence.

Various combinations of joint appointments in business, classics, economics, law, medicine, philosophy, political science and other subjects are far from unusual outside the UK, and make sense: each of these disciplines may benefit from greater interaction with others.

Joint appointments are not the only path to fostering such interaction, but they might help to build more lasting bridges between disciplines than funded research projects. Projects come and go, but such appointments will often last far longer and potentially have a far greater effect on relevant fields of study and the university teaching and research environment.

By failing to offer joint appointments, the UK actually suffers a competitive disadvantage in relation to North American universities.

It is time to reverse this state of affairs. If our universities, research funding bodies and government remain sincere about their desire for greater collaboration between disciplines, one significant and highly welcome step forward would be to open the doors to joint appointments. And the sooner, the better.

'Observergate' and academic freedom[56]

The 'Observergate' saga began with an essay published in the *Observer* on 27th March that included the claim that political pressure was exerted upon the Arts and Humanities Research Council (AHRC) to include the 'Big Society' in its funding plans. It was claimed that inclusion was even 'non-negotiable.' This was met with a strong denial by the AHRC. It claimed that no such pressure existed and that its 'Connected Communities' research theme – one of its six areas for strategic research funding priority – had been agreed long before the last general election. The denial was very specific: there was no pressure on the AHRC to adopt any particular research theme.

My concern was that this denial did not extend to a fundamental issue reported by the *Observer*: should the political party campaign slogans be included within research council funding documents? The AHRC nowhere denies the repeated mention of the 'Big

56 '"Observergate" and academic freedom', *New Statesman* (15 April 2011).

Society' in its current delivery plan. This plan states that its 'Connected Communities' research theme will 'enable the AHRC to contribute to the Government's initiatives on localism and the "Big Society" ' (sect. 2.4.4). The AHRC delivery plan also states that it aspires to make a 'contribution' to 'the "Big Society" agenda' (sects. 3.10, 3.12). The 'Big Society' is mentioned five times in total.

If we believe the AHRC and reject allegations of political interference, there remain significant concerns with regard to the decision to include the 'Big Society' within the delivery plan and especially as an illustration for where funding for a strategic research funding priority area might be directed. It has been revealing that such a concern went unnoticed both in the original decision to include the 'Big Society' in its delivery plans and its response to the *Observer*.

This situation led me to draft a petition on behalf of fellow members of the AHRC Peer Review College, AHRC funding applicants, and others with an interest in AHRC activities in response. The petition is based upon a position of principle, not politics: research councils should not direct funding to strategic areas which overlap with any political party slogans. This is not a petition against the 'Big Society' but against political campaign slogans becoming incorporated in funding documents spelling out funding priorities. The petition clearly states that we would all have equally opposed the 'Third Way' receiving the same attention after the 1997 election: this is not at all a comment on government policy, but on the inclusion of party slogans in research council delivery plans. We have called upon the AHRC to remove all references to the 'Big Society' in its delivery plan with immediate effect.

The petition attracted over 1,000 signatures in less than twenty-four hours with more than 3,000 at present and growing. Those who have signed the petition come from across political and disciplinary divides and include fellow members of the AHRC

Peer Review College, Fellows of the British Academy and Royal Society, Fellows of the Royal Historical Society, the Academy of Social Sciences, and many other learned societies demonstrating clear and widespread support.

Some may argue the petition's success is based upon a mistake or that it wrongly accepts a contested allegation. However, the petition does not take issue with what the AHRC contests (e.g., the allegation of political interference). Moreover, the petition is not critical of the 'Connected Communities' theme nor does it reject the idea of a 'Big Society.' There need not be any opposition to colleagues seeking to conduct research into the 'Big Society' within the 'Connected Communities' theme. Academic freedom is to be protected. This is precisely why we should unite to oppose the AHRC's decision to illustrate how funding applicants might successfully contribute to the 'Connected Communities' research through research related to the 'Big Society.'

This is a mistake. If this matter were left unchallenged, then the possibility would arise that the use of including political party campaign slogans within research funding delivery plans might become more common. Some may argue that we must speak the language of our politicians to best demonstrate the 'impact' and funding importance in this age of austerity. Our response should be that inclusion of political party campaign slogans is a move too far. The ability to communicate our funding priorities need not rely on explicitly linking them with such slogans.

I emphasize that the petition is based upon principle, not politics. No matter our political or disciplinary differences we can unite around the idea that political party campaign slogans have no place in research council funding documents spelling out strategic priorities. The AHRC can address this satisfactorily by immediately removing all references to the 'Big Society' in current and future documentations.

We should constructively support the AHRC to make the right decision and enact this important change. This might better enable a positive platform from which we may join together in defence of the arts and humanities. Failing to do so would be to choose both a failure of principle and furthering unnecessary division at the worst possible time. If the AHRC is correct to claim mention of the 'Big Society' in its delivery plan is trivial, then it should hasten its removal from all research funding documents rather than delay.

Government should make greater use of university academics as specialist consultants[57]

Central government spent over £500m on consultants and staff on short-term contracts across seventeen departments in 2012/13. This figure was reported to be about £800m if staff 'off payroll' were included. This is not surprising.

Modern governments require specialists to assist the effective management of complex programmes. Specialist consultants have a valuable role to play for government. The 'newsworthiness' of this story is that the figures appear relatively high despite pledges by the Government to reduce the use of consultants.

The challenge is how to more effectively support the use of consultants benefiting improved efficiencies and reducing burdens on taxpayers. The current model has been to recruit fewer specialist consultants and offer less remuneration. But there is a better model that can and should be embraced: the greater use of university academics as specialist consultants.

57 'Government should make greater use of university academics as specialist consultants', Impact of Social Sciences (23 September 2013).

University academics are a largely underutilised resource for Whitehall. Recent years have seen the launch of a new so-called 'impact agenda' rolled out by higher education bodies, such as HEFCE and RCUK, where research 'impact' is assessed and a factor in determining higher education funding. The role of this assessment of research impact has been contested and some argue it presents higher education funding with problems difficult to avoid.

These activities operate against a backdrop of supportive rhetoric by successive governments for university academics to demonstrate their research impact as one important part of what public funding for higher education should demand. The increasing importance of impact in British academia should be broadly welcomed and can benefit research even in areas thought vulnerable to neglect in such a climate, such as philosophy and the humanities, as I've argued elsewhere. Nonetheless, many academics complain that interacting with government and civil servants remains far too constrictive: government rhetoric in support of academics demonstrating research impact is not met by governments providing academics with a greater space to create impact in good governance and public policy.

This has been an opportunity lost. Most university academics I know are eager to contribute to policy areas, if only there were more opportunities. There are multiple potential future benefits. The first is that university academics are well-placed to provide the kind of specialist advice governments have acquired from consultants because it is often these academics who helped train the consultants. A second potential benefit is many university academics are in a position to provide such assistance through funded leave from their teaching or between teaching terms. For many academics, this engagement will provide real benefits for their current and future research through first-hand interaction at the policy coalface. Plus, there could be real benefits for their teaching of students, as they would benefit from the first-hand knowledge their lecturers would acquire.

Finally, university academics would likely cost much less than the specialist consultants used by successive governments – and there could be innovative ways of supporting funding. I conclude with one possible model. University academics could form research policy units both within and across institutions that could bid for specific short-term projects in Whitehall. The application process should be as simple and transparent as possible. Teams could then be accepted for work on specific tasks assisting government over the short-term. This might help open up work for government far beyond London permitting greater inclusiveness of research teams across the country and this is a further potential benefit for such a scheme. It might also serve as a useful 'top up' to funding received in relation to research impact that can be targeted for specific funding.

If governments want more efficient and cost-beneficial ways to secure effective specialist advice, university academics are an invaluable resource that has been underutilised. It is time Whitehall looked more closely at how opportunities can be created so that academics might provide the policy impact and good advice that government demands.

Demanding universities name their Brexit teachers is a bizarre attack on academic freedom[58]

A few weeks ago Conservative MP Chris Heaton-Harris wrote to all Vice-Chancellors seeking information about their staff. First, he wanted 'the names of professors' involved who taught European affairs 'with particular reference to Brexit.' Secondly, Heaton-Harris

58 'Demanding universities name their Brexit teachers is a bizarre attack on academic freedom', *The Daily Telegraph* (24 October 2017).

requested copies of their teaching materials and any 'links to online lectures' connected with Brexit.

None of this might have come to light if the Vice-Chancellor of the University of Worcester – David Green – had not made public the MP's letter written on House of Commons stationery he received three weeks ago. Green made clear he'd refuse this request and rightly so. I would do the same if asked.

This is not about Brexit. Universities might be seen as 'soft' targets filled with academics who voted overwhelmingly for Remain, but that doesn't apply here. Not only am I quoted with approval by the Electoral Commission, recommending changes to the EU Referendum's wording to remove pro-Remain bias, but my Law School's alumni includes several distinguished MPs who are all Tories, including Robert Buckland QC, Graham Brady and until 2017 James Wharton.

The issue is academic freedom and possible abuses of power. We need to ask several questions. First, why would Heaton-Harris believe it appropriate for such a letter to be sent to all university chiefs? Information about modules taught is easily found online. If the MP wanted to make a list of them, he did not need to contact VCs.

Discovering who is teaching on specific areas can be more difficult. It is not unusual for colleagues to teach on different modules from year to year and some will be engaged in externally funded research off-campus.

It's the request for individual names that my colleagues find chilling raising a second question: what is the purpose behind this? Why are some academics being singled out?

Ironically, only a few days ago the universities minister Jo Johnson criticised higher education institutions for stifling free speech on campus demanding Vice-Chancellors do something about this. Now we learn that every Vice-Chancellor was contacted a fortnight earlier to provide details about their teaching staff with the issue of their pay in the background. Mixed messages like these enmeshed with potential threats is no way to influence universities that are the envy of the world.

While Heaton-Harris has since tweeted his support for academic freedom, his actions give little reassurance. Not only did he ask for names, but their teaching materials – and even links to their being delivered to students.

It's difficult to see the purpose being anything other than acting like some kind of thought police. MPs should not be snooping in our classrooms looking to expose ideas they disagree with. Nor should such materials be available to anyone not involved with the module. If he wants to know more, he can apply like anyone else.

A final issue concerns who Heaton-Harris is. He is an assistant government whip. MPs in his role don't go rogue: they keep colleagues in line rather than blur lines always seeking to support the Government in getting its policies approved.

So what knowledge or support did Heaton-Harris have when writing to all Vice-Chancellors? Did they agree or condone his activities? Where did this idea to send letters originate – and did it come from the top?

It is difficult to see how a junior government whip could act like this without some endorsement or consent from those issuing commands to the party's parliamentary rank-and-file. We need answers to these questions to understand where this potential attempt to intimidate lecturers for purposes still unknown by a government whip – and who gave the orders.

Our universities are a tremendous asset not least for providing an engaging, critical space where ideas are created and challenged. Whips have no place trying to close debate or dictate what is discussed because they – or senior ministers – are uncomfortable with the conversations. If they allow us to flourish, they might even learn something.

'In place of external examining as it currently operates, let's introduce more rigorous programme reviews'[59]

External examining is no longer fit for purpose.

The problem is not the increasing numbers of student assessments to review or degree programmes to check. It is the failure of universities to increase their resources for external examination in proportion with the sector's expansion. They largely still pay the same paltry fee for the same few hours of externals' time as they always did.

The result is that, apart from for dissertations, externals can rarely alter individual marks any longer. They simply don't have the time to go through them all. So they are limited to either agreeing with everything, warts and all, making some systematic adjustment to marks, or calling for everything to be done again. In my experience, they typically approve just about everything without change, confining themselves to making various comments – usually enormously helpful – on how modules and programmes might be improved further.

Some colleagues argue that we should turn back the clock. If external examining is becoming too much of a rubber-stamp process, we need to increase the powers, time commitment and remuneration of externals, so they can do the job they once did. However, it is unclear how many colleagues would be willing to take on such an onerous task, even with greater compensation.

The right-of-centre think tank Reform argues that national standards should be guaranteed by pegging the distribution of degree classifications on particular courses to their students' performance in national final-year assessment for each subject. This would seemingly cut out external examiners altogether, but it

59 'In place of external examining, as it currently operates, let's introduce more rigorous programme reviews', *Times Higher Education* (26 July 2018): 41.

is a thoroughly bad idea as it would stifle innovation in curriculum design while encouraging teaching to the test.

Universities all claim to engage in some form of research-led or informed teaching. Yet many regulators and managers place research and teaching in different silos. If teaching should have parity with research, then it is high time it was considered in tandem with it.

So I'd propose a US-inspired approach. Let's leave the annual ritual of marking and exam boards to academic departments and universities. In place of external examining as it currently operates, let's introduce more rigorous programme reviews, involving external input, every five or so years. Crucially, these would consider a department's teaching and research strategies together, in terms of how they cross-pollinate to shape the curriculum.

Such reviews could feed into departmental planning and be of even more use than comments in the truncated tick-box forms used by examiners at present. What we have is formal sign-off that all is well; what we need is genuine challenge to improve.

Bureaucratic micromanagement for its own sake is not the road to climbing international league tables, reassuring students that their education is world class, or assuring employers that our graduates are ready for any challenge. It's time we moved on.

A super-exam for solicitors will close doors for those who want to join the profession [60]

It is time for law firms publicly to challenge the Solicitors' Regulation Authority over its plans to introduce a 'super exam' before it is too late.

---

60 'A super-exam for solicitors will close doors for those who want to join the profession', *The Times* (18 December 2018).

I regularly visit law firms of various sizes and I have not found a single partner in favour of the new route to qualification as a solicitor in England and Wales, which is set to come into effect from 2021. And it is easy to understand why.

A significant part of the stated rational for the move is to make the process more open and socially diverse. But this does not stand up to scrutiny.

The SQE involves a multiple-choice exam covering select areas of legal knowledge. It will be a first test for students and their prospective employers that could play a decisive role in career planning.

Multiple-choice exams are easier and less costly to assess for large groups, but not the best or most effective way of discerning ability. Potential is better captured through a diversity of assessments. Putting all eggs in a single basket gives an advantage to the students who need it least.

Under the SQE scheme, a top law programme will be judged more on whether its factory-produced students pass a standardised test instead of innovative excellence in delivery of world class pedagogy.

It will be tempting for struggling schools to drop the qualifying degree and so a route to the Bar to cut costs by reducing the number of modules run annually. Therefore, while it is designed to increase access, the SQE will close doors.

The SRA claims the legal practice course 'gamble' costs students more than £16,000. Yet the SQE tests are up to £4,500 not inclusive of any supportive tutoring that will surely become the norm. The SRA is replacing one gamble with a worse one.

There is a simpler way. Universities, for example, are under intense pressure to open access and be more socially diverse. A target to be met for offering a law degree would ensure all programmes were maximising access.

Some might dismiss these concerns as the expected grumblings of a university don fearful for the effect on his business model. Nothing of the sort.

My university has no plans to launch a legal practice course of or SQE cram school. Law schools like mine will thrive because we can afford to innovate and be world class despite counterproductive pet projects like the SQE.

It is easy to see plans as inevitable when pushed for so long. But few, if any, outside the SRA are convinced these reforms are for the best. Now is the time to raise our voices publicly.

Let us open doors and raise standards, but work together getting it right. Future generations of lawyers – and, most importantly, the public – will thank us.

Foreign students aren't just cash cows – they're saving British universities from Brexit's destruction[61]

University applications are up significantly. In particular, applications from China which have risen thirty per cent since last year, exceeding those from Northern Ireland for the first time. Higher education is in a period of increasingly financial uncertainty as the Augur Review and Brexit lurk in the background.

These latest student figures will delight many institutions which have come to rely more heavily on the higher student fees that international students can bring, especially from China.

It can be tempting for universities to open their doors more to such students in order to protect themselves against feared funding cuts on the horizon. It is easy to view the value of foreign

61 'Foreign students aren't just cash cows – they're saving British universities from Brexit's destruction', *The Independent* (12 July 2019).

students in terms of the extra fees they bring, but also a mistake that could imperil a crucial opportunity to maintain world leading educational standards.

As a former student originally from the United States, I was struck by how little the increasing global diversity of my classroom impacted on the internationalisation of what was being taught. Such a model values foreign students for their income, but not necessarily their global perspective that might enrich the educational experience of all staff and students.

This situation challenged me when I became dean of a leading law school and needed to find some new means of better valuing the diversity of our students by improving our curriculum. With most of our graduates studying for a qualifying law degree in England and Wales, it is not immediately obvious how internationalising the programme will enhance it.

Regularly meeting with employers changed all this. For even modest sized firms, their legal work in the UK stretched out across borders with China a key emerging market.

A fit for purpose education to train the next generation of lawyers successfully now requires exposing students to other legal systems, especially the Chinese legal system. One 'magic circle' partner said he would hire everyone taking a class in Chinese law given its growing presence in everyday work in the City.

This showed how to transform a traditional curriculum towards a new, more global direction adding modules in areas of Chinese and US law alongside more familiar topics. We've also launched the largest Centre for Chinese Law and Policy in Europe.

Our realignment has been greeted warmly by our growing list of partner law firms and chambers for improving the employability of our students. It has embraced the internationalisation of our undergraduate students – our programme has the most non-EU students in the sector – within the design of our programme. This, in turn, makes our school more attractive to a growing cohort of academic staff from multiple legal systems in a virtuous cycle. Foreign students can see their diversity matters in preparing more effective future lawyers for a heavily competitive market.

If such a transformation can be achieved in a subject like Law, it can succeed in others too. A more global student body in Philosophy can drive the much needed diversification of its canon, bringing into conversation ways of thought familiar to our students that can enrich and progress academic staff research as well.

Such a model is easily replicated in other subjects, if not already, that continue to change our approach to education in universities that better acknowledges the increasing internationalisation of our campuses – and in a way that improves on our current practices.

British higher education continues to prosper from the high regard it is held across the world. We must not be complacent about our privileged position at a time of high competition and funding uncertainty. International students are central to many institutions for the financial benefits they bring. This is best maintained when we value even more the global perspective they add to our classrooms by internationalising our programmes.

We should aspire to creating a curriculum that requires global diversity for its educational benefits more than any additional income it brings. Anything less takes present student interest for granted with negative longer term consequences for our universities in general.[62]

62 'Foreign students aren't just cash cows – they're saving British universities from Brexit's destruction', *The Independent* (12 July 2019).

Labour should make better use of supportive academics[63]

Whoever wins the leader and deputy leadership contests will have a difficult task unifying a Labour Party still in mourning after the 2019 defeat. Adding to that challenge, there is now less money to support expert advisors because we won fewer seats. The Government can rely on the civil service to support its programme of reforms, yet the mountain an opposition must climb is more arduous, with less resources for additional advisors to help it hold the Government to account and develop plans for taking power.

Labour is only beginning to unlock the enormously potential of its huge membership, and a relatively untapped part is the significant number of pro-Labour leading academics. They could be put to greater use, funded through other resources, bringing further benefits to policy development while remaining cost neutral. Recently, the Government advertised for experts and 'weirdos' to apply for a series of positions in select areas via Dominic Cummings' blog. The plan was to have a formal recruitment round in various roles, including policy experts. This has costs that may be within reach of a newly-elected government, but beyond what an opposition relying on limited funding can spend. The issue then becomes how the opposition can similarly benefit from extra policy experts, without the additional resources to pay for them.

The answer can partly be found in making better use of leading academics who are Labour members or supportive of Labour's policy goals. University professors and lecturers are more pro-Labour than pro-Conservative by a large margin across academic fields, providing a wide-ranging talent pool to draw upon. This is,

63 'Labour should make more use of supportive academics', *LabourList* (5 February 2020).

in my view, not a product of bias but of following evidence – which often overturns conventional, traditional thinking in favour of progressive, new solutions to old problems.

There is a strong incentive for academics working in higher education and their universities to provide free policy advice and expertise. This incentive comes from the Research Excellence Framework (REF), a competitive national framework assessing the quality of research in every academic department across all universities. Assessments happen every six to seven years with the next exercise ranking departments in 2021. The better the quality of a department's research in the REF, the greater the share of new income they receive each year until the next one. The exercise ranks departments across every academic subject, from first to last, with those at the top receiving more research funding than any below it.

A department's REF score is determined mostly (*c.* sixty per cent) by the quality of its publications as judged and scored by a panel. The department's general research environment is also taken into account – looking at research funding, PhD student completions and other factors (*c.* fifteen per cent). A significant portion of a department's REF score is determined by its research 'impact' (*c.* twenty-five per cent). And research impact is defined as follows:

- *impact includes, but is not limited to, an effect on, change or benefit to:*
- *the activity, attitude, awareness, behaviour, capacity, opportunity, performance, policy, practice, process or understanding;*
- *of an audience, beneficiary, community, constituency, organisation or individuals;*
- *in any geographic location whether locally, regionally, nationally or internationally.*

A department needs one impact case study for every eleven research-active staff members – for example an academic department with thirty-three staff or more would require three impact case studies.

But the numbers here are not the important part of this story. The greater the impact generated by an academic or team of academics on a certain project, then the higher their score – which will support a stronger REF performance and the added financial support for the institution that comes with it.

Universities, as charities, cannot discriminate between political parties or provide funding – and rightly so. However, universities can and do support fringe events at party conferences and much more. Universities also regularly provide funding to support academics to make regular visits to Parliament, as mine has done. This is not to promote any particular political view, but to support the advancement of the research-led impact of its scholars on policy development, without supporting any one party to the exclusion of others. Most universities would make such funding available for their staff because it can literally pay off in earning extra funding through creating a strong impact case study that boosts a positive REF performance.

There is an opportunity to create a new 'academic Labour network', launching a ready team of policy expert advisors drawn from the university sector. They would provide additional support in areas or topics relevant to Labour's future policy development, acting as part-time advisors and at no cost to the Labour Party. Its launch would require minimal organisation beyond targeting the areas of expertise required.

Experienced policy advisors like me can assist in supporting the location of funding from institutions to attend meetings as required and to support training and continued mentoring, so that all work together and understand their role and specified areas for making a contribution. This work can include drafting brief policy reports as directed, recommending written questions for tabling, providing advice ahead of oral debates, additional scrutiny of proposed legislation and more.

This network can be utilised to do much more than be an extra set of policy advisors – it could be the heart of a new educational and training organisation. Recent calls by Keir Starmer to create a 'Labour Party college' delivering accredited political education, campaign training, leadership skills and online courses would be transformative. And an academic Labour network could bring together pro-Labour scholars that have the know-how and ability to make a Labour Party college, and its hugely positive and ambitious programme for change, possible.

The UK is home to some of the world's leading universities – and the most talented academics, the majority of whom are supportive of Labour if not party members already. This is a talent pool that is underused but could be unlocked at no cost to the party and at much potential gain. It could easily be used to address the needs of the leader's office and front bench, with training and mentoring from an experienced, policy-interfacing academic already in use. Such an academic Labour network would provide much beneficial support to whoever wins the leadership contests.

Don't launch solicitor super exam during a global pandemic[64]

Working remotely has gone from optional to mandatory within a few short weeks. Our workplaces are temporarily closed and the

64 'Don't launch solicitor super exam during a global pandemic', Legal Cheek (7 April 2020).

court system has been seriously impacted as well. Law students have now gone home from their universities as their professors switch from teaching in ever larger lecture theatres to Zoom.

In virtually every area of our lives, we see planned reforms paused and put on ice so that something as close to 'business as usual' can be maintained. A global pandemic is not the time to consider the future of the Qualifying Law Degree, but rather ensuring the existing system can be maintained through the current crisis.

The main regulator for becoming a solicitor – the Solicitors' Regulation Authority (SRA) – has conceded temporary changes of how assessments are conducted may be unavoidable under these extreme circumstances. An enormous amount of effort and time will be spent getting this right for the sake of students and the wider profession.

But it is now time for the SRA to go one step further and postpone its plans for the Solicitors' Qualifying Exam (or SQE) – widely referred to as the 'super-exam' – for at least six months. The SRA is expected to request formal approval from the LSB this summer.

It is unreasonable and unnecessary to divert attention from the major challenges posed to all education providers by the pandemic to respond to any such submission. To potentially require significant changes to how law is taught – on top of the virtually overnight shift for most providers from traditional lectures to online learning – would be enormously and avoidably disruptive.

Putting the SQE on the backburner until the coronavirus outbreak is under control does not entail the exam must be abandoned as a result. If the SRA wants to launch it, then its plans should receive proper scrutiny and the providers who are to prepare students for whatever these plans might be must have time to succeed. Neither is possible now.

Many see the SQE as a gamble not worth the risk at the best of times. I am a vocal opponent of the SQE while a passionate advocate for wider legal education reform. I worry that a top law programme will be judged more on whether its factory-produced students pass a standardised test setting a threshold instead of innovative excellence in delivery of world class pedagogy. I also have concerns about the costs and doubt the SQE solves the problem of access and quality that motivate its introduction. But now is not the time to have this crucially important debate. COVID-19 has changed timescales in virtually all areas of life – this should be no different.

If a global pandemic is not a sufficiently strong reason to postpone SQE plans until next summer, then it's not clear what would. I call on the SRA to hold off on the SQE so we can work together on getting this right after this crisis is over.

Metrics would ruin the REF[65]

At the end of every research excellence framework (REF) cycle, the question is asked whether a more metrics-driven system could simplify and improve what is undeniably a complex, time-intensive exercise. This time around is no exception; since submissions closed at the end of March, there has been a flurry of articles addressing this question, and it is certainly a discussion worth having. However, it seems to me that the answer remains the same: no.

The REF aims, among other things, to identify the relative world-class strengths of UK academic departments, scoring them according to output produced, impact generated and their research environments. It seems likely that high output scores reflect the

65 'Metrics would ruin the REF', *Times Higher Education* (5 May 2021).

strongest research environments, in terms of protected research time, availability of research funding and frequency of research leave. So one simplification might be to do away with outputs and score the REF entirely on environment (which is much less labour-intensive to assess than outputs) and impact.

However, the incentives that doing so would introduce might damage quality. Departments might divert scarce resources to supportive measures but without maintaining sufficient regard of what they helped produce. Moreover, the correlation between quality of input and quality of output is hard to definitively prove, and if our aim is to assess the quality of the research produced, anything less than a close look at the outputs themselves would seem to be second best.

But could the burden of assessing outputs be lightened by switching from peer review to some form of metrics? I think not. Every metrics-driven model I have seen for assessing research quality tends to focus on what can be counted – and all are very imperfect proxies for what needs to be counted: quality.

Take journal rankings. Different academic fields disagree (including internally) about whether there is or could be a definitive ranked list of the best journals. In most, if not all, fields in the arts, humanities and social sciences it is not uncommon for different journals to approach the same referees to assesses the same piece of work; specialist expertise is scarce, after all. Sometimes those approached recuse themselves if they have already reviewed the manuscript for another journal. Sometimes they don't. Either way, the supposed 'best' journals certainly don't have a stranglehold on the best reviewers or the highest standards. Rather, in my experience, the 'best' journals are generally considered to be those most commonly available within universities – and those tend to be the oldest titles.

What about other possible metrics? Grant income (and the need for it) varies enormously by field and scholarly approach.

Citations, meanwhile, are a particularly unreliable indicator of quality in the humanities. In my own work, for instance, I cite work that I find mistaken as often, if not more so, than work supporting my points, since I aim to offer something new. Does that matter at an aggregate level? After all, universities are assigned funding based on the entirety of their REF submission, so you might ask how much granularity we really need. However, the minutiae of the rankings do matter enormously for those involved. Cutting corners might save time, but if it short-changes certain departments and institutions it isn't worth it, in my opinion.

Perhaps a metrics-based approach might be more relevant to the sciences, and there is nothing to say, a priori, that all disciplines must be judged in the same way; I am aware that, in Australia, for example, a hybrid approach is used depending on the discipline. But if we do want a universal approach, the worst option apart from all the others would appear to be peer review.

While it might be difficult to improve on the REF as a mode of national research assessment, I do worry that it is so utterly divorced from the assessment of teaching quality. This seems particularly misguided for those research-intensive institutions that champion their research-led teaching.

Some might worry that bringing teaching and research together would create more administrative workload. This is an important concern, and I agree with those who argue that we need to focus more on doing research and teaching rather than filling out reports about it. Yet it is also important that we think clearly about what we do and why we do it.

In this case, I don't think the administrative burden need increase at all. We in the UK already spend a lot of time on teaching quality through assurance exercises, periodic departmental reviews and annual reviews of teaching – not to mention the teaching excellence framework (TEF) itself. How difficult would it be to reorient these exercises so that strategic planning about teaching focuses on research-led teaching excellence? After all, the staff and students who create and benefit from research and research-led teaching are whole human beings, so why should our institutional research and educational strategies be run by separate teams, each with their own future plans?

Of course, any joined-up assessment of research and its contribution to world-class education would probably lend itself even less to a metrics-driven approach than the REF does. But what I propose would, I believe, produce a far more holistic, far more useful measure of departmental and institutional quality.

We can and we should do better that the current approach – but not by grasping for low-cost, low-quality metrics.

The Labour Academic Network is here to offer a reliable reservoir of experts[66]

Solid expertise and a sound grasp of the evidence has never been more important than now. Although this government once prided itself on being able to 'super-forecast', it has never acted in response to events until after the damage was done. And never before have we seen such a mess. One minute we are told the Government is simply following the scientists, the next their warnings appear to go unheeded. There is no strategic vision and policymaking seems evermore removed from evidence.

The Government seems to be aware of this problem. Former chief adviser to the Prime Minister Dominic Cummings called out for policy experts to contact him with possible jobs on offer,

66 'The Labour Academic Network is here to offer a reliable reservoir of experts', *LabourList* (5 January 2021).

reporting to him, a year ago. It probably did not help that he specifically wanted 'weirdos' and 'misfits' – and it would appear his plans for a new 'super-brain' policy unit have come to nothing.

At the time, I believed that Labour could do far, far better than this with a new policy network that could plug a crucial gap. Last February, I set out a pitch on *LabourList* for a new group: the Labour Academic Network. This network will bring together the academic expertise of Labour members and supporters across all key strategic areas on a voluntary basis to supplement and support Labour's frontbench.

The idea is simple. Having lost seats in 2019, Labour has also lost short money and, thus, can support fewer advisers. There is a clear need for finding additional expertise that can fill this shortfall of those working with the leadership with an emphasis on harnessing the expertise and evidence base to support policy-making. This aligns with Labour's focus on competence under Keir Starmer's leadership.

The network requires a reliable reservoir of experts that can provide support where needed. It is a means by which experts can be brought together and called upon to provide an extra layer and level of expert advice. Labour has championed education since its founding and an inspiring body of talent is in the party, waiting to be harnessed and utilised effectively. The issue has been how to best draw on this talent.

Anyone can have their say in Labour's policy process through various existing forums, which are vital to our movement. This collective know-how and experience is invaluable, and I have been an active contributor since the day I joined the party. An academic network will only amplify the various ways that members and supporters can contribute.

As founding director, I am proud to announce that the Labour Academic Network has been launched. I have heard from over two hundred interested individuals wanting to contribute via our new website. This is not a campaigning organisation; the only side it takes is supporting Labour to win the next general election.

The role of the Labour Academic Network is to provide the party with evidence and expertise, in confidence, from among the incredible members and supporters we have. Over the coming years, the network will bring together, train and support a global network to provide expert advice on legislation, recommend draft amendments, provide talking points and serve as expert witnesses, organise focused round table discussions and provide policy reports in confidence and on request. This work is already underway and making a difference.

The Labour Academic Network opens a new, exciting chapter for members and supporters for the new year. I encourage anyone with an interest in taking part and with expertise in any area of policy to get in touch with me via our website. Labour is under new leadership and the network is one of many means to support its work.

Big problems about Borders

Immigration has been a top public concern since I first moved to the UK in 2001. This is mostly a problem of perceptions which the financial crash only fuelled.

Migrants became easy targets – readily blamed and lacking a voice – politicians on mostly the ideological right, but also some otherwise espousing left-wing sympathies, who scapegoat them as a matter of routine. Everything from education and housing to health and transport was blamed on migrants.

Undoubtedly, chronic underinvestment in public services which austerity helped drive did lead to insufficient resources for schools, NHS under strain, not enough affordable housing especially for younger families and so on. The pressures on people were real.

But what was rarely highlighted was the fact that migrants were far more likely to be in the NHS queue as the doctor or nurse than as patients. Reducing their number meant, yes, there would be fewer migrants on the patient list – but also fewer medical professionals to help the patients. Fewer migrant doctors means queues get longer, not shorter. Same with other areas: migrants don't only live in housing, but build it – and that migration helps fill the places of much needed teachers, lecturers, classroom assistants, laboratory staff and public transport teams. Fewer migrants doesn't make these problems go away.

When preparing for my permanent residency application about a decade ago, I discovered that I needed to sit and pass a Life in the UK citizenship test – an exam that I had never heard of before. I promptly failed an online practice test, purchased a copy of the handbook – after all, I was going to have to study for it – and headed home. That evening the leader of the British National Party was on BBC's *Question Time* programme. Everyone made sure to say how they disagreed with his views, but then made clear how they nonetheless harboured views that migrants crossed the border too easily, that few checks were made and the system was essentially offering migrants an open door. And all of it was rubbish.

I made a commitment to myself that night – when I became a British citizen, I was going to speak up for migrants everywhere in the country. This was because on that programme and countless others there are plenty of folks who are called 'experts' on immigration. But it's striking how few have ever been a migrant themselves – it's virtually never the case – and their knowledge of immigration rarely transcends having a political view, but almost never a grasp of the rules. There was a clear gap in the media market for an immigrant who knew the system and its rules first-hand. I've tried to fill that role ever since.

These essays cover a range of topics and overlapping themes. Their content comes from my personal experiences and research on the topic. I'm especially proud to have been at the forefront of highlighting the points-based system already in place (a fact seemingly still lost on the Prime Minister who claims he wants to start one). I broke the story of how the Home Office had a form to report ex-lovers, few have written as much about the problems of using net migration targets, I have followed the money and helped expose the up to nine hundred per cent profits raised by the Home Office off the back of application fees, I'm the only one to have noticed that granting the Cornish protected minority status meant the citizenship test did have to change, I have argued for half a decade and more than anyone else against the health migration surcharge (which isn't even spent entirely on health) and have been a lone voice for many years stating that Labour can win with a progressive immigration vision. The essays chart the ebbs and flows over nearly a decade about immigration – and demonstrate how many of the problems and gaps in understanding when I started have continued to plague Conservative Governments since.

The 'Life in the UK' Test has morphed into a barrier to immigration[67]

The Life in the United Kingdom citizenship test has become an integral part of British immigration policy. One million tests have been taken since its launch in 2005. About 150,000 people sat the test last year. Passing the test is a requirement for permanent residency and citizenship. Alternatively, a short course, 'English for Speakers of Other Languages with Citizenship', may be completed although this can take much longer and is more expensive. The Life in the UK test takes forty-five minutes and it has twenty-four questions. Applicants must answer eighteen or more correctly to pass.

I published the only comprehensive report into the test and its uses for immigration policy in June. The report launch was held in Durham Castle and uploaded on YouTube. My findings were covered in over three hundred newspapers and media outlets across the UK and internationally, including Comedy Central and Mock the Week. However, my report was no laughing matter for the

67 'The "Life in the UK" Test has morphed into a barrier to immigration', *The New Statesman* (16 July 2013).

Government as I revealed the test to be impractical, inconsistent and contain significant gender imbalance rendering it 'unfit for purpose' and like 'a bad pub quiz.'

The Life in the UK test has always included what many of us might consider trivia. Information such as the number of MPs in the House of Commons or how to claim a National Insurance number is not probably known by most British citizens. But the test has gone from a test about practical trivia to the purely trivial. Information about how to contact an ambulance, how to report a crime or how to register with a GP has been removed. Instead, applicants are required to know the year that the Emperor Claudius invaded Britain, the approximate age of Big Ben's clock and the height of the London Eye in feet and metres. Consider the following dates in the life of Sake Dean Mahomet that must be memorised by rote: birth (1759), first came to the UK (1782), eloped to Ireland (1786), opened first curry house (1810) and death (1851). Furthermore, it must be known that he married a woman from Ireland named Jane Daly, that his curry house was called the Hindoostane Coffee House and it was established on George Street in London. The test has never included so much impractical information before – and the new handbook has about three thousand facts to be memorised. And remember: only twenty-four will be covered on the test.

Curiously for a handbook written and approved by politicians, the number of MPs has always been a bit of a problem. The first edition was published in late 2004 and stated there were 645 MPs. This was untrue: there were 646. So why this mistake? The best explanation I found for this was that only 645 constituencies were contested in the 2005 General Election. This was because a candidate in the 646th constituency – Staffordshire South – had died and so that election was postponed. But there were still 646 (and not 645) MPs. In 2007, the second edition of the test handbook was published. This time the Government confirmed the correct number of 646. However, this soon changed to 650 MPs and this change was never incorporated on the test. It was the case – when I sat the test in 2009 – that the 'correct' answer to this and many other questions were factually untrue.

The new handbook published this year has solved this problem through omission. Applicants are no longer required to know how many MPs sit in Westminster. Many of us might think this a welcome change: after all, if MPs have been confused about this, why expect the British public to do any better? And why should this information be a requirement for citizenship anyway? Nevertheless, all applicants are still required to know the number of elected representatives in the Welsh Assembly, Scottish Parliament and Northern Ireland Assembly.

The inconsistencies do not end there. Various courts from youth courts and beyond are mentioned, but the UK Supreme Court is left out. Another inconsistency concerns telephone numbers. It may be hard to believe, but the new test handbook requires applicants to memorize telephone numbers. There are five to know and none are 999 or 111. The five include the National Domestic Violence Helpline and the HMRC self-assessment helpline. The final three are the front offices of the House of Commons, the Welsh Assembly and the Scottish Parliament – omitting (forgetting?) the Northern Ireland Assembly at Stormont in Belfast.

The Life in the UK test suffers from serious gender imbalance. For example, the new test includes a substantial chapter about British history. This chapter lists the dates of birth for about thirty men, but only four women. Neither of the Queen's birthdays is included. No women artists are mentioned: we are required to know Damien Hirst won the Turner Prize, but no note of who is Tracey Emin. No women musicians or singers are noted. No women poets have any lines for memorising among the several scattered throughout the handbook. No women are included in a long list of famous scientists and inventors. Nor are these the only strange omissions: L. S. Lowry is left out and there are no lines included by Robert Burns.

Nor does this gender imbalance appear to be a simple oversight. A Home Office announcement on the day the new test launched commented on how the test now includes a chapter about British history. The Home Office announcement states the importance for immigrants to know the achievements of the people who have shaped Britain – naming nine men and no women.

My report provides twelve recommendations for how the test can be reformed and avoid these problems in future. These include the need for greater care to be taken to ensure greater balance and consistency. I also recommend the need for a public consultation. This is now long overdue. There has been no such consultation since the test was launched in 2005. The test has now undergone three editions with one million tests sat. It is high time some effort was made to re-examine whether the test has lived up to its promise and how it might be further improved. Any such consultation must include engagement with people like me – immigrants to Britain who have sat the test. It is shocking that no public effort has been made to consult with those who have sat the test and become British citizens. Many of the mistakes we can find in the test might have been avoided if ministers had experienced immigration first-hand and sat similar tests.

Finally, it is worth reconsidering the purpose of the test. One model is a barrier where the test serves as an obstacle to citizenship. A second model is a bridge where it is more of a formality confirming common membership. Should the test be a barrier or a bridge? For the moment, it is neither fish nor fowl or platypus. To best reform the test, we must ask what purpose we want it to serve. I believe a sensible discussion about this is possible and the positive, widespread coverage of my report gives me hope for the future. If we wait any longer, the test's problems will only be exacerbated. The time to act is now.

Immigration arrests are not a spectator sport[68]

In the week that saw the British press rightly condemning the use of Twitter to send violent threats to several women, the Home Office started to use the social media site to publicise operations to carry out its threat to expel more illegal immigrants.

The Home Office has been tweeting images of enforcement officers apprehending through force people suspected of working illegally in the UK with their faces gently blurred. A running feed of Home Office tweets celebrated triumphs including the discovery of 'suspected visa overstayer' (surely, no greater threat to the security of our fragile borders) at the most unassuming of locations: a 'Swansea nail bar.' Each tweet congratulated a rising tally of arrested undesirables: first 62, then 94 and soon 139 people were claimed to have been carted off in a series of raids.

The backlash was instant, with several high-profile Twitter users criticising the feed. Comedian David Schneider mocked the Home Office for its coverage of the 'preliminary rounds of the UK Hunger Games', while journalist Charlie Brooker likened the live updates to a 'tweet-a-long-a-stormtroop gallery.'

The Home Office's decision to use social media in this way seems mistaken and potentially dangerous. Perhaps we might expect tabloid newspapers to distribute images of individuals when arrested and prior to any conviction but it is highly disappointing

68 'Immigration arrests are not a spectator sport', The Conversation (5 August 2013).

to find a government department following suit. In one tweet, the Home Office even went a step further by identifying fourteen of those arrested as, to use the hashtag, #immigrationoffenders, rather than suspected immigration offenders.

These images are distributed to all 98,000 of the Home Office's Twitter followers and freely accessible to the wider Twittersphere with millions of potential readers. It would appear that every person apprehended has been convicted before any trial or legal confirmation that, in fact, they truly are an illegal immigrant. We should demand that the Home Office does not treat anyone as guilty before charged. And it will be interesting to see if anyone captured in the photos is innocent after all.

A further problem is the idea that this is the kind of activity that the public wants to see. The idea rests on a mistake that we, the public, so concerned with immigration, will sleep better and feel greater security if the Home Office broadcasts its activities as if its staff were the stars of a new series of COPS.

It is highly doubtful that releasing images and a few numbers on Twitter will make any substantive effect of addressing the public's concerns about immigration. Most do not make any use of Twitter. So distributing these images under the banner of 'immigration offenders' does not achieve any wider goal save attributing guilt before it is due. The images shame people not as individuals, but as a class – the unwanted, the immigrant offender – and without confirmation of wrongdoing. Such stigmatisation of a group is a kind of disintegrative shaming that contributes to mistrust and feeds suspicions that are ill-suited to a decent society.

If the Home Office wants to tackle fears about immigration, then it should focus on the problem of the general anxiety that feeds these fears. A major challenge for all political parties is the problem of overcoming insecurity about employment, housing, crime and declining standards of living. It is insecurity over these issues that contributes to concerns about immigration. Immigrants are blamed for problems in unemployment, rising crime, housing shortages and other social challenges all independently of the fact that immigration may contribute little, if anything, to these challenges.

But the worst outcome is to feed public insecurity about several complex social challenges through the lens of a common enemy, the immigration offender, by celebrating tough cops as they pounce on potentially innocent people. Sometimes looking like doing something is worse than doing nothing at all.

Bad Data underpins health tourism report[69]

A new report into so-called 'health tourism' makes for a shocking read. Not because the costs of migrants deemed to have travelled to Britain primarily to enjoy free NHS services on British taxpayers has spiralled to £2 billion, but because it exposes serious concern about the Government playing politics with both immigration and the NHS.

Consider the facts. The Government has yet to provide a reliable estimate of how many such migrants have actually used the NHS. In July, Health Secretary Jeremy Hunt admitted on the BBC Today programme that 'the truth is we don't know the number' of health tourists in Britain.

This failure to know the number of migrants benefiting from the NHS without contributing to its costs hasn't prevented Hunt from claiming that health tourism costs the UK about £12m – a figure manufactured from the rounded-up sum of £11.5m, which related to unpaid charges for treating migrants. When we talk

69 'Bad Data underpins flawed health tourism report', The Conversation (23 October 2013).

about the costs of health tourism, what we're actually talking about is any use of the NHS by migrants for any reason. And so we begin to expose the mythical health tourist problem.

The new report, published by the Department of Health, makes for interesting reading. Its purpose is clear: to provide a more reliable evidence-base for estimating the number of migrants using the NHS and associated costs.

The report was celebrated in the *Daily Mail* for providing the 'true cost of health tourism' and claimed this was now up to £2 billion per year and far beyond previous estimates. The Home Office plans to introduce a levy of £150 on foreign students and £200 on temporary migrants to help recover these costs.

The problem is that the report is a product of considerable guesswork where assumptions drive the data. This is clear from the first few pages. It claims to consider only 'the expected uses of services' but not the actual services that were used. These assumptions about predicted uses were then 'weighted to adjust' according to the assumed 'demographic profile' and estimated 'health needs' of health tourists to determine the costs incurred.

And it gets worse. The report admits its figures on illegal migrants is 'very uncertain' and lacks 'up to date statistics from the Home Office.' It likewise claims the number of health tourists – you guessed it – is also 'very uncertain' and the report's 'numbers should be used with caution.' In fact, the estimates used in the report to provide a figure on the cost to the NHS by migrants are 'based on incomplete data, sometimes of varying quality, and a large number of assumptions.'

And there's yet more. As every student in my lectures about public policy knows, any cost-benefit analysis must not only include the costs, but also the benefits. All migrants studying at universities in the UK are permitted to work and would pay National Insurance contributions. Most migrants in the UK possess a visa permitting them to work and they also would pay these contributions.

A serious flaw of this report is its failure to note any benefits paid by migrants through National Insurance contributions that also financially support the NHS. Any cost-benefit analysis must include these contributions in its estimates.

The failure to include benefits, such as National Insurance contributions, in assessing the costs of so-called health tourism seriously undermines the value of this report to inform debates. It is deeply concerning that such a fundamental omission could go unnoticed by the Department of Health and the mainstream media.

It is bad enough the Government continues to lack secure statistics about the numbers of migrants and that it would trumpet as fact assumption-fuelled speculation about migrants and the NHS. But it is even worse where cost-benefit analysis is a consideration of costs alone.

If we want to expose the reality of migrants' use of the NHS, then we require better data and less guesswork. And the Government would do this debate a great service if it showed half as much care in trying to identify the benefits that migrants contribute to the NHS as it is on claiming costs. Otherwise, the Government appears more willing to peddle myths as facts to push policy change.

'Polish precedent' won't work to forecast future EU migration [70]

David Cameron has received a strong rebuke from the Bulgarian president, Rosen Plevneliev, who revealed in an interview yesterday that he had confronted the British prime minister at an EU summit over his Government's 'actions, language and plans' about the

70 '"Polish Precedent" won't work to forecast future EU migration', The Conversation (23 December 2013).

likelihood of a mass influx of Bulgarian migrants to Britain after restrictions are lifted on January 1 next year.

In an interview in *The Observer*, Plevneliev said: 'Bulgarian people are raising a lot of questions today about the democratic, tolerant and humane British society. Are we in Great Britain today writing a history of a switch to isolation, nationalism and short-term political approaches?'

Migrants from Bulgaria and Romania will be allowed to take advantage of free movement of labour within EU countries next year – a step which has prompted a great deal of speculation by press and politicians that Britain will be overwhelmed by migrants from those countries. But the truth is that most leading migration experts agree that providing any precise figure is difficult, if not impossible. We're dealing with something best called, to follow Donald Rumsfeld's apt description, a 'known unknown.' We know there will be migrants – but what we don't know is how many will arrive when current restrictions on living and working in the UK expire at the end of this month.

Some think tanks offer guesses with hard numbers. One particularly widely cited figure is an estimate by Migration Watch that we should expect about 50,000 migrants from Romania and Bulgaria to enter Britain each year from 2014. That's about 250,000 over five years. The problem is that these numbers are based on a flawed analogy that doesn't work.

Let's examine the figures used by Migration Watch. They claim we can model how many Romanian and Bulgarian migrants will come to the UK based on how many Polish migrants have already migrated to Britain. But there's a problem. Poland has a population of 38 million people, much larger than Romania's 21m and Bulgaria's 7.5m combined. Without much justification, Migration Watch lumps Polish, Bulgarian and Romanian citizens together, arguing it's logical to estimate the number of new migrants from

Romania and Bulgaria by assuming they'll migrate to Britain in the same proportion as Poles did.

So we scale our figures in proportion to known migration to Britain from Poland and – presto! – we have our estimate of Romanian and Bulgarian migration: nothing more than a share of migration from a different country over a period of time in the recent past. Rather like saying that if I'm one-fifth bigger than you, you'll consume one-fifth less than me. Or something like that.

The big question is whether the 'Polish precedent' can point us toward a clear estimate of migration numbers. Unfortunately for Migration Watch, it cannot.

Poland's situation is very different from Bulgaria's or Romania's in various ways. Poland is much bigger, and the UK was among the first in the EU to open its doors to Polish migration. In contrast, the UK is now in the last group to open its doors to Romanian and Bulgarian migration. This means that migrants from those countries keen to work and live elsewhere have already had opportunities in other EU states. This was not true in Poland's case.

Polish migrants also came to Britain in larger than expected numbers at a particular time in history: the economic boom years of the mid-2000s. Once the economy began to falter, migration numbers decreased significantly. Restrictions on Romanian and Bulgarian migration will be lifted while the British economy remains weak with little growth. The economic conditions that attracted Polish migrants from 2004 therefore simply do not apply to Romanian and Bulgarian migrants from 2014.

Using known migration numbers from the boom years as a proxy for future migration during stagnation therefore relies on false equivalence – between very different countries, in very different circumstances, at very different times. As should be obvious, this is hardly a basis for a sound statistical forecast.

But I don't disagree with everything Migration Watch says about this topic: as they themselves have conceded, 'There is no purely statistical basis on which one could estimate the likely future flows of migration from Romania and Bulgaria.' This is something we might all agree on – although it calls into question their decision to release an estimate anyway.

The question of how many Romanian and Bulgarian migrants really will come to the UK from 2014 is clearly an important one. But the answer is a known unknown. While we can all appreciate the need for useful figures, the numbers we're given simply don't add up.

Immigration Ministers need to know more about immigration[71]

Mark Harper MP was a junior minister making a name for himself. He oversaw the publication of the Government's controversial 'Life in the United Kingdom' citizenship test – likened to 'a bad pub quiz' – and he supported the equally controversial 'Go Home' vans that were driven through London in a brief trial.

Harper had been the champion of a new immigration bill making its way through Parliament. The bill would require GPs and landlords to check the immigration status of their patients and tenants, and would double the fine for hiring illegal immigrants from £10,000 to £20,000. Critics claimed the bill would create confusion by turning citizens into border agents, but without the appropriate training; still, the bill is a key part of the Government's programme on immigration reform, and Harper had proven an effective advocate for its progression in Parliament.

---

71 'Immigration Ministers need to know more about immigration', The Conversation (11 February 2014).

It is then deeply ironic that he has so readily become an example of why critics oppose it. Harper has now resigned as Immigration Minister after he discovered that he had been hiring an illegal immigrant as his cleaner. While he claims to have been shown documents appearing to confirm her indefinite leave to remain, it now appears her papers were fakes.

Harper's critics ask why, if the Minister for Immigration can't ensure his staff are legal immigrants, we expect everyone else to do better? GPs, landlords and employers might soon face significantly increased fines if they fail to take steps an immigration minister himself could not take. There may still be political ramifications: the public doesn't look kindly on politicians who push for plans and regulations they can't honour themselves.

It is unsurprising to see these revelations, clearly a real embarrassment for the Government, used to support opposition to the Immigration Bill. Critics can point to Harper's folly as proof the new law would create problems. We can also expect the bill's opponents to remind us about this case for as long as the law is debated.

But while commentators may be quick to draw attention to the irony of Harper's conduct, there is a crucial question all have overlooked: what does it say about the immigration debate that the Immigration Minister cannot recognise the correct documents certifying that someone is permitted entry to work in the UK? It is striking that someone in his position could be so easily fooled by false documents, given that few should be expected to know better what they should look like.

This case is just one of a long list where ministers have proven more focused on headline-grabbing announcements than on practical realities. Harper's relatively successful efforts at winning media coverage for a new citizenship test, the 'Go Home' van pilot, and his support of the Immigration Bill were all instrumental in attempting to help the Government appear more 'tough' on immigration. But each has been subjected to scathing criticism without any convincing response.

Few accept the 'Life in the UK' test as an unproblematic exam for citizenship; the 'Go Home' vans proved ineffective at encouraging illegal immigrants to leave the UK and were decried as deeply offensive. Now Harper has become his own best proof that requiring employers to confirm the lawful immigration status of employees is more challenging than the Government has conceded.

The Harper resignation is not an isolated case of government policy moving in the wrong direction, but an example of a much wider problem. Ministers simply seem to know too little about the realities of immigration. They have so far failed to engage with and learn from the experiences of immigrants who have come to the UK and built lives here. They also need to look far more closely at the process of immigration and understand it intimately. Immigrants should not be the only people who know what a valid indefinite leave to remain visa application looks like.

The problem is that engaging with the very groups they wish to control better is either unappealing or thought unnecessary. But until such interaction is launched in earnest, I fear we can expect to see more mistakes from a government that is increasingly out of touch – even with issues it claims to take especially seriously.

Calais Migrant Crisis must be a problem shared between France and Britain[72]

Calais might be in France, but it is the front line of Britain's battle to control immigration. Yet the Governments of both countries

72 'Calais Migrant Crisis must be a problem shared between France and Britain', The Conversation (1 September 2014).

continue to pass the buck between each other and very little progress has been made since the Sangatte refugee camp was closed a decade ago.

Surveys of UK public opinion paint a mixed picture and while there is significant support for reducing migration, views about why this is important vary considerably from reality. Pollsters Ipsos-Mori found that more than sixty per cent of the public believed refugees made up the largest group when it comes to immigrants entering the UK. Respondents to a survey on the subject in fact overestimated the number of refugees coming into the country by as much as four times the real figure. Most migrants to the UK are actually students.

This gap between public perceptions and official immigration figures is nothing new. The difference between the facts and opinion often creates distortions that make it difficult for the Government to reduce migration while simultaneously carrying public support. Calais is the perfect example of this problem – its problems indicate a failure to calm public concerns about tackling immigration.

Now, a crisis has erupted. French riot police have stepped up their efforts to close illegal camps housing up to 2,000 foreigners who mainly come from the developing world hoping to enter Britain. French officials estimate at least thirty-five migrants succeed in crossing the Channel every day. About 19,000 illegally attempted to enter Britain from Calais last year.

Britain requires immigration checks to the UK to take place in Calais. This is why so many people wait to try their luck at entering illegally. While this policy makes it easier for the UK to control entry from Calais, it also creates an increasingly dangerous environment and it is not clear who should be responsible.

The UK government supports the status quo. A Home Office spokeswoman recently said, 'The conditions of any camps in France and the policing of them is the responsibility of the French authorities. If individuals have a genuine need of protection they should claim asylum in the first safe country they reach.' The view is that the camps are based in France and are therefore the responsibility of the French government. It should not direct blame to others for its own problems.

It is true that many people living in Calais camps want to enter the UK to claim asylum. While international law does not require refugees to seek asylum in any particular country, there is a longstanding principle that an asylum application should be made at the first available opportunity. In other words, refugees may have a right to asylum but not to have full discretion about where they apply. This is consistent with the UK Government's position: if individuals in Calais wish to claim asylum, then they should do so in France and not the UK.

But it is also true that the UK's policy is under pressure. Today, it is reported that lorry drivers are being ordered to avoid Calais altogether since they could end up confronting what the *Daily Mail* calls 'knife-wielding illegal immigrants who are trying to get to Britain.'

The tightening of border controls by recent UK Governments coupled with the razing of refugee camps by the French authorities might have contributed to a more dangerous environment as migrants attempt more desperate, and violent, measures to cross the Channel.

It is clear the status quo and current stand-off should not be allowed to continue. No major British political party would support lifting current border restrictions in Calais given the state of public opinion but the problem of growing unrest in Calais will not be solved by ordering drivers to avoid the area. This will only relocate the problem and may even make things worse.

It's a difficult problem but we need to start looking at immigration as an opportunity rather than a problem. We live in a world in which states compete with each other for people and skills more fiercely than ever before. Immigrants can bring significant economic and cultural benefits to a country, as was recently confirmed in a report by the House of Commons Treasury Select Committee. In a race for economic competitiveness internationally, it is important that every state is able to find new talent. It should have well managed immigration policies that support that goal. Better to have more than enough individuals to create jobs and wealth than too few.

Yet, the public continues to view immigration as a threat. UKIP's Nigel Farage is even on record saying he'd oppose immigration even if it hurt the British economy.

People only seem to want policies that support their preconceptions, even if they are inaccurate in the first place. The economic case for migration is therefore rejected or ignored.

There is no ready solution to the crisis in Calais. But it is clear the UK government must do more than bury its head in the sand. There is a pressing need to begin a national conversation about migration control rather than continuing to develop policy on the hoof, in reaction to tabloid headlines.

The UK should also aim to view France as a partner and develop a common framework for managing migration across the Channel that improves access to and from Calais. This is in their shared interests and should not get lost in the pursuit of looking tough on immigration. This is a crisis that can be managed but only if there is leadership and a more constructive partnership between the countries involved.

Cornish pasties must be added to the UK Citizenship test[73]

The UK government has agreed to extend protected minority status to the Cornish – a status already granted to Scots, Welsh and Irish. This will require the Government and public bodies to factor in the Cornish when considering the impact of decisions. The aim is combat discrimination and promote equality.

But questions remain about the significance the new status will have, and so the development has been greeted with only cautious enthusiasm. Most commentary denies the new status will bring major changes. There will be no new investment in job creation or infrastructure in Cornwall, for example. Perhaps the status was expected to be more symbolic in recognising the wider diversity within the United Kingdom. Even Loveday Jenkin, the former leader of Mebyon Kernow (the Party for Cornwall) had difficulty articulating the changes this new status for the Cornish might bring.

The new protected status for Cornish can and should have a significant impact. But perhaps not where anyone – least of all Mebyon Kernow, or even the UK Government – might have expected: the Life in the United Kingdom citizenship test must now be substantially rewritten.

The UK citizenship test is a requirement for permanent residency, not just for British citizenship. More than one million tests have been sat since it was first launched in 2005, and more than 150,000 people take it each year. So the test matters. It is an integral part of British immigration policy, and none of the major parties has called for it to be scrapped.

73 'Cornish Pasties must be added to the UK Citizenship Test', *The Conversation* (25 April 2014).

The Government published the current third edition of the test last spring. I exposed serious omissions and inconsistencies in the test, finding it to be 'unfit for purpose' and akin to a bad pub quiz – as laid out in my June 2013 report, the only comprehensive examination of the test available.

The protected status of Cornish identity makes the omissions and inconsistencies I identified in that report all the more pressing.

My new research has found the test does not include the Cornish – not even Cornish pasties. Cornwall's relevance is limited to the Eden Project. That is all – this in a 180-page test handbook, a 143-page study guide and a 408-page official practice book. It is almost as if the Cornish and Cornwall don't exist.

Their absence isn't new either. The first citizenship test handbook published in 2005 contains no mention at all of the Cornish or Cornwall. The 2007 second edition includes only a single mention of Land's End in Cornwall, but locates it as part of the 'South-West of England.'

Protected minority status for the Cornish requires urgent revision of the citizenship test, and the possible changes are far-reaching. For example, the test will have to include some element of Cornish history and culture, Cornish traditional foods (such as the Cornish pasty), the Cornish national flower (which, interestingly, is a contested title), the Cornish language, the Cornish flag, and inclusion of the patron saint of Cornwall, St Piran and St Piran's Day (March 5). The current citizenship test includes these for the English, Scots, Welsh and Irish; it should include them for the Cornish, too.

This is not all. The only Cornish individual mentioned is William Golding, who is not identified as Cornish. No other Cornish person is noted for their British contributions to art, literature, music, science or sport, unlike various Scots, Welsh and Irish greats. This omission might be filled by including mention of Captain William Bligh, the scientists Sir Humphrey Davy and William Gregor, the painter Walter Langley, John Nettles, Rick Stein and of course, rugby union's Phil Vickery.

The protected minority status of the Cornish matters – but not in ways the Government and others might have predicted. This change creates a greater urgency for a new citizenship test to be published.

Labour should lead on reforming citizenship rules[74]

Citizenship rules have changed significantly over the past decade. The use of citizenship tests, the revised guidelines for 'good character' and the start of citizenship ceremonies across the UK are only some of this change—and all introduced by Labour.

In 2002, then Home Secretary David Blunkett established 'The 'Life in the United Kingdom' Advisory Group led by his former university tutor, Sir Bernard Crick. The Group's fourteen members came from a diverse background of education, ESOL service, police and community workers while London-centric. They met with people from across the UK leading to the publication of an important report *The Old and the New* on how citizenship rules should be reformed. Many in the group went on to help draft the first citizenship test.

Crick's Group made an important start. Its members had the expertise and experience to develop key reforms, many of which were adopted and remain in use today. The Group engaged with a wide range of citizens working with migrants that helped identify policies that were informed by those working on the frontline.

74 'Labour should lead on reforming citizenship rules', *LabourList* (24 February 2015).

The problem now is much has changed since for the worse. For example, many of the recommended reforms that became official policy have not been subjected to any proper consultation or review since. The resulting revisions of immigration rules we've seen have been made piecemeal and ad hoc.

Over one million citizenship tests have been sat since its launch in 2005. The current test is in its third edition. The test has shifted away from its focus on questions about practical trivia to the purely trivial and likened to a bad pub quiz. I published the only comprehensive report about the test revealing it as impractical, inconsistent, gender imbalanced and generally unfit for purpose, requiring urgent reforms. It is shocking that all changes to the test have been made without any consultation with those of us—like me—that sat the test and became naturalised British citizens. It is a matter of fact that past tests have included 'correct' answers that were factually untrue, such as claiming there were 646 MPs when there are 650 or asking about Educational Maintenance Allowances after that programme had closed.

UK citizenship requires qualifying applicants to attend a citizenship ceremony. These take place at public buildings such as civic centres across the country. But there is little shared in common between them beyond the oaths stated and fees charged. Much more should be done to ensure these events receive the importance they deserve through sharing good practice, improving standards and engaging—at long last—with the many of us that have taken part in them.

It is time for a change to get this right. Immigration has rocketed to become a leading concern for many voters – something that was not the case in 2005 when much of what we have today was originally introduced. Immigration law has exploded in size to cover over two thousand pages. And that's before you consider UK Visas & Immigration guidance documents. A review of citizenship rules is urgently required.

Labour should call for the creation of a Citizenship Advisory Group sharing a similar focus and expertise with Crick's Group. The new Group's aim should be to advise a future Labour Government on how current rules can be made more fit for purpose. Their work should include:

examining the 'good character' guidelines required for permanent settlement and citizenship to remove anomalies and recommend improvements to avoid problems in its application;

ensuring the citizenship test delivers on its objectives;

consider recommendations on reducing current exemptions from English language proficiency tests and developing joined-up regulation and oversight of test standards; and

develop good practice and raise standards for improving citizenship ceremonies.

Most importantly, it must engage with people like me – immigrants to the UK who understand naturalisation first-hand and became British citizens: the people the British public trusts most on immigration.

Supporting a Citizenship Advisory Group is more than good sense. It can provide new reassurance to voters that Labour takes immigration seriously. But it does so by championing Labour's leadership on this issue that is so often overlooked, such as the lasting influence of the citizenship reforms found in the original Advisory Group's report.

Let's debate immigration this election, but let us not forget Labour's past achievements that delivered an important first-step in the right direction. We must now finish the job we started. A Citizenship Advisory Group can play a pivotal role in making this happen.

New migrant 'health surcharge' – an election stunt full of loopholes[75]

The Government announced yesterday that migrants will be subject to a new 'health surcharge.' The fee comes into effect next month. The surcharge is £200 per year payable upfront with students required to pay £150 annually.

The health surcharge is an election stunt full of loopholes. The policy begins on 6 April – a week after Parliament is expected to dissolve and during a national election campaign. The timing of it is hardly coincidental.

But the bigger problem is this: government rhetoric fails to meet reality. The public are told the surcharge will offset the costs to the NHS from treating migrants. However, thousands of migrants will not need to pay because of several exemptions and restrictions. It's a clear case of government saying one thing, but doing another.

The health surcharge will only be imposed on non-EEA citizens in the UK temporarily for more than six months. EEA citizens from Europe are unaffected. There are eleven different exemptions from the surcharge: these include anyone visiting the UK for under six months, intra-company transfers, children under eighteen years in care, and nationals of Australia and New Zealand.

There are further concerns that the funding raised may not be used effectively. Migrants paying the surcharge must do so upfront and the money collected is distributed to the relevant health department in England, Wales, Scotland or Northern Ireland. The problem is that migrants don't always stay in the same place. If a migrant moves from England to Wales, the funding raised by the

75 'New migrant "health surcharge" – an election stunt full of loopholes', *LabourList* (22 March 2015).

surcharge does not appear to follow the individual. This will mean the new funds might not go to the authorities that need it most.

It is true that migration has put pressure on public services, such as the NHS. But it is also true that the Government lacks concrete figures about the actual costs that migration adds to the NHS bill. If health tourism is about migrants dropping in for free procedures and then leaving the country, this is not tackled by the new health surcharge as it does not affect anyone coming to the UK for less than six months even if a visa is required for entry.

A better alternative would be to bring back the Migration Impacts Fund launched by Prime Minister Gordon Brown in 2009. Like the new health surcharge, the Migration Impacts Fund was a levy on application fees paid for by non-EEA citizens. Over two years, it helped raise £70m to provide English language training, extra support teachers and improve emergency services. Local authorities would submit bids and the funding would go to those areas where support was needed most. It wasn't ideal, but it was a step in the right direction.

The Government ended the programme shortly after entering 10 Downing Street. Baroness Hanham CBE said that 'In light of the overall fiscal position the Government concluded it was not a priority funding stream.' And so it was stopped. But while the Fund was terminated, the levy remained with the extra funding going to other programmes.

The upshot is that the pressures on public service have not gone down while government support for relieving such pressures – through instruments like the Migration Impacts Fund – were cut. If our health service requires urgent support because of migration, then the Government shares some of the blame for too quickly scrapping a useful programme.

Moreover, migration-related pressures on public services are not confined to health services alone, but also education, transport and other areas. The Migration Impacts Fund was a programme that addressed all of these areas. The Government's new health surcharge speaks to only one and leaves the others exposed.

The Government should have considered a new Migration Impacts Reduction Fund, as I have called for recently. A small levy of £25 on immigration fees could raise an extra £11.7m of new funding to help provide necessary services without increasing costs for hardworking taxpayers while improving public services for all. Instead, the Government's health surcharge might not support the NHS in the way it has been announced – and it will do little to improve public confidence in either the seriousness that government officials take migration issues or in championing the many genuine contributions that migrants bring to the UK. And I should know first-hand: I am a migrant to the UK (and British citizen since 2011) who has paid into the Migration Impacts Fund. So I do not advocate a programme I haven't contributed to myself.

The Government should stop seeing immigration as a political football and instead as a serious policy area that deserves far more serious policymaking.

Why control of immigration is not just for mugs[76]

Immigration policy is a popular target for criticism. Often the proposers of new ideas are called mugs, but here the problem is highlighted by a particular mug, of the ceramic kind.

The Labour Party is issuing new mugs that are branded with one of five new key pledges. Greatest attention has turned to the mug bearing the fourth pledge – 'controls on immigration.' *LabourList*'s Maya Goodfellow wrote recently that the problem is that the mug is a painful reminder of 'just how wrong Labour are on immigration.'

76 'Why control of immigration is not just for mugs', *LabourList* (1 April 2015).

To be fair, Maya and I agree on several things. We agree that immigration has benefited the UK economy. We also agree that Labour needs to work harder to convince the public they have the best immigration policies to choose from.

But I disagree strongly that immigration control should not be a major pledge – and I fully support Ed Miliband on this. Let me explain why.

Fair controls on immigration are not about ending it. Nor is it about peddling myths, half-truths and worse to stoke unwarranted public fears.

Launching Labour's election campaign, Miliband rightly said that 'the Labour Party will never cut ourselves off from the rest of the world, but we are a party that believes in rules which protect working people.' These rules include ensuring everyone working in Britain receives no less than the minimum wage and migrants must have at least two years' residency before claiming benefits.

These policies do not assume migrants are benefits scroungers any more than they do migrants work only for scraps. But they rightly link fairness for some to fairness for all. Fair immigration controls are a key and integral part to the idea of One Nation Labour.

The debate over immigration is one that Labour should win. Alternatives largely seek to tweak what Labour introduced. This fact needs to be broadcast more loudly. It was Labour that introduced the UK's first points-based system, the formalisation of English language requirements, the launch of the citizenship test, codifying the rules on immigration requirements like good character to improve Home Office decision-making and the start of citizenship ceremonies. These are only some of the many policies that Labour Governments introduced and are here to stay. When the Tories transform the citizenship test into a bad pub quiz or when UKIP call for an Australian points-based system, call them out on it. Labour has forged widespread agreement across parties on the fundamentals.

It is true that other parties have indulged in tweaking with the consequence of making things worse. There is the citizenship test debacle rendering a potentially helpful tool for integration I support unfit for purpose in its current form. There is also the Coalition Government's poor judgement in scrapping the Migration Impacts Fund that raised funding from a levy on immigration application fees used to target areas of greater need to reduce migration-related pressures on public services. I'm not pretending the system is perfect, but it is worth fixing – and building upon the fair immigration controls that Labour introduced.

People are usually surprised to hear Labour did so much on immigration. One reason why is because these achievements aren't trumpeted enough. The next government – of whatever party – urgently needs to launch a Citizenship Advisory Group to engage the public more so they know more about UK policies and so that these policies better reflect the public – it's a two way street and time we minded the gap.

My interest is somewhat personal. I am a migrant. Worse, a non-EU migrant. I know about the Migration Impacts Fund because I paid into it. I know about the citizenship test because I took it and I've attended a citizenship ceremony, not as a spectator, but as a participant. I have serious concerns about negative stereotypes and inflammatory rhetoric. I recognise the importance of controls, but also their transparency and fairness.

And so this is why I support a future Labour government. I believe it is best placed to deliver the kind of fair controls we need. We shouldn't be embarrassed to talk about controls because the rules in place are largely of our own making – we can trumpet our achievements and how little the Government has done with this other than make things much worse.

Now that I'm a UK citizen, I'm even more motivated to ensure we have a system that works – and is fair for all. Whatever our disagreements about coffee cup slogans, surely this larger picture is something we can be united on. The only mugs I dislike are those who say Labour has nothing to contribute on immigration policy.

Australia should tread cautiously on UK-inspired English language tests[77]

One reform the Abbott government is considering as part of sweeping changes to Australia's citizenship regime is the introduction of English tests for all new citizens.

Migrants learning English can be crucial to integration, whether in Australia, the UK or any other Western country. But Australia should be cautious in how closely it follows the UK in this reform.

Britain has formally required for more than a century that all new citizens know English. The Secretary of State had to be satisfied that new citizens had a satisfactory knowledge of English and 'life in the United Kingdom.'

The latter became the 'Life in the United Kingdom test' for citizenship. Launched in 2005 by then-prime minister Tony Blair, I have previously likened the test to a bad pub quiz for its long list of errors and omissions.

The UK's requirement that new citizens know English was not formalised into a test until more recently. New citizens had to pass either the citizenship test or an English for Speakers of Other Languages (ESOL) with Citizenship course.

77 'Australia should tread cautiously on UK-inspired language tests', The Conversation (2 July 2015).

The latter course taught English through citizenship lessons, in an odd introduction for anyone coming to study English for the first time. The first quiz asks about the Houses of Parliament instead of how to greet a stranger or how to order lunch from a menu.

The UK tightened its policy almost two years ago. The level of satisfactory English all must demonstrate was raised, aimed at making it more difficult to qualify for citizenship. Previously, someone with no English need only improve by one level of competency. Now, all must prove they have conversational English at an intermediate level.

This will be a more challenging hurdle for many to pass. And this will be especially true for people who are illiterate in their native tongue, but must exhibit literacy in a new language. Applicants must normally pay their own way – and a higher standard will mean greater costs for many.

The Government claims improving standards will further integration. And maybe they will. But the problem is how the UK government manages this requirement. Australia should learn from the UK's mistakes if it is to take this leaf out of its book on citizenship reform.

The new English language rules are subject to about a dozen exemptions. Some of these are reasonable for children, persons aged sixty-five years and above or victims of domestic abuse. Anyone meeting these criteria is exempt from having to prove knowledge of English.

But many other exemptions are not reasonable. One set of exemptions is for nationals from a list of countries. Some on this list are de jure English-speaking countries, like Australia and New Zealand, where English is the official language. Others on the list are de facto English-speaking countries, like the US.

What's unreasonable about this exemption is two-fold. First, a person's nationality is no guarantee of English fluency. The US has tens of millions of citizens for whom English is not a first or even second language. The UK's new rules would deem them sufficiently fluent in a language they might not know well.

Second, there are no clear criteria for how countries were selected. Not all de jure countries are included (such as India) or de facto countries (like Singapore). If there is to be an exemption on nationality, then there should be some clear rationale for choosing some and not others. But this is not given.

A further problem is that there is an additional blanket exemption for individuals who hold a degree taught or researched in English, even if the degree is obtained in a university not on the nationality exemption list. This is even more surprising given the variability of English competence that will be held to satisfy the English language requirement.

With so many degrees awarded in English around the world, this may permit individuals to be exempt from the requirement because of a false assumption about English fluency.

The lesson Australia can draw from this is to introduce a standardised English language test that is subject to fewer restrictions, and show the UK how it should maintain a fairer and more consistent policy.

One way Australia might do this is by not endorsing exemptions based on nationality or for holders of degrees taught in English gained elsewhere. If the goal is to better guarantee more new migrants possess some competency in English language skills, this would be one important step to achieving this goal.

Maybe then the UK could learn lessons from Australia when it sees how this more fair, consistent and strategic approach works much better.

The Tory budget forgets immigration [78]

George Osborne finally came clean on where the Government will apply substantial cuts making working people worse off. In the words of Harriet Harman, 'The great Northern Powerhouse is starting to look like the great Northern power-cut' as the Government pulled its plug on railway electrification that it promised to deliver during the election. Let's hope voters in Berwick-upon-Tweed, Hexham and Stockton South don't forget this in 2020.

Osborne's budget has been dissected by commentators left and right. But there remains one surprising fact no one's noticed: immigration is forgotten. And that's a mistake. The budget is 123 pages long. But there is only a single mention of 'immigration.' It is used just once to refer to non-doms. Nowhere else. Nada. Zilch. This is not enough and it's surprising to see this from a government that claims to take immigration seriously. There's no mention of borders or Calais either.

At a time of increasing pressures on public services, the Government should be looking to reintroduce a Migration Impacts Fund through a new surcharge on visa applications. This is an opportunity lost. My research has shown at least £11.7m could be raised by a £25 levy that could be bid for by local authorities to reduce pressure on public services supporting English language training, extra support teachers, public transport and improve emergency services.

The Government's 'health surcharge' introduced during the election campaign is an election stunt full of loopholes, as I've argued before for *LabourList*. This is a new £200 annual surcharge and £150 for students to address the concern that there are health

78 'The Tory budget forgets immigration', *LabourList* (16 July 2015).

tourists costing the NHS considerable sums. These add up to big sums for the NHS, but don't look for them in the budget.

But this fee is collected only from non-EEA nationals and not all migrants, there are nearly a dozen exemptions altogether and money directed from this surcharge to local NHS services will not follow migrants should they move elsewhere. Given that migrants are much less likely than British nationals to use the NHS, this may seem like a ploy intended not to offset migrant use of the health service, but instead provide a new income stream to top up the NHS budget. But this still leaves other public services under pressure like schools and transport where the Government remains too slow to act.

The Government's problems don't end there. The newly rebranded 'living wage' might make the UK more attractive to increased migration. This policy may be aimed at a domestic audience, but have an impact beyond our borders. This may raise new headaches for the Government's attempts to achieve reduced net migration. I wonder if Iain Duncan Smith will be triumphantly waving his fists and shouting 'fantastic' when the figures are in!

Ed Miliband received a lot of criticism for what he didn't say at our last party conference. George Osborne should get his fair share of criticism for forgetting the importance of migration. It's time the Government began listening to migrants – and to voters.

Some fencing and a few sniffer dogs in Calais is just not enough[79]

The Calais crisis is a problem the Government saw coming. It didn't happen overnight. Observers have talked about the increasingly

79 'Some fencing and a few sniffer dogs: it's not enough', *The Journal* (Newcastle) (15 August 2015): 39.

difficult situation as a 'crisis' for months, some as far back as September last year.

The only thing unsurprising is the Government's poor response. This is something we've seen before. First, the situation reaches a breaking point. Next there is some extra staff and fencing along with vague assurances everything is under control. Calm is restored temporarily. Then repeat, but only things are worse than before.

The crisis hasn't gone away. In fact, it has deepened. About 4,000 migrants are believed to live in squalid conditions near the Eurotunnel entrance in France. The area isn't called 'the Jungle' for nothing.

Every day more than a thousand and as many as 1,500 or more attempt to breach the barrier to hide inside a lorry en route to the UK. A surprising number actually make it over, risking life and limb. Recently, one migrant from Sudan was arrested in Folkestone after evading French security and dodging fast-moving trains running much of the thirty-one mile tunnel before getting caught.

I don't know if the risks they are prepared to make are more shocking than the appalling efforts to contain the crisis and bring a humane end to it.

It isn't like the UK is bearing the brunt of the wider refugee crisis facing Europe. Over 150,000 refugees reached the EU during the first half of 2015. Both Greece and Italy received more than 60,000. Only a small number of these will make the long journey to Calais.

Many make claims for asylum although success is difficult. The UK rejected sixty per cent of all asylum claims received last year and we are below the EU average, far behind Germany and Sweden. Others may enter the EU through illegal human trafficking.

The Government doesn't seem to have a grip on the Calais crisis. Efforts to breach security have continued apace while the Jungle camp only grows larger.

Home Secretary Theresa May was quick to point the finger at the French first. Many of the migrants are believed to lack valid residency permits and want to apply for asylum. The EU member states agreed that asylum claims should be heard in the first safe EU country a claimant came to. This is clearly not happening and the French need to step up their security, or so May argued.

The French were quick to respond that these several thousand people all want to enter to the UK and they're only in Calais because the UK wanted to have its border checkpoint for the Eurotunnel in France. Clearing the area and processing claims will be costly and risks creating clashes. If the UK doesn't like it, then it should help out.

This very public spat reveals how poorly UK and French relations are concerning the Calais crisis. Each is more keen to blame the other than share responsibility. A problem shared is a problem halved.

The UK's inadequate response has shown the sheer poverty of the Government's thinking. Marie Antoinette was rumoured to have said 'Let them eat cake.' Cameron now says let them have sniffer dogs and a bit more fence. The French have sent about a hundred extra police.

This is remarkably short-sighted and will do no more than bring temporary relief. Even if all refugees in Calais were moved to the place of their choice, more will continue to come. This is because this is a problem that only the EU can fix. If Europe's borders are not better secured, refugees will continue to come to Calais and seek entry to Britain.

I've been asked a lot recently about what should be done. The fact this is a problem the EU can fix is all the more reason why the UK must remain at the heart of Europe. Our EU membership gives us a seat at the negotiating table. Maybe EU policies on asylum seekers and refugees can be improved. They will no more be to our liking if we're not part of this critical club.

We need a more coherent and effective policy that only EU membership can deliver. We may be concerned about Calais, but other member states have their own Calais-like issues. Too much is left to the discretion of member states and more must be done to change incentives to tackle the crisis in a fair and consistent way.

One small step in this direction would be to launch an EU-wide migration impacts reduction fund. This could be raised from a surcharge on visa application fees and be distributed according to need without adding a penny or a pound to the British tax bill.

EU states like the UK and France must stop the finger pointing blame game now. It has done little but create a political stalemate while the crisis continues to grow. Both sides must work together and build a more effective joint security force.

A lesson here might be the Port Authority of New York and New Jersey handling critical transport and trade routes in the greater New York City area.

Cameron's government must stop placing responsibility for this mess on others. Lorry drivers should not be penalised for wanting help removing unwanted stowaways that have broken into their cargo. They deserve protection and that should not be in short supply.

Cameron said he wanted to send potential refugees a message. But plans to target landlords who rent to illegal migrants won't be heard. Cameron's former Immigration Minister, Mark Harper, once mistakenly hired an illegal migrant as his cleaner. If government ministers can't do proper checks, it seems wrong to shift more responsibility onto citizens and with more penalties. Landlords should not become virtual border agents.

The Calais crisis is in no one's interest, not least the migrants hoping for a better life. Assisting refugees is not a problem. Needlessly condemning desperate people to an avoidable limbo is.

EU migration crisis: we have offered so little to those who have lost so much[80]

Europe faces its biggest crisis in a generation. States came together to form the European Union intended to forge a lasting peace between neighbours and end old rivalries.

Few could have forseen that the greatest threat to European stability is not the effects of conflict in Europe, but the effects on Europe from conflicts elsewhere.

Today, we are witnessing the largest numbers of refugees in Europe since the Second World War. An estimated 300,000 people thus far have knocked on Europe's door. This is often at grave risk to themselves and several thousands are believed to have died on their desperate journey.

Syria, Libya, Eritrea, Afghanistan. These are only some of the countries from which refugees have given up everything but hope as they flee from persecution and civil war.

European leaders have been anything but leaders in name with the exception of Germany. Each speaks in a different voice sending out a clear message of incoherence and chaos. Some like Germany, the Netherlands and Sweden have been more welcoming. Others like the UK are more cautious.

It is clear that too little coordination at the EU level is in place. This was made evident by the fact the refugee crisis that continues to grow in Calais had not been witnessed by a UK minister until recently, when the announcement of a joint Anglo-French policing force was made there years after it should have been launched. 'Too little, too late' is an apt summary of British immigration policy.

But so too is 'warning: another u-turn ahead.' It's bad enough

80 'We've offered so little to those who have lost so much', *The Journal* (Newcastle) (12 September 2015): 39.

that different European leaders are sending out mixed messages. David Cameron's government has incredibly achieved something worse: sending mixed messages all on its own.

Tragically, the current EU refugee crisis is a powerful example of this. The UK receives far fewer applications for asylum or humanitarian protection than other European countries.

Part of the reason is the so-called 'Dublin Regulation' whereby EU countries agreed that asylum seekers should have their claims assessed in the first safe EU state they enter. Refugees are more likely to reach countries on Europe's boundaries before reaching Britain.

This has led some EU states to argue the UK must now take its fair share. And it's not to say all who apply will receive residency: it's a little known fact that sixty per cent – yes, sixty per cent – will be rejected.

The Prime Minister's position was repeated on several occasions: we would not be taking on a greater share of Europe's refugees. EU member states face extraordinary challenges, but Cameron's UK was too happy to pretend life goes on as usual. Or so it seemed.

A photo of a dead boy on a Turkish beach then changed everything. Young Aylan Kurdi never made it to the UK. But he had an immediate and profound effect on British politics.

Only days after the Government failed yet again its nonsensical 'net migration' targets that counts British citizens returning home after time abroad as migrants to the UK, the Home Secretary made clear that efforts will double to bring net migration down.

But after photos of Aylan's lifeless body circulated – a chilling symbol of the desperation and deadly risks refugees endure to reach Europe – the Prime Minister announced a new U-turn.

The Government now agreed it would accept additional refugees. We only knew at first that it would be in the 'thousands.' Several days later we learn the Government will accept 'up to

20,000' during the current Parliament. That's no more than 20,000 over five years. Or about a dozen per day. Maximum.

Such is the big heart and generous spirit of the Government to assist – even temporarily – people who've lost everything but the desire to live without fear or persecution. Their crime is to have lived at the wrong place and at the wrong time. So little to help those who lost so much. Perhaps compassionate conservativism is dead in Westminster. You know the Tories are out of touch on migration when UKIP comes out more strongly in favour of accepting greater numbers of refugees. And as they should.

But the Government's U-turn is more timid than you think. This maximum of up to about twelve refugees per day over five years are to come from a programme that's only managed to help a grand total of 216 people. From 216 in a lifetime to 20,000 over five years. If you're sceptical about the Government's resolve, please join the queue after me.

The Home Secretary Theresa May said that this programme is selected because it processes people near the Syrian border and so makes it easier and less costly for people to return should conflicts cease, and it was important to send the message out that people should avoid taking deadly risks in fleeing to Europe.

It's uncertain at best how clearly refugees evading persecution and civil war and willing to risk their lives to do so will be moved by May's comments stated only in English to a British audience, and doubtful they'll be heard. If you genuinely need to flee as refugees do, there is no time to catch up on the latest speeches in the UK's House of Commons. After all, most refugees don't want to go to Britain anyway.

The real message May's comments send is directed at European countries who think we're doing too little and too late. They state our commitment to take on larger numbers, but crucially not a single refugee of the hundreds of thousands already in the EU that need help already.

Top marks to Labour's Shadow Home Secretary Yvette Cooper who argued that the Government should go further in its announcement and agree some fair deal on accepting refugees already in Europe as a means to doing necessary social justice and to aid talks negotiating the UK's relation to the EU ahead of a referendum next year. Cooper is probably the only frontbench politician showing leadership on this leading issue of the day.

Europe's refugee crisis isn't going away and may get worse before the situation improves. But already we see signs of a continent divided and a government stumbling from one light touch statement to the next. U-turns are only really a problem if you know where you're headed – and I don't believe this government does.

But where it could start is by making a clear statement to the British public about why accepting refugees is not only a legal obligation, but the morally right thing to do. It takes courage to do what's right sometimes. The question is whether the Government has the courage of its convictions or simply hoping for this humanitarian crisis to blow over leaving everyone else to pick up the pieces. Time will tell.

Immigrants don't contribute? Think again, Mrs May[81]

Earlier this week, the Home Secretary Theresa May addressed the Conservative Party conference. She delivered a long-awaited speech on immigration expected to continue her increasingly hard line. May did not disappoint.

May told the cheering party faithful that mass immigration was

81 'Immigrants don't contribute? Think again, Mrs May', *The Journal* (Newcastle) (9 October 2015): 23.

a bad thing. It brought no economic benefits and it was not in the public interest.

There is no denying that immigration is the top concern for voters. While polls show support for less migrants than more, a key worry is that the Government simply lacks control over the UK's borders.

Theresa May has argued vociferously for reducing net migration to the tens of thousands without any special allowance for students.

She firmly believes that the public must have confidence in the migration figures and refusing to count some – like foreign university students – could undermine that confidence by making it look like ministers were playing games.

May's reluctance to quit her support for a net migration 'target' – recently downgraded to an 'aspiration' – is all the more surprising given her abject failure to achieve it. It is on her watch that net migration has hit a record high of over 300,000 people.

This is not the fault of any Labour Government. May has served as Home Secretary for over five years and now two Governments. She has had time to pass new laws – which the Tories have – aimed to help reach their target and they seem to miss it by larger amounts each time you look.

The truth is that net migration is the wrong approach. It is determined by counting everyone who comes and goes irrespective of their nationality. If 100,000 British citizens return to the UK and 1,000 non-British nationals leave the country, that leaves a net migration of 99,000.

But public concerns about immigration are not a call to keep British citizens from returning home. Yet that is what net migration can demand. As the economy has slowly improved, fewer British citizens have left to find jobs in Europe and this has helped drive up net migration.

Net migration is not a number you can control. You can manage different pathways to the UK. You can limit student visas for non-EU citizens or cap the number of non-EU workers, but you cannot control how many British citizens choose to come or go. Net migration is more a ghost than a holy grail. Nor is it clear that anxieties about existing migration will somehow disappear if net migration was 100,000. Zero might not be low enough for some people playing a numbers game – and it would be a great mistake.

The problem is that May is plain wrong that migrants do not contribute to the economy. They do. Who says? Her own department. Government figures from the Treasury and OBR show a modest, but positive effect on economic growth. Migrants do not take jobs: they make jobs in a market that is not zero-sum. It is true that different parts of the economy are affected very differently and the picture – and the pressure – on manual labourers is not the same. And it is safe to say that much of the NHS would screech to a halt without the foreign-born doctors and nurses working incredibly hard for a great British public service. May is either being selective about immigration's effects on the economy – or she is ignorant of them.

All the more incredible in May's speech to the Tory conference was her focus on refugees. Asylum seekers were the group getting most of her attention and she plans to clamp down hard.

May never admitted to the audience that refugees make up one of the smallest groups of migrants and sixty per cent of applications for asylum are routinely rejected already. So her big plan to cut down on refugees – the most vulnerable people fleeing civil war and persecution – to reach an arbitrary net migration target she continues to miss is the biggest farce of all.

In the twelve months up to March, the Government received 25,000 applications for asylum. Only about ten thousand will likely be successful. Even if all were rejected, May's target will still not be reached.

If the Home Secretary is so concerned about winning public confidence, she could start by being honest about the deception she is trying to sell the country. This is not about getting tough or meeting targets, but simply being mean to human beings in a desperate situation to score a few points with the Tory backbenchers.

But this is more than mean-spiritedness – it is hypocrisy. Anyone listening to what she told the public will hear how bad immigration has been for the country. This is not at all what she sent me in a letter I received when I became a British citizen at a ceremony in Gateshead a couple years ago. Theresa May said: 'Her Majesty the Queen has asked me to welcome you on behalf of Herself, the British Government and your fellow citizens into our national community.'

She continues: 'The talents, background and experiences you are bringing are very important to us. As a full and equal citizen I know that you will help to make the United Kingdom a more prosperous, generous and open society.' Says one thing to the country when everyone is watching, but something very different when the cameras are turned off. Principled? Hardly.

There is a last point. May raised concerns about migration on public services. This is an issue for many communities, but she conveniently kept silent about yet another secret kept from the British public. Under Gordon Brown's government, the previous Home Secretary Jacqui Smith rolled out a Migration Impacts Fund. This was money raised from a levy on immigration applications used to helped divert funding to where there was pressure on public services. Local councils, health trusts and educational institutions could apply.

Within only a few months of coming to office, May scrapped the Fund but she kept the cash. Millions raised since have not gone into reducing the impact of migration over the last five years. Instead it was used to pay for other government pet projects instead.

In sum, you don't always get what you see. We heard a tough-talking speech, but it is undermined by her actions and poor choice of targets. Immigration need not be a problem and it can be controlled, but not when it continues to be some kind of game for ministers concerned more for their promotion than the public.

Breaking up is hard to do – especially when you have to fill out a government form [82]

The British government has published documents for people to use to report the end of a relationship to immigration services.

When your relationship breaks down you are expected to use these forms to confirm that it's over and give the name of your partner to the Government. They ask you to declare that you 'do not live with them' and 'do not intend to live with them' in the future. These forms ask for the names of who is confirming the break-up and the estranged spouse or partner. These are then to be filed with the Home Office.

The purpose of all this is to provide information to UK Visas and Immigration, the Home Office department in charge of managing deportations. Spousal visas can become invalid when the holder's relationship with a British citizen ends. The new form appears designed to help identify individuals overstaying their visas.

According to the latest International Passenger Survey, 45,000 non-EU nationals migrated long-term to the UK to accompany or join others with the intention of residing one year or more over the past twelve months. This is a decrease from 53,000 in the previous year.

82 'Breaking up is hard to do especially when you have to fill out a government form', The Conversation (7 January 2016).

The Home Office's new forms take a clear aim at exposing bogus marriages but the Government no doubt hopes that more estranged people will come forward to inform the Home Office when their real relationships end.

The problem is that the Government has not thought this through. The flaws in these forms are startling. For one thing, they fail to ask for the contact details of the person submitting the form. Any submitted statement cannot be verified before it is investigated.

But there is more. The forms don't ask for the estranged partner's contact details or nationality either. This makes their discovery and potential removal all but impossible. Without an address, phone number or email account, these new forms are all but meaningless.

And it gets worse. The Home Office also appears to have forgotten to note where the form should be submitted. It provides no address, email or fax number leaving completed forms with nowhere to go. In my many years of working in immigration policy, I have never seen such a shambles before.

So why do this at all? These forms seem directed more towards looking tough than being effective. The public will wonder why the Home Office produced a form that no one can use – and that can be sent nowhere.

Usually such forms are accompanied by a press release to help communicate new measures introduced by the Government. But remarkably, the Home Office appears to have forgotten to produce one. It's almost as if it did not want the public to know about this new measure aimed at getting the public to rat out their ex-lovers.

And really, this form should never have been released in the first place. There will rightly be concerns that it could be used to intimidate non-European citizens into remaining in relationships they wish to leave for fear of removal from the country. This could make these forms more a tool for abuse than the public good.

If the Home Office wants to identify terminated relationships, it can begin by checking the courts for divorce announcements for a start. Ministers would do better to use common sense and raise their game by becoming more knowledgeable about how the system works before making yet another policy change that may well make necessary detection more difficult. This isn't rocket science. But it is people's lives, and the public deserves better.

Cameron's immigration strategy is to govern through gimmicks[83]

I've never accused David Cameron of lacking an immigration strategy. He clearly has one – to govern through gimmicks. And there are so many to choose from.

This week Cameron announced £20 million of 'new' funding that will fund 'English language tuition' to help 'combat social isolation for some Muslim women.' Did you notice his use of 'combat' there, too? This is no slip of the pen. The Prime Minister thinks the road to tackling extremism runs through people sitting more English lessons.

But the Prime Minister is playing the public for fools. His Governments have cut funding for English instruction through deep hits in 2011 and 2015 estimated at about £45 million. The 'new' £20 million doesn't make up half his cuts.

Funding used to support any individual that needed it. But now the new money will only go to some – and not all. While Cameron says the target of this funding programme will be 'Muslim women' it's not focused that narrowly, but will be available to help women

---

83 'Cameron's immigration strategy is to govern through gimmicks', *LabourList* (19 January 2016).

requiring support more generally. No doubt Muslim women may benefit from this help, but it is curious that he singles them out without reference to the women of other faiths who may benefit from this funding support, too.

Let's return to Cameron's mention of 'combat.' He has set his sights on improving English language skills in order to 'combat' social ills like 'gender segregation and discrimination.' Cameron said in a statement that better English skills will help foster 'women's empowerment' that will 'break down barriers' and guard against 'radicalisation and extremism.'

Andy Burnham, the Shadow Home Secretary, got it right in his response when he said that Cameron's plan was overly simplistic – tackling extremism will take more than better access to English lessons. This isn't to deny better English helps drive integration. It is easier for anyone to become involved in their local community if they can easily communicate in English. But knowing how to order at a restaurant or ask for instructions when driving are no guarantee that people can feel a part of Britain – especially when we're constantly reminded about the problems, not the future prospects, we bring.

Let us turn to the fine print. Cameron's announcement claims it is 'new' and will tackle barriers to participation by women in English language learning by funding classes in 'homes, schools and community facilities.' Here is some news for the Government: many English for Speakers of Other Languages (ESOL) already do this. It's not new, only underfunded and undervalued by 10 Downing Street.

The Government says that those applying to settle permanently in the UK must now be able to speak intermediate English and pass the UK's citizenship test – a test I've previously likened to 'a bad pub quiz' in the only comprehensive report about it in 2013. Here is some more news for the Government: it has long been part of Britain's common law that citizens possess a knowledge of life in the UK and English. This was incorporated into statute as far back as the British Nationality and Status of Aliens Act 1914 over a century ago. Formal tests for English language and knowledge about the UK were launched by Tony Blair's Labour government. And, yes, the test had questions about Britain's history. I should know – I had to take it! So nothing new here either.

Finally, the Government says that anyone on a spouse visa will be tested for English language skills after they have lived for two and a half years in the UK. Showing no progress won't mean deportation, but it might lead to a future visa extension or application for permanent residency being rejected. Sounds tough, doesn't it?

That's only because the Government is moving towards Labour's policy a decade ago. Spousal visas used to require a residency of two years. After this period, a spouse could apply for permanent residency – and would be required to confirm some command of English. The Coalition Government changed the rules. It made the residency period five years. That meant instead of many spouses getting checked in two years, this was delayed for much longer. So bringing up checks to two and a half years is almost as soon as it was under Labour.

It's easy to think the Government has simply lost its way on immigration. It has. The problem with making policy only by reacting to the right wing media is that you'll never win. There is no leadership. Every announcement is a gimmick that anybody with a smattering of knowledge about immigration rules can see for the charade that it is. And the only reason they do it is because they can get away with it – few people need ever become familiar with two thousand pages of primary and secondary legislation on immigration. If the public don't know, maybe they might even believe the Government's fairy tale. All the more reason why migrants need to call this out for what it is.

I don't enjoy exposing the Prime Minister's immigration policies as one gimmick after another with so much hot air it could send Sir Richard Branson around the world in record speed. It's because when we get a constant stream of rhetoric without substance it does no one any favours. The public grow more sceptical about what politicians can and should deliver – and migrants are left to pay the price personally (and financially).

If the Prime Minister is generally worried about building 'a strong society', he should reflect more on how his policies make this noble ambition fall further out of reach.

David Cameron must apologise for his 'bunch of migrants' comment – it's not US versus THEM[84]

Prime Minister's Questions can often yield heated debates. Much can be – and is – said in exchanges that might never be said at other times. The prime minister has had a problem before with his 'flash man' moments, including his telling a female Labour Party MP to 'calm down, dear', which obviously did anything but calm tensions.

One of the biggest issues of voter concern in the UK is immigration. It is popular politics these days to look and sound tough. But sometimes a line is crossed and an apology becomes needed.

At Prime Minister's Questions on 27 January, David Cameron told the House of Commons that Labour Party leader Jeremy Corbyn met 'a bunch of migrants' in Calais that he'd love to bring to Britain. As if helping children without relatives stuck in an anarchic 'Jungle' was somehow worthy of contempt.

84 'PMQs: David Cameron must apologise for his "bunch of migrants" comment – it's not US vs THEM', *International Business Times* (27 January 2016). This column is the only piece I've written entirely on my smart phone – and while sitting in the House of Commons' public gallery, too.

We have heard this language before. Margaret Thatcher once spoke of Britain being 'swamped' by migrants. Now they become 'a bunch': nameless, faceless, dehumanised. A bunch that Britain is better off without.

And that's how migrants can be thought of. As a swarm, a tsunami or tidal wave. In every case they are a problem – a mass – to be feared and kept out. The kind of flood that government really does want to keep out with proper defences.

This language is offensive and potentially incendiary. Us versus them. This is not the language of a statesman but a coward – cowering to our worst instincts of a Little Britain afraid and distrustful of the world outside.

If Cameron thinks it is acceptable to demonise a minority, maybe he will rethink his comments when he considers that many of them – or perhaps should I say 'us' – are British citizens too. I am a migrant. I immigrated to Britain. The UK is my home and I worked hard to integrate, to give something back to society and become a British citizen.

When migrants are demonised or belittled, it says much about who we are. And it can be easy to forget that many of 'them' are also many of 'us.'

Cameron should apologise to the House of Commons for his remarks without delay. Enough is enough. If he cannot respect the humanity of our fellow human beings, then maybe he might listen to the migrants who became British. We all deserve better.

How the Government set us on the road that led to the red doors of Middlesbrough[85]

Our region is making the news for all the wrong reasons. Welcome to our part of the Northern Powerhouse – otherwise known as the lands that the Government forgot.

This week came news that in Middlesbrough the homes of many asylum seekers were marked by their red doors. Except this was not new.

Refugees claiming asylum had made complaints before in 2012 and 2014. But nothing happened. Things changed as more came forward to talk about the abuse they had endured, as they were easily targeted by their distinctive red doors.

So what did the Home Office know about this? James Brokenshire, the Tory MP and Immigration Minister, said he first heard about this about two weeks ago. He didn't know because he hadn't been told. But why did he need to be told? Surely, as the Immigration Minister, he should take an active interest in matters like how asylum seekers are handled, right? Wrong, or so we are led to believe.

This almost makes sense – as a creature of his Government's creation. The Tories decided they would privatise several public services – and the management of refugees claiming asylum is one of them. Instead of being a direct responsibility of ministers and their civil servants, now matters are handled on the front line by contractors

While refugees wait for a decision on their claims for asylum, their housing and living needs were now managed directly by companies. One of these – G4S – looked after asylum seekers in the North East, including Middlesbrough.

85 'How Government set us on the road to the red doors', *The Journal* (Newcastle) (29 January 2016): 27.

But there is a twist. G4S won the contract to save the taxpayers – that's you and me – money. We now learn that G4S, in fact, subcontracted some of this work to another firm who looked after asylum seekers instead and stands accused of leaving many, if not most, doors of asylum seekers painted red.

So the twist here is that the Immigration Minister is no longer directly responsible for managing asylum seeker support while they await a verdict from the Home Office – and no longer merely one level removed, but a full two steps removed. Don't shoot the messenger or his contractor, but the subcontractor. This is what the new politics means in Whitehall – and it isn't pretty or accountable.

And there is more. Middlesbrough isn't only a place where many asylum seekers' homes have been marked in bright red. It is also in breach of national guidelines for the number of asylum seekers it is home to.

A few years ago, Middlesbrough was not alone. But in a Parliamentary debate last week, Brokenshire admitted that today only Middlesbrough is in breach of national guidelines. Nowhere else in the UK.

Let me be very clear and unambiguous about what the problem is. It is right that the UK grants asylum to individuals who meet strict criteria – and all areas should do their fair share.

The problem is that where there is a disproportionate number of new people this will add avoidable burdens on local public services and increase the costs of fostering integrated communities.

The right thing to do is for the Government to ensure all parts of the country are not disproportionately burdened – and if they are to provide some funding support. When he was at last shamed into action, Prime Minister David Cameron provided emergency relief to Middlesbrough that went to assisting integration efforts and supporting public services.

This appears to be a one-off. Now a few years later, the situation has improved for everywhere else but not here. It would be deeply wrong to move people somewhere else adding to their disruption and severing what local connections they have been able to create. And they bring value to our communities – something too rarely acknowledged by ministers.

Yet this is not without costs – and the Government should either provide this funding or consider demanding that G4S or its subcontractors responsible for breaching national guidance contribute.

It was not always like this. There used to be a Migration Impacts Fund. It was created by a surcharged levied on immigration-related applications when Jacqui Smith was Home Secretary. I should know – as an immigrant to the UK myself, I paid it. This Fund could then be tapped into to provide funding relief where it was needed.

But the Fund is no more. While the Government kept the high application fees – set to increase by up to twenty-five per cent in April – they also kept the cash.

What is it spent on now? No one is saying, but it is not a ready, funded reserve to help local communities better acclimatise to migration-related impacts. The Coalition Government scrapped it within months of coming to power. At least they had priorities – and immigration was not one of them.

Asylum seekers are victims of the worst stereotyping. Many still believe that most migrants are asylum seekers. But they aren't. Asylum seekers typically make up no more than about eight per cent of migrants. And sixty per cent will have their applications for asylum rejected and be earmarked for deportation. Most migrants are a lot like me – students and people in full employment.

Every speech about immigration by this Government starts the same. The first sentence or two says that we're all proud to be a place of safety for the most vulnerable of the vulnerable – but without once saying why. That might get in the way of ninety-nine per cent of every speech typically focused on why migrants are unwelcome and unwanted.

No doubt a sentiment that many will feel – and I don't pretend that the overall positive effects of immigration on Britain's economy and culture have been positive for all. They haven't.

But nor will they be when you have a government that will no longer let immigrants pay into funds to help local communities better handle migration-related impact. Or when the Government doesn't know or care that contractors, or their subcontractors, are branding vulnerable refugees with red doors or red wristbands making them ready targets. Or a government that defends banal 'British values' determined by a committee of special advisors and bureaucrats with no input from the public. Or where the Government is satisfied with a citizenship test few British citizens can actually pass. Or a Government committed to a net migration target that might be reached if more British citizens are encouraged to leave and not return.

How did things come to this? Simple – this is government without principle directed only by short-term headlines where their acting is hoping others act for them. The public is played for fools and everyone is worse off – not least asylum seekers who may be among the very worst off.

Can Labour win on immigration? [86]

Immigration is an issue that continues to challenge the Labour Party. The official report by Dame Margaret Beckett into why the

86 'Can Labour win on immigration?' *LabourList* (2 February 2016).

2015 general election was lost concluded that Labour's 'failing to convince on benefits and immigration' was one of four key reasons behind its defeat.

Labour's manifesto included a pledge to ensure all customer-facing staff at public authorities speak fluent English – a policy pinched by the Tories and in the current Immigration Bill – and a commitment to linking residency with contribution. But these positions became quickly overshadowed by mugs declaring 'controls on immigration' that appeared more gimmick than concrete for critics.

The choice for Labour is how it might develop and defend an immigration policy consistent with the Party's fundamental values that can win public confidence. If this key electoral liability is not dealt with, it will impose limits on what Labour can deliver in future contests – and time is not on our side with major votes this year.

This is no easy task. We need more than specific policies, but crucially we need a narrative. The public need to understand not only what we believe – but why believe it.

There is virtually no issue that lacks dissent. A welcome development in Labour is Jeremy Corbyn's insistence that the 'new politics' is about a constructive dialogue that brings people into politics rather than shuts them out by declaring official policies from on high.

This dialogue is set to launch with Keir Starmer QC and his national fact-finding tour over the next three months. Keir will visit constituencies across the country to gain a clearer picture of the different perspectives and impacts of migration.

This is welcome not least because no such immigration review has taken place in many years – and no detailed policy since at least the White Paper 'Controlling Our Borders: Making Migration Work for Britain' in 2005 under Tony Blair when Charles Clarke was Home Secretary. And the fact is that Labour should be trying to complete what it started and not begin from scratch.

It was a Labour government that introduced:

- a transparent points-based visa system
- English language tests for all who want to become permanent residents
- fixed penalty fines on employers for each illegal worker employed
- pre-boarding electronic checks on all persons entering or leaving the UK by air
- increased residency requirement for permanent settlement
- The Life in the United Kingdom citizenship test
- grant temporary leave for refugees opening a clearer pathway to permanent residency and citizenship
- reduced abuses of the asylum system.

Some of these achievements will surprise. I lost count of how often Nigel Farage claimed a vote for UKIP was to choose to launch a points-based immigration system – despite the fact the UK has had it for years. I should know. I am an immigrant and met the points-based criteria allowing me to work here. The online calculator you can use is perhaps as informative as it is entertaining.

We should start conversations about Labour's immigration policies by making clear that the best parts of the current system were created by a Labour government. The importance of knowing English for long-term residency, raising the bar for employing non-EU workers, requiring knowledge of British life set out in a test to improve integration, citizenship ceremonies to celebrate becoming British and reducing abuses of the asylum and immigration system.

Labour also spelled out in new guidance tough measures restricting residency for non-EU migrants with convictions and tests for 'good character.' These policies are popular – and Labour made it happen. We need to communicate much better how Labour created today's border controls that the Tories seek only to tweak with ineffective gimmicks.

And we can go further still. The public's concerns about immigration is that it is too much and too fast. Labour should continue to reject the Government's use of net migration and instead focus on different numbers. Net migration counts people in the wrong way. It finds success when British citizens choose to leave or not return.

But that's not the kind of migration that concern the public. They worry about migrants taking benefits without paying their fair share – and they worry about the pressures on employment, housing and public services. An important first step is to reject net migration and its discrimination of UK citizens – and stop counting students as migrants because they are not part of the public's concerns.

Instead we should look to ensuring that those who can work and contribute can do so. One of the first measures David Cameron scrapped was the Migration Impacts Fund. This was a pot of money paid into only by migrants through a surcharge on immigration applications. The fund help support integration and provided relief on public services affected by migration-impact. The Coalition Government ended the scheme, but kept the high application fees using this money to plug holes elsewhere while turning a blind eye to the impact of migration on local communities.

Labour should bring this back – and call on the EU to establish an EU Migration Impacts Fund that has the same goal on a wider scale. This would be funding distributed across EU member states to help relieve impacts on public services, such as in schools, housing, health and public transport.

Labour is about work – as they say, the clue is in the name. We should be tough on creating full employment and the ripe conditions for it. Taking migration-impact more seriously is a key part of this. Those who worry Labour is more on the side of taking benefits than doing work will be shown to have it very wrong – and on immigration, too.

When Labour launched citizenship tests and ceremonies, it did not accept a proposal at the time that migrants already settled in the UK – such as naturalised British citizens – could serve as voluntary mentors to help enable the integration of newly-arrived migrants. Integration remains an important issue where Britain can do better. Requiring people to learn English – usually at their own expense – is necessary. But it is not sufficient.

Other EU countries like France and Germany provide integration classes, usually incorporating some language instruction into their curriculum. Attendance can be mandatory in order to receive any benefits and programmes must be completed for long-term residency. Something along these lines is well worth considering for the UK – and it would fit in our history of achievement on immigration which has always welcomed contribution and integration over separation and isolation.

These are only a few ways in which Labour can develop an immigration system that is fair and fit for purpose. Our Clause IV is clear: 'by the strength of our common endeavour we achieve more than we achieve alone' – and it is this that can help flesh out our narrative that provides the why to the what: why we believe in what we want to do.

Migration should not become something that happens out of control but instead there should be a plan for ensuring a fair and transparent system that does not turn a blind eye to those refugees needing our urgent help – but nor be deaf to public concerns about the impact migration has or is perceived to have on them and their communities.

I warmly welcome Keir Starmer's national fact-finding tour as a moment whose time could not come soon enough. Labour can listen and learn from the public on immigration – we clearly do not have their trust on this issue. Doing nothing will do little to help improve our electoral chances in future and we need to perform better.

Perhaps surprisingly, we start from a stronger position to set the record straight and move forward. Labour has done much to create what is right about the UK's immigration system. But we must go further, building on Labour values and in the spirit of Clause IV make a stronger Britain more confident in itself and its place in the world – rather than create gimmicks dressed up as 'policy' that does much to increase people's worries without doing anything substantive about solutions.

Why is the UK ramping up costs for potential Australian migrants? [87]

Australian citizens make up one of the largest groups entering the UK each year. More than 21,000 Australians received entry visas in 2015 – the fourth highest number of visas for any nationality after China, India and the United States. But this looks set to change as Australians get swept up in Britain's efforts to reduce net migration.

In 2015, the UK government introduced a healthcare surcharge for all non-EU arrivals on visas longer than six months. The surcharge is added to most immigration applications and paid up front. It costs £200 (or roughly A$400), or £150 (roughly A$300) for students per year.

A family of four on three-year visas would be required to pay a health surcharge of £2,400 ($A4800) on top of other application

87 'Why is the UK ramping up costs for potential Australian migrants?' The Conversation (24 February 2016).

fees – all of which have risen much faster than inflation. Some are set to rise by twenty-five per cent this northern spring.

Australians had, so far, been exempt from this charge. This was due to reciprocal agreements between Australia and the UK that allowed citizens of one country to use most healthcare services in the other country for free. Exceptions are made for services with a fee, like dental treatment or prescription medicine.

But, from April 6, Australians will no longer be exempt from paying the health surcharges. This means the higher upfront fees will be required for all UK visa applications. The UK Government claims this is being done out of fairness to other nationalities. But important questions as to the Government's motivations remain.

While Australians coming to the UK must pay the new surcharge, it is unclear how this affects existing agreements for British citizens travelling to Australia.

The health surcharge is meant to offset the expected costs for treating migrants in the UK's National Health Service (NHS). However, the UK government has only recently begun collecting data on how much different nationalities actually use the NHS. This means the Government is conjuring up the charge almost out of thin air before reliable data is available.

One former UK Home Secretary told me the charge was likely being used to plug holes in the NHS budget caused by government cuts – and not by migrants.

The UK's underlying motivation for this change is its continuing struggle to reduce net migration. This has reached record highs under the Cameron government despite continuing promises to reduce it to under 100,000 a year. It is currently more than three times this at 336,000.

The UK government has become increasingly desperate to find any means it can to reduce numbers. It also plans to increase the required salary for work visas to £35,000 (roughly A$70,000). This has raised fears that Australian citizens could be hit hard and damage the long-standing close relationship between Australia and the UK.

Relations have become increasingly frayed over the last two years as Australians are abandoning the UK 'in their thousands.' The number of work visas issued to Australians by the UK Home Office has halved since 2006 and is now fewer than 15,000.

Between 2011 and 2012, the number of Australians resident in Britain dropped by nearly 10,000. A key factor in this decline were new visa restrictions brought in by the UK government in 2011. These measures included a cap on non-EU migrants permitted to acquire sponsored work visas.

It is likely that the health surcharge to be levied on Australians will continue the trend of fewer seeking work in the UK to avoid spiralling costs. Meanwhile, new labour statistics suggest another rise in EU migrant workers, who have free movement to work across Europe and are subject to few restrictions.

Not only are Britain's increasingly restrictive measures ineffective at achieving short-term political goals, but there is little serious discussion about the longer-term consequences – including the UK's relationship with Australia. As fewer go to the UK and work, and instead choose to go elsewhere, this once-close bond may become difficult to repair.

What should Theresa May do about immigration? A six-point plan[88]

Immigration poses a crucial challenge to Theresa May as she settles into Number 10. David Cameron failed to reduce net migration as

88 'What should Theresa May do about immigration? A six-point plan', *Daily Telegraph* (22 July 2016): 20.

he vowed repeatedly he would do and support for less immigration played a key role in Leave's success. There are five things that May can do about this:

First, Cameron set himself the wrong target. 'Net migration' includes all persons leaving and entering the UK for a year or more. About one-third are foreign students and over 80,000 are British citizens. The public has legitimate concerns about long-term migration, not students or British citizens. Omitting them from a new target will cut the official figure in half—and provide a more accurate picture.

Secondly, migration puts pressure on public services. In 2010, Cameron closed the Migration Impacts Fund using its surplus for the debt. Migrants paid into this through an additional charge on immigration applications: I know—I paid it as a migrant at that time. Local councils, health trusts and charities could apply for support covering more nurses, teaching assistants and buses. May should resurrect a new Migration Impacts Reduction Fund like the original to cover areas of need like education, housing and transport.

Thirdly, more should be done to ensure migrants speak English. The Government supports that all those in public sector public-facing roles are fluent in English. May should go further and make most, if not all, public sector staff meet this standard over the next five to ten years. She should also close unnecessary loopholes in satisfying English requirements like exceptions for nationality.

Fourthly, the biggest secret about Britain's immigration system is that we've had an Australian-styled points-based system for over a decade: again, I know – I had to pass it. This system applies only to non-EU citizens. There are exceptions for jobs where there are shortages, but this list only gets longer each time it is reviewed. May should have this list made more fit for purpose.

Finally, it has been ten years since Sir Bernard Crick led an Advisory Group recommending reforms to improve integration and foster citizenship. Their report led to a citizenship test now sat over two million times and citizenship ceremonies. There has never been a review into how these reforms are working and no migrant or naturalised citizen has been consulted.

In researching my book *Becoming British*, I found that many of the policies designed to promote integration of migrants had the opposite effect – and there has never been a review with citizens or migrants alike. A new, national conversation is long overdue and it can help heal the social divisions we've seen over the last few weeks – alongside increased funding for immigration officers struggling to tackle a threefold spike in human trafficking into Britain by illegal 'lorry drops' that puts pressure on the ability of border agents to reduce illegal working and sham marriages.

Theresa May has an opportunity she can seize to reform immigration policies. The consequences could be political gold.

In the age of Byron Burgers, we are all border agents [89]

Dozens of migrants working illegally at the Byron hamburger restaurant chain were caught by immigration officials, in welcome news for the new Home Secretary Amber Rudd. She will hope these headlines continue.

The previous government under David Cameron made it more difficult for migrants to work illegally. They did this by requiring new checks for work, renting property from a private landlord, opening a bank account and acquiring a drivers' licence. Applicants have to prove their lawful residence. The plan was to make everyday

89 'In the age of Byron Burgers, we are all border agents', *International Business Times* (29 July 2016).

living in the UK too difficult for illegal migrants. Eventually, they would be found out and could be subsequently removed.

The logic behind this is that most illegal migrants are discovered after they cross the border – not at the border itself. A travel or work visa may expire, but the Government lacks the tools to know where these people are. Its plan is to expose them when they engage in everyday tasks like renting a home, using the bank or driving a car.

Some industries are targeted by immigration officials more than others. One area receiving significant attention is the restaurant industry, especially takeaways, where illegal working is rife. The Government has been increasing its searches of businesses where illegal working has been a problem historically, given the limited resources for such work.

Yet it remains unclear how much the Government's tougher residency checks contributed to exposing the Byron burger chain. Byron had already checked the residency papers for its staff, including the thirty-five people found to be working illegally from countries like Albania, Brazil, Egypt and Nepal.

The checks were lawful, but the documents provided were not. We have now learned that these employees had submitted false documents.

This poses a real challenge for the Home Office. It has effectively devolved much of its immigration enforcement efforts to us. It falls to employers, private landlords, banks, universities and others to do the document checking. Many of us are now de facto border agents.

The problem is that we may act like border agents, but we are not them: we lack their training, their experience and resources to make the full checks available to the Home Office. They are better placed to uncover false papers, yet it is us who do this important work.

I strongly suspect the 'intelligence' that led to this exposé was a tip-off from the local community and that this brought about the result, and not any of the Government's recent measures to tackle illegal working. This does not mean these measures aren't worth having, but that immigration officials are in a difficult position trying to tackle the known unknown of illegal workers in our midst armed with a lack of resources and people on the frontline to provide the checks necessary.

This highlights the need for greater public investment in immigration officials to carry out proper checks to enforce existing regulations and keep the community safe. The public needs action backed by resources, and not gimmicks that may come to nothing.

Prime Minister Theresa May is in a strong position in her new role to get this right and help make the Home Office fit for purpose. The public is concerned about immigration more than any other issue, precisely because it lacks confidence in the Government's ability to exercise control over our borders. Improving efforts to tackle illegal working can both promote protecting the public and rights in the workplace, while getting the balance right on migration. She should act decisively sooner, rather than later.

This is personal: why Corbyn was right to pledge to revive the migration impact fund[90]

Immigration is a concern for most voters. But what should be done?

David Cameron and Theresa May have seen this as a wake-up call for fewer people to come to Britain. They have tied their Governments to an arbitrary number of net migrants. Those who think there are too many migrants will be no more satisfied by 100,000 than 110,000. There is no rational or sentimental argument for why less net migration will bring more public support.

90 'This is personal: why Corbyn was right to pledge to revive the migration impact fund', *LabourList* (29 September 2016).

And then there is the question of what counts as net migration. The term lumps together very different groups from economic migrants and asylum seekers to foreign students and British citizens (nearly 80,000) returning from a gap year or working abroad. Remove students and our citizens and net migration is down about forty per cent.

When people express concerns about migration, it isn't returning fellow citizens and students they are thinking about. So removing them from an arbitrary target brings down the number but not, rightly or wrongly, the concerns held by many voters.

Cameron and May misread public concerns about migration levels as a problem about a numerical target they have missed and that fuels a sense that the situation is out of control.

Jeremy Corbyn's speech at this year's conference was a welcome move in the right direction. Our focus should not be on numbers, but on impact. What concerns people about migration levels is the scale of change and impact on local communities and public services. If Labour gets this right, it can address the core concern that people have about migration.

This has been spun by some parts of the media, like the *Daily Mail,* as Labour supporting unrestricted migration. That is nonsense. Labour's focus on impact is not separate from numbers. The greater the numbers, the more of an impact this can have.

But it's not true that raising barriers to migration will lead to better public services – that often rely on migrants for providing the world class education, health care, housing and public transport that we all enjoy. Migrants contribute to Britain. They are not an enemy, but our friends and neighbours.

Labour knows that migrants contribute to making Britain great. A Labour government launched the Migration Impact Fund. This was created by a modest surcharge on immigration applications that provided financial support to be made available where it was needed most. The fund made possible more teaching assistants, more nurses, more buses and beyond – migrants funding migration measures without any added costs for British taxpayers.

This is personal for me. I paid into the fund when I was a migrant prior to becoming British – and I have been campaigning for its return since it was scrapped by the Tories, only weeks after they returned to power in Coalition with the Liberal Democrats.

Corbyn's pledge to bring restore the fund is a welcome first step on the journey back to winning public support.

There is more to be done. Too many of our communities – both new and old – feel alienated from the mainstream. Britain isn't working for them or providing the support they need or deserve. This isn't only about doing more to ensure migrants can become integrated into British society, but must be about integrating all segments of society. People won't do this if society scapegoats the few to please the many. We need to build stronger, healthier and sustainable communities.

Labour can do this on immigration by focusing on the impact – not on arbitrary numbers – and get results that help local communities that need it most. This is a direct challenge and alternative to the hollow solutions that Tories offer Britain on immigration.

Public confidence won't be won overnight. But the usual 'solutions' aren't helping. We need to offer something different – and something that is fair that can be delivered. Policies like a migration impact fund that reduce the pressure on public services can make a difference to local communities and ensure public services support all those who need them. Everybody can win and – to quote Corbyn – 'it's the Labour way.'

The sooner we have a national conversation about migration and citizenship, the better[91]

Immigration is the problem that won't go away for Theresa May's government.

After committing to reducing net migration, it continues to remain at record highs. 'Net migration' counts everyone coming or going to Britain. Despite repeated claims that Labour lacked sufficient border controls, net migration has never been higher than since the Tories promised to bring it down. This post-truth politics of saying one thing but doing another fools no one.

This problem could be partly avoided by a better means of counting the number of migrants to restore the public's faith in the immigration system. Net migration counts many people as 'migrants' like 80,000 British citizens and many more full-time foreign students at our top universities – people who few would consider migrants.

It is fundamentally wrong to have an immigration target where the Government can reach its goals by encouraging more British citizens to leave or not come back so that 'net migration' can be reduced. This is not what the public voted for when it wanted to take back control with Brexit.

Pledges to reduce numbers mean little when they are routinely missed – and they don't hit the real issue. Migrants bring many benefits in shaping modern Britain beyond their contributions to the economy through paying taxes or student fees, but these are not cost-free and this is too readily overlooked. Voters were making clear long before Brexit that they have concerns with how poorly successive governments have helped support creating cohesive communities despite population changes.

91 'Immigration has to work for the whole of society', *The Journal* (16 December 2016): 25.

Dame Louise Casey's new report on integration is long overdue. Theresa May deserves credit for helping commission it over a year ago when she was Home Secretary. Many of its findings are welcome, but it should have gone much further.

First, Dame Louise is correct to prioritise the promotion of English skills. A shared language is the key to creating a sense of community. The Government could improve cohesiveness if it was more pro-active in better providing support to areas that require it most urgently. Real term cuts for English support since 2010 has been counterproductive.

It's a mistake to think that only migrants are in need. Why not support British citizens as well? Too many in Britain are functionally illiterate – possibly as high as sixteen per cent of the adult population. If English proficiency is a good thing for gaining employment or integrating communities, support shouldn't be restricted to migrants but made available for citizens old and new alike. So let's see more support for all, rather than a few. This will benefit all in Britain and help bring us together. The Government's review should have recognised this better instead of being too narrow.

Secondly, the Casey Review recommends schools and local communities work more closely together to provide opportunities for pupils to mix with others from diverse backgrounds. More can and should be done. British values should receive greater attention in classrooms – even if it seems bureaucrats, and not the British public, are the ones defining what these values are. This democratic deficit should be addressed. These proposals in the Casey Review should go much further. Bringing together people from a local area has many benefits for breaking down barriers between neighbours. Communities shouldn't be isolated from each other or unable to come together.

Yet these plans can also be more ambitious and extend to the country as a whole. Our young people should see more of what makes Britain great beyond their backyards alone. Let's have a more open horizon – and help bring our country closer.

Finally, Dame Louise supports reviewing the route to British citizenship. This is long overdue, as I've argued for some time. The last review was completed over ten years ago by Sir Bernard Crick, at the invitation of his former university pupil, the then Home Secretary David Blunkett. Yes, that long ago.

Crick's report came to similar conclusions about language, values and integration that we find in Casey's Review – and with some different policy recommendations. While not all Crick's proposals took hold, none have been subjected to any review since and are now long overdue.

As the Casey Review makes clear, its time has now come. Migrants should expect better than a bad pub quiz for a citizenship test – and citizens deserve greater confidence in how the immigration system works for all, rather than only a few. This could herald a more fair and trusted policy that the public craves, and waits for its deliverance.

Theresa May deserves credit for commissioning this review on integration. And while the Casey Review has its flaws, it should not become an opportunity missed to tackle this most pressing of public concerns. The sooner we have a national conversation about migration and citizenship, the better – and we can't wait much longer.

As a migrant I know Labour must have a coherent and compassionate policy on immigration if it is to win again[92]

A long overdue debate is opening up in Labour about its position on immigration. It will be difficult for Labour to win the next

92 'As a migrant I know Labour must have a coherent and compassionate policy on immigration if it is to win again', *LabourList* (5 January 2017).

general election if it can't do better than rock bottom on what is the public's number one concern.

The debate is seen as a choice between freedom of movement and reducing numbers. This isn't quite right because it assumes freedom of movement is unrestricted – and this is untrue. EU citizens can be deported after six months and prevented from re-entry under certain circumstances although these powers are rarely used. In researching my book *Becoming British,* I discovered that 2,731 Europeans were removed in the year up to June 2014 and only nineteen allowed to return over a year later.

Labour MPs including current Shadow Home Secretary Diane Abbott, and Yvette Cooper, one of her predecessors, are developing new ideas about what a progressive immigration policy might look like for the party. Here are four key principles they should consider:

Firstly, a progressive policy is shaped by the past and looks to the future. We should not romanticise a past monolithic Britain that never was. Turning back the clock turns our back against our shared history. Respect for our differences in a modern, multicultural Britain is not a tolerance of the status quo but a recognition of what Britain is. This should be embraced, not overlooked.

Secondly, Labour should focus on reducing impact and not look only at numbers. Kicking migrants out will not make the problems of impact go away. Immigration is a concern for many because of pressures on public services like healthcare, employment, education and housing. Relief through a migrant-funded migration impact fund is a step in the right direction – cutting numbers so there are fewer doctors, employers and teachers will only make a bad situation worse.

Thirdly, integration is not a one-way street. While the new report from the APPG on social integration has many welcome recommendations, its focus is too narrow and we should not see integration as something that immigrants are to do by themselves alone. This is how the system works for many at present. As a migrant from the US, for example, I first learned about television licensing when I had a knock on the door from an enforcement officer. If we want migrants to integrate, we must provide support so they can.

Building fair, sustainable communities works both ways. New citizens must engage with their new localities for sure, but we gain new members and have responsibilities to them too. If knowing English helps create better integration and employment prospects, we need to tackle functional illiteracy for citizens old and new – including the left behind. Supporting high English standards is not for migrants alone but for everyone, with benefits for all.

Finally, becoming British shouldn't be alienating. All permanent residents must pass a citizenship test that is more like a bad pub quiz. It's scandalous that a knowledge test few British citizens can pass is the bar for new members to join the club. My research exposed that instead of helping new citizens become more positive about becoming British they were instead left feeling more cut-off. Becoming British should not be done in isolation – new members are joining a community.

Failing to listen or even care about whether the current system helps migrants integrate shows how impoverished the system has become. But keeping it in a form few understand sells short the strong community spirit Britain has and progressives celebrate.

How Theresa May ended up to the right of Enoch Powell on immigration[93]

It almost happened. Theresa May has been under constant pressure from Labour's frontbench to remove international students from the Government's net migration target.

Net migration is determined by the total number of people who enter and leave the UK. May has consistently argued – and maintains – that net migration includes all who come and go not least students and so they should remain in the Government's net migration target. She is refusing to change her mind and claims she has no choice. This is untrue.

May is correct that net migration statistics currently include foreign students. But it is incorrect for her to claim that the Government's target must be inflexibly tied to one statistic. It is just as easy to say the target will look at migrants, but not foreign students. But this is a political decision – May is not required to do this. She is choosing to do this.

By failing to remove foreign students, she risks damaging one of Britain's greatest cultural and economic assets – our world-leading universities. Of course I would say this as a professor and head of a distinguished law school, but it's also true. May's decision has been called a 'mystery' – not least because cutting students damages not only the funding of higher education, but even more importantly damages the vibrant intellectual culture our universities are best at globally. Where Britain retreats, others will step in.

The biggest surprise to me is this. Enoch Powell is not someone I would normally cite approvingly – and especially not from his outrageous 'Rivers of Blood' speech, because looking at his words can leave me feeling ill – but in researching my book *Becoming*

93 'How Theresa May ended up to the right of Enoch Powell on immigration', *LabourList* (26 April 2017).

British, I discovered by closely reading his speech this comment about students: 'They are not, and never have been, immigrants.'

So the big question we must ask the Tories: if even Enoch Powell – in his most infamous of infamous speeches – accepts that foreign students should not count as migrants, why has Theresa May decided they do?

Any government that is to the right of Powell's 'Rivers of Blood' speech on migrants should be seen for the outrage that it is. While it may be wishful thinking, it is not too late for May to do the right thing – and change her mind on students.

Labour must increase the pressure on May to stop using students to meet her arbitrary targets. The Government tries to address public anxieties about immigration by blocking a group the public does not view as immigrants. If the public and even Powell don't see this, it's hard to believe that May's government does.

If May is serious about Britain continuing to keep its door open to 'the brightest and the best' as she said in her Brexit speech, then Labour must hold her to account. We need to shine a bright spotlight on May's record and let her lack of action speak louder than her empty promises. Labour can defend a progressive immigration policy and win public support. Removing international students from May's migration target is a first step in the right direction.

Theresa May's strict immigration rules are keeping numbers down – by driving British citizens out[94]

In order to win public confidence on immigration, the Conservative-led Coalition Government, under the then Home Secretary Theresa

94 'Theresa May is driving British citizens out of their own country', *The Independent* (26 April 2017).

May, imposed a new requirement that anyone wanting to bring a spouse and any children to the UK needed to earn a minimum of £18,600 a year. The policy was designed to ensure that family members brought to the UK did not become a burden on taxpayers, labelling their partner a 'sponsor' who would, by their own earnings, pay for any benefits they qualified for.

As we head into a general election in which immigration numbers will play a key part, the Prime Minister will be attempting to paint this as one of her crowning achievements. But the policy simply doesn't work.

First, it doesn't make any practical sense. Migrants from outside the EU, children or spouses included, are not entitled to any public benefits. 'Sponsoring' them to compensate taxpayers makes little sense; it is a cheap gimmick to fool those who have little understanding of our immigrants and benefits system. I should know. I am an immigrant, and my visa is incredibly clear: I am entitled to nothing.

The second problem is that this policy does not account for the wealth of an incoming spouse. If one worker earning £18,600 or more is sufficient to guarantee their family will put no further stress on the UK's public services, why must that worker be British? If someone from the UK married a non-citizen as wealthy as Donald Trump, they are still considered a drain on the state. It's a meaningless test of self-sufficiency.

The flaws in this policy have created real hardships for many British citizens who are married or have children with non-UK nationals. In researching my book, *Becoming British*, I spoke to Britons who shared with me depressing accounts of their desire to live in their own country and raise their children, but that the income threshold – designed to reduce net migration overall rather than thwart the life chances of existing citizens – prevented them from exercising their right to a family life in the UK.

Some described the Home Office as going well beyond their role, interfering in personal lives by determining who does, and who does not, have the right to fall in love with a non-British citizen based solely on their income, and with no consideration given to the integrity, strength and commitment of their relationships.

A UK Supreme Court case challenged the minimum income requirement earlier this year, giving such families fresh hope. The court ruled that the income requirement was permissible, but the Government – now, of course, a Conservative majority administration, at least until 8 June – was required to consider more substantively the income of those affected.

So why did the judges conclude that the current scheme could nonetheless continue while these considerations took place? Though they agreed that minimum income requirements were acceptable in principle, they raised serious concerns about their use in practice. That should warrant at least a temporary freeze until the Government can measure and better understand the damaging effect of breaking up legitimate families and preventing some British citizens from raising their children in their home country.

The Government claims its policy is necessary to address a public interest in reducing net migration. And that long-promised reduction is happening because these inhumane rules are forcing British citizens and their families out. Net migration figures are down by 49,000, but 54,000 extra British citizens chose to leave the UK. Is Theresa May really 'getting it right' on immigration?

The form was intended as a way to provide evidence over invalid spousal visas, but it was clearly unfit for purpose. In the rush to get this out, the Government forgot to include a line where informants could give an address to verify what they were reporting; they forgot to ask how to contact the person identified as illegally in the country; and they did not provide an email or postal address for where any paperwork required could be sent.

Its biggest failing, however, was that it put spouses at risk of domestic violence. Abusive partners could potentially record their spouse as in the country illegally as an act of aggression or control, despite their possession of a valid UK visa.

The Government is clearly desperate to reduce net migration and the public supports this general aim. But breaking up families and putting vulnerable women and children at risk is no way to improve public confidence in the Government or the Home Office and its ability to manage our borders.

Our immigration policies should support British citizens, not encourage more of them to leave their country, and their Government, behind. Theresa May, now is your chance to prove that you're listening.

The manifesto pledge that the Tories have never – and will never – deliver on [95]

Despite strong hints by Home Secretary Amber Rudd it wouldn't happen, the Tories have confirmed they will stick with their pledge to reduce net migration to under 100,000 for the general election.

It's a pledge that the Tories love to break. Despite repeated promises since 2010, net migration hit record highs under Tory-led Governments and on Theresa May's watch as Home Secretary and Prime Minister. No matter how often May blames Labour, the inconvenient truth is that it's the Tories seeing higher migration levels than at any point under New Labour.

Even the *Telegraph* has said 'if ever a manifesto pledge had failed to be delivered then this is it.' Simply wanting numbers to go down is not enough to make it happen. Not then and not now.

---

95 'The manifesto pledge that the Tories never have – and never will – deliver on', *The Independent* (11 May 2017).

But the problem with the Tory pledge isn't only that they haven't kept their promise once for seven years and counting. It's that using net migration is unworkable and probably counterproductive.

Migrants are not all the same. Some are wealthy entrepreneurs, many are in professional employment while others are here as students or spouses. More select categories like these can help government plan around local labour markets, school places and housing. Lumping them together makes planning more difficult – the short to medium term impact of a thousand foreign university students is very different from a thousand foreign university lecturers (I should know – I've done both).

Targets can work in a more selective approach than a blob – especially when you look beneath the surface to discover who is counted as a 'migrant.'

In counting everyone coming or going as a 'migrant', British citizens are included. That's you and me. The last quarterly net migration statistics in February showed a 49,000 drop overall. Ministers cautiously praised themselves for turning a corner with the first news of net migration being less instead of more.

However, ministers have little to celebrate. Hidden in the migration figures – that I exposed – was the fact that the 49,000 drop was partly due to 54,000 more British citizens choosing to leave or not come home. Any immigration target that includes local citizens as foreigners is unfit for purpose. If the only way to reduce net migration is by more of us leaving or not returning, then we need a new way to count immigration. Net migration is past its sell-by date. Where fewer British citizens helps meet net migration targets, something has gone terribly wrong with how the Government is showing it's listening to the concerns of the British public.

Perhaps the biggest problem of all is that even if net migration cuts happened, they would probably be counterproductive. It's because it is confusing fewer numbers with less impact. This might look obvious, but the two don't always go together.

For example, reducing the number of migrants may not lead to shorter queues at A&E when migrants are more likely to be doctors and nurses than patients. Or having fewer migrants might not mean more affordable housing when there are fewer migrants to build them. If there were fewer international students in further and higher education, this would not mean UK students would see the same or better resources available to support their education. Voters have genuine concerns about the impact of migration on public services, but looking at reducing migrants willy nilly could lead to longer NHS waiting times, less affordable housing and fewer resources for education.

Scrapping net migration targets does not mean giving up. A rational policy should not be fixed to an arbitrary goal. If targets are to be set, they should be evidence-based and specific to different categories of immigrants such as workers and students. The Government does not need to wait for Brexit to reduce numbers if it really wanted to. There is control over non-EU migrants – and free movement of EU nationals is not unrestricted: we can do more to enforce existing rules than at present, but this will require the Government taking responsibility instead of giving blame.

The Government could also address the real concerns voters have around access to public services by launching a Migration Impacts Reduction Fund paid for by a surcharge on immigration applications. Funds earned could be targeted at areas of greatest need benefiting citizens without costing a penny.

Either way, failing to meet unrealistic expectations on immigration will do nothing to improve public confidence in border security or move the country forward. The sooner this is realised by the Prime Minister, the better – and while there's still time to change the Conservative Party's election manifesto.

The Home Office makes huge profits from immigrants. So where is the money going to?[96]

As Theresa May's Government makes plans for Brexit, there are increasingly serious concerns about the economy if there is a hard Brexit and fewer migrants filling skilled work shortages.

Little attention has focused on how new immigration policies will be paid for as the costs of Brexit go up and extra funding proves harder to find. This might be because Theresa May has other plans for the money raised from immigration applications – and so starving the immigration system of much need cash.

Migrants pay increasingly high fees to apply for visas and citizenship – and most of this goes into the Government's back pocket. Prices have soared in some cases by twenty-five per cent – many times the inflation rate – over the last year. It can cost £2,297 to become a permanent resident and an additional £1,282 for citizenship – and that's after passing a citizenship test that's more like a bad pub quiz, meeting five year residency requirements and no access to public funds. The Home Office has even started charging £5.48 for emails.

According to their own data, the actual cost to the Home Office of making decisions is only about £135 per application. This means the Government is quite literally soaking migrants for a hefty profit of nine hundred per cent or more on many applications. And there is no sign that immigration fees will do anything but rise after Brexit. This cannot be right.

Not only are migrants paying more than necessary for their applications to be processed – in a service regularly criticised for being unfit for purpose – but the money raised isn't being used

96 'The Home Office makes huge profits from immigrants. So where is the money going to?' *The Independent* (13 September 2017).

to help address immigration-related issues where it could provide welcome relief. The Government has cut the number of border agents by several thousand despite receiving large sums in immigration application fees. Funding is available and not being used.

What's even worse is that part of these high fees was specifically earmarked to reduce migration-related impact. In 2009, Home Secretary Jacqui Smith launched a Migration Impacts Fund. This was a £50 fee added to migration applications that went to a common pool distributed to local communities most affected by migration impact such as supplying extra nurses, teaching assistants and buses where required.

Within six months of coming to office, the Tory-led Coalition scrapped the fund in 2010 – but kept the funding for different pet projects. The fee remains high, but we don't know where the extra funding goes except it isn't to reduce migration-related impact. This means millions are still being paid linked originally to a fund to reduce migration impact that has been diverted for over seven years. Communities affected by migration impact have lost out on much needed support – and migrants are left paying the bills for unrelated Tory pipe dreams. A lose-lose situation.

This money could help May in enforcing migration controls she says that she wants. Her government is committed to reducing net migration – the numbers leaving or returning to Britain – to under 100,000. It is within her power to place heavy restrictions on visas for entrepreneurs, skilled professionals and students from outside the EU that could help her achieve her target without affecting a single EU citizen. Her failure to meet her Government's net migration target is not the fault of the EU, but a political choice made in 10 Downing Street – just like the decision to use migration fees to fund non-migration policies – undermining further the immigration system the Prime Minister promises to protect.

So when the Government claims there is no magical money tree, know that migrants are making the Home Office massive profits that the Government is diverting outside an immigration system where it could be put to better use. It's time we all challenged the Government to explain the high fees, large profits and yet chronic underfunding in the immigration system. This isn't a problem caused by Brexit, Brussels or anybody else: it's poor decisions made under this government. Let's get it fixed.

We can detoxify the immigration debate by making fees on migrants more transparent[97]

Last week's Budget by Philip Hammond was a disappointment on several fronts. Britain faces another seventeen long years of falling incomes, rising debt and low productivity plus all the uncertainty his government has created over Brexit – the pictured painted by the Tories could not be more disappointing.

If Philip Hammond cannot promise more than producing a lost generation, it's time for him to go – and Labour must continue to generate the exciting new ideas like those found in its 2017 manifesto if we are to enter 10 Downing Street.

Whatever Brexit will mean in terms of any final deal, there is a strong likelihood it could profoundly change how the immigration system works. This is no bad thing. The Home Office requires urgent reform and public support for new immigration controls helped win the referendum for Brexit.

Change is necessary.

But these changes come at a cost. Britain will need to fast find

97 'We can detoxify the immigration debate by making fees on migrants more transparent', *LabourList* (1 December 2017).

funding support for more border agents and new border controls, especially if Britain is out of the EU single market and customs union. No free movement from Europe means restrictions to and from Britain must work differently. It was recently reported that the Home Office might be forced to hire European workers to register EU nationals without increases in staffing. Yet problems remain for where the funding might come from without increasing taxes on the public.

I recommend taking a bold step: make the immigration system fully self-funded on a sustainable footing. If the administration could stand on its own feet funded entirely by fees on immigration-related applications, this could help raise the profile of migrants by ensuring they do not take a penny from taxpayers.

The system's fees are big business. Immigration-related income raises over £2bn each year. At least £106m was raised and spent on non-immigration matters in a consolidated fund according to the Home Office's annual report of accounts for last year. If John McDonnell, as future chancellor, is looking for cash that could help pay for more agents or new controls post-Brexit, then the current immigration system could pay for itself in a sustainable way at a critical time.

Home Office figures show how reliant it has become on immigrants to fund non-migration services. For example, the annual surplus earned from border, immigration and citizenship services in 2014–15 was more than £468m. This was enough to absorb an overall deficit of £266m leaving an overall surplus of £200m or more. The truth is that immigration isn't just helping sustain the British government, but their application fees keep the Home Office afloat with much of the funding earned spent on anything but migration. This is a mistake.

Plus, these application fees are where the migration impacts reduction fund – a modest surcharge that could be used to reduce migration impacts on public services – would come from. Creating a sustainable, self-funded immigration system could manage distributing such funding more easily.

Of course, immigration fees are also sky high. I should know – I paid them as a migrant to Britain. The immigration system is not transparent enough in the cash it raises or how it is spent. If it was self-contained, then the true costs – and surpluses – would become clearer as would the case for reducing immigration fees which I would favour strongly. Left unreformed, the current system does not make this easy as too much raised in fees is diverted elsewhere. This is why change is needed to protect immigrants, reduce fees and improve the immigration system overall – and all of which is achievable from the political left.

The public has voiced concerns about uncontrolled immigration long before the vote for Brexit. Britain's leaving the European Union will impose costs at least in the short-term for border management and security whatever the new deal in place might be. Britain must be prepared and part of its plans must include funding reserves that can enable the delivery of a new immigration strategy.

Labour should argue for a ring fence around immigration as a self-funded zone – a system that must live within its means on a sustainable basis with no recourse to public funds. This is a promise we should make for a system that needs more of the money it is already generating to support significant reforms. The only question is whether there is enough political will to act now before it is too late. The consequence will be ending the view of migrants as a cash cow to be milked for other pet projects. This is a price worth paying.

Labour must take the lead on immigration after new report shows government failure[98]

The Home Affairs Committee published its latest report about the Home Office's handling of Brexit, and it is damning. It focuses on the much promised, but yet to be delivered, immigration white paper spelling out the Government's plans on immigration. Publication of these plans has been delayed at least four times by the Government and still no firm date has been set.

The urgency is obvious: EU nationals in the UK need to know now what their status post-Brexit will be – and, critically, the Home Office needs to be prepared to handle whatever this arrangement becomes. The failure to decide next steps creates confusion and anxiety for UK based EU nationals, their workplaces and friends and families, but also keeps the Home Office in a state of limbo it can ill afford. A perfect storm is brewing for genuine chaos. The Home Affairs Committee is now the latest body to begin sounding the alarm as March 2019 is just under one year away.

Unnecessary delays

The report begins by highlighting that the longer delays continue in providing certainty for EU nationals in the UK, the greater the anxiety this will cause for them and the more unnecessary confusion for British businesses. The Home Affairs Committee accepts that a final arrangement may be subjected to negotiation and the importance of receiving feedback from the Migration Advisory Committee. But it was unequivocal that 'the Government has a responsibility to Parliament, the public, EU citizens who will

98 'Labour must take the lead on immigration after new report shows government failure', *LabourList* (15 February 2018).

be affected, employers and public servants it expects to deliver the policies to provide some urgent clarity on its intentions.'

But the Home Affairs Committee could have gone further. It is the Government that announced there would be a new immigration bill in this Parliament term that would include new rules for EU citizens. The Prime Minister can hardly blame a Brexit process she triggered or waiting for talks to end so she can produce a bill her government promised last summer. Blame can only fall on her Government and it is important Labour repeatedly makes that point.

While the Migration Advisory Committee has an important role to play as a source of independent advice for the Government on immigration, it is also too narrow in its scope and remit. It can only advise on what it is asked to consider – and its membership consists of a small handful of economists. It is ripe for substantial reform to be more active in providing evidence-based advice on a broader range of migration-related issues, but desperately needs an expanded membership to include expertise in law and social policy. Immigration policy is about more than economic costs and benefits; it is also about social impact on communities, which is routinely overlooked and undervalued. Labour should change it and therefore gain better advice than currently available.

Registration chaos

The Government plans a dual registration system. The first will register EU and EEA nationals already resident in the UK before Brexit – and the second will register those nationals coming afterwards. The Government intends to permit those who have been resident for five years to apply for what it calls 'settled status' permitting permanent residency. But we know little else.

The Home Affairs Committee raises concerns on several fronts. First, it is unclear exactly how many EU and EEA citizens qualify for this 'settled status', making it difficult to determine what resources the Home Office requires to make a success of it. Secondly, it is unclear how the Home Office will enforce registration. I suspect the Prime Minister will be up to her usual tricks in turning you and I into border agents in all but name. We've already seen this with identity checks to open bank accounts – touted as an effort to smoke out migrants here illegally, although it has not actually identified a single individual not already known to be here illegally.

'Settled status' is something the Government talks about as a done deal, but it doesn't yet exist. It needs to be passed in the immigration bill, the white paper for which we're still waiting to see. This was originally sold as permitting EU or EEA nationals here within the rules to receive this status. That would have excluded many thousands, perhaps tens of thousands. Why? Freedom of movement rules require some categories of EEA nationals to arrive with comprehensive health insurance or risk removal. This has not been policed much at all and many, if not most, probably don't know they are in breach of it either. While it is welcome the Government will provide an amnesty and not require anyone to have this insurance to have settled status, we still don't know if some – or many – might be excluded. This is the kind of certainty we need urgently.

We also need to know how someone gets this status now or in the future, what would happen to those who qualify now but for whatever reason do not register before next March or during the transition period, and how this system can be run with so many unknowns.

What law will still be law?

The Home Affairs makes an important point about relevant law. The Government has said in withdrawing from the EU the UK will incorporate EU law in a new way (as of course it is already incorporated) with the UK Supreme Court taking precedence in place of the ECJ. Much of the debate now is how this might be amended in future.

But as every law student in my class knows, the law is more than the statute books – it also includes case law, sometimes lots of it. This can be an important source for clarifying the application of legislative principles in the concrete. What is the status of case law such as under Zambrano, Metock and Surinder Singh post-Brexit? This seems entirely overlooked and shows the incompetence of the current 'plans.'

Life after Dublin

Finally, the Home Affairs report raises a concern about what is called the EU's Dublin III Regulation. This is perhaps one of the better known migration principles in force and the most popular with the public. It is many things, but the part I will refer to is that when a migrant makes a claim for asylum in any EU country it must be in the first safe EU country they enter. If it can be shown that person entered another country first, he or she can be returned to it. This has meant a number of migrants have been sent from the UK to Greece, Italy and other EU countries on the eastern and southern borders.

The Home Affairs Committee is concerned that there be 'no diminution in the UK's approach towards meeting its international humanitarian obligations as it leaves the European Union.' It notes the importance of making provision for unaccompanied minors and much more. Sadly, this area of policy seems woefully underdeveloped with seemingly no plans at all for life after Dublin III, which the UK will exit with Brexit. There could be a new agreement – perhaps a Dublin IV – and growing interest in Europe for one. But whether the UK could become a part of it outside the EEA remains unknown.

In short, the Home Affairs report doesn't tell us anything new, but it could act as a wake-up call for the Government. Brexit is about much more than trade deals that have yet to happen and substantive immigration reform is necessary whatever happens next.

This will require vision, sound evidence and a commitment to making real change. The potential benefits are huge for creating certainty for businesses, building public confidence and, most importantly, providing clarity for affected individuals. All of this is in short supply under May's government – and provides a critically important time for Labour to take the lead.

Good luck with the citizenship test, Meghan Markle. It's a mess.[99]

Meghan Markle is on a fast track from Hollywood to British royalty. She'll certainly be joining the royal family from the moment of her marriage to Harry in May. And yet, if she wants to remain permanently in the UK, even the wife of the Queen's grandson must pass a citizenship test.

The test has been sat more than two million times since its launch in 2005. Anyone applying must correctly answer eighteen or more of twenty-four multiple choice questions to pass – and the test costs £50 for every attempt.

It's like a bad pub quiz: the test for British citizenship that few Brits could pass. One candidate failed sixty-four times before finally passing the test, and if you look at what the Government's quiz asks, it's easy to see why. How many of us know the height of the London Eye, the age of Big Ben's clock tower, or that Sake Dean Mahomet introduced curry to the UK when he opened the Hindoostane Coffee House on George Street, London? These are some of the nearly three thousand facts in the 180-page test handbook anyone wanting to stay in Britain is expected to know.

99 'Good luck with the citizenship test, Meghan Markle. It's a mess', *The Guardian* (1 March 2018).

The absurdity doesn't stop there. The test requires knowledge of the numbers of elected representatives in each regional assembly, but not in the House of Commons. Candidates need not know how to report a crime or register with a GP, but must know the approximate size of the Lake District and about 278 historical dates including when the Roman emperor Claudius invaded Britain.

If the citizenship test is meant to help migrants 'integrate into society and play a full role in your local community,' there is little evidence to show it succeeds. The test has appeared in three editions and been used for more than a decade, but there has never been a formal consultation on whether its aims are being achieved. So I did it for them.

My 2013 report exposed serious failings, including the test's impracticality and the many mistakes and omissions. My report made a dozen recommendations for how these problems might be fixed. Despite being raised in Parliament, the test remains unchanged.

For my book *Becoming British*, I interviewed citizens across the UK about the citizenship test. Almost no one believed it helped their integration into a British society where few had even heard of the test. Instead of building bridges, most saw the test as another barrier whose main purpose was to extract additional fees. The lesson to learn here is that the test is currently damaging integration more than it's enabling it.

There is an opportunity now to get this right as Britain changes its immigration policies after Brexit. Either the test is substantially modified to become a less trivial and fairer test of knowledge required for citizenship, or it should be thrown on the scrap heap.

A citizenship test is not obviously necessary to demonstrate a knowledge of life in the UK or British values. People could instead be tested informally without an exam, for instance by satisfying existing requirements for lawful residency, avoiding a criminal record, paying taxes owed and the like. These are ways in which people do show an understanding of living in this country in harmony with others.

But if the test is kept, change is needed – and a first step would be to make the answers freely available. Displaying knowledge about living in Britain shouldn't require buying a book with the information in. And rather than the test remaining a block, it should be relaunched as something that is primarily of symbolic importance. In the US, the test is the last step to citizenship with zealously non-partisan questions about who was the first president or which side won the American civil war.

In contrast, half the UK's test information on education is about setting up the Government's then flagship programme of free schools, but without any mention of a national curriculum, A-levels and more. Such partisanship needs to go. A test aimed at formally recognising the belonging someone has already earned is clearly preferable to what we have.

And if it is revised, it's critical that there is a public dialogue about what is included. The Government imposes this test of Britishness in the public's name, but it is so alien as to render it absurd. People need to have confidence in our immigration system again, and imposing arbitrary knowledge tests won't solve it.

Finally, migrants shouldn't have a veto, but they deserve to have a voice. If the test doesn't support integration, this needs to be fixed. Second-guessing the experience of migrants like me – who have passed the test and become British citizens – only continues the problem.

Theresa May's hostile environment strategy just isn't working[100]

The heartbreaking stories emerging of people from the Windrush generation have been shocking. Invited to Britain, then targeted for deportation many decades later based on a mistake, shattering lives and creating public outrage. The cause is Theresa May's 'hostile environment' approach to immigration that saw everyone as guilty unless proven innocent and where the Home Office helped destroy evidence that would have helped those it made victims.

Apologies have been offered, but the Government is refusing to see the Windrush scandal as a bad policy, only a poor implementation of a good one. But we don't need to look too far to see how malign and pernicious May's hostile environment has become – and ineffective, too.

Sham marriages have been a persistent concern for the Home Office, although the actual figures are hotly disputed. The previous Chief Inspector of Borders and Immigration, Sir John Vine, called bogus weddings a 'massive loophole' with many going undetected. In late 2015, the Home Office published a little noticed proposal to crack down on sham marriages as part of their creating a hostile environment. Unusually, there was no accompanying press release to celebrate its launch. It's easy to see why.

May's new plan was to get citizens to 'inform UKVI of a relationship breakdown.' The first part is a public statement form that a relationship with a migrant is not ongoing. Anyone signing the form must declare: 'I give my permission for the Home Office to use the information referred to above.' The second part is a consent form where signatories confirm that they give 'permission

100 'Theresa May's hostile environment strategy just isn't working', *LabourList* (23 April 2018).

for the Home Office to use the information provided' in the public statement.

Both forms ask for the names of the person submitting the statement and consent form and of the migrant being identified to the Home Office. But they also include several large practical omissions. Neither ask for the contact details of the person making the statement to verify the information reported. Neither asks for the nationality of the person making the statement or the ex-spouse. This is surprising for several reasons.

Relationship breakdowns will only be of potential interest where it involves a migrant, especially where he or she is on a spousal visa. Its terms would be breached if a relationship was no longer active and had come to an end. This would be equally true for a migrant making the statement about a British ex-spouse as it would be a Briton making the statement about a non-UK ex-spouse. Yet neither form asks for any nationality or contact details of the ex-spouse.

The implication of these practical gaps is simple, but no less dangerous. It makes it almost impossible for the Home Office to actually inform anyone named in a public statement that someone has reported him or her to the Home Office – while providing it with the consent to use this information for activities that would include terminating spousal visas and deportation.

This is a potentially serious use of personal data by the Home Office that it might store about individuals without their consent and with content that may be untrue, as it is almost impossible to verify given the absence of any contact details. Unlike the reported misuses of personal data uncovered about Facebook and Cambridge Analytica, this is a plan orchestrated and launched by the Home Office under May.

But did it work at cracking down on sham marriages? The answer is no. Labour peer Lord Rosser asked the Government for the number of forms received since 2016. The Government's answer was that the Home Office was unable to provide the data. When he next asked how many arrests or deportations had resulted from the use of this form, the Government gave the same reply: it couldn't provide the data.

Perhaps the Home Office is receiving these forms but leaving them in a storage cupboard in Whitehall unread, or maybe they've been lost or destroyed. Either way, they serve no clear purpose in tackling sham marriages, have not exposed a single sham marriage and are potentially open to serious abuse.

Nor did the Home Office pay much regard to problems the forms could cause. Further parliamentary enquiries have revealed that, in fact, 'no formal assessment has been made' for use of the public statement or consent form. For a Prime Minister who has called herself a feminist, this is hardly a good sign given the risk in the hands of abusive partners.

May could have done something else much easier, less open to abuse and without any misuse of personal data. When couples begin to divorce, a migrant's spousal visa becomes invalid at the point a decree nisi is confirmed by the court. Both parties will be aware of this formal proceeding.

The application might be amended to indicate whether one or both parties are non-British and, if so, reported to the Home Office, which can then declare the spousal visa invalid. This would avoid all the problems the public statement needlessly creates while also ensuring that relationships that really have come to an end are so recognised.

Such joined-up thinking should not escape the imagination of an experienced senior minister, not least any Prime Minister. This public statement farce must end now.

The Home Office already has a poor track record on tackling sham marriages with devastating consequences for innocent people when it has got it wrong. Turning ex-lovers into covert Home Office informants is among the new lows of the hostile environment Theresa May has fostered and developed since 2010. It's time her government put this bad idea in the bin where it belongs – and for May to take responsibility for getting this so badly wrong.

Sajid Javid is right – the British citizenship test is like a bad pub quiz. So what is he going to do about it?[101]

Speaking at his party's conference this week, the Home Secretary Sajid Javid criticised his own Government's British citizenship test, describing it as like 'a pub quiz' that is not fit for its intended purpose.

Javid is not the first to realise this. In 2013, I published what is still the only comprehensive report into the citizenship test, in which I criticised it in those terms – and this was discussed in Parliament. So it is pleasing to see my campaign for changing the test has the Home Secretary on board.

It's about time. The test is a key part of the immigration system for permanent settlement. Over two million tests have been sat since it launched in 2005. Immigrants sit a multiple choice exam with twenty-four randomly selected questions and must get eighteen or more correct to pass the exam. It costs £50 for each attempt – and one person was known to take it sixty-four times.

The test's intended purpose is to help confirm that an immigrant has successfully integrated into British society. This might be thought best achieved by checking for any criminal record or tax arrears over an extended residency period (which are also part

101 'Sajid Javid is right – the British citizenship test is like a bad pub quiz. So what is he going to do about it?' *The Independent* (3 October 2018).

of the process), but the test is supposed to add something extra beyond this. And here it categorically fails.

If you pour over the roughly three thousand facts covered by the test questions, including about 280 historical dates spread over 180 pages, it is difficult to see what practical use the citizenship test has. Its handbook does not say how to contact emergency services, register with a GP or report a crime. There is no mention of 999 or of how many MPs sit in the House of Commons. But you must know how many elected representatives sit in the Welsh Assembly, Scottish Parliament and Stormont in Northern Ireland. The handbook requires memorising the height of the London Eye and the age of Big Ben. And while you must know about starting a free school, there is no mention of the national curriculum.

Unsurprisingly, the test is regularly seen as the test for British citizenship that few British citizens can pass, with many migrants seeing it as an opportunity by the Home Office to extract increasingly more expensive fees through a test of random trivia meant to make more fail.

Instead of ensuring new and old citizens were coming together, my research found the test was actually moving them apart – and doing more harm than good at confirming integration.

In June this year, a House of Lords Select Committee on citizenship and civic participation agreed with me, endorsing seven of my recommendations, including the need for a new test and an advisory group engaging with the public to close the gap between public expectations and what any such test should cover. While Javid's remarks acknowledge the citizenship test's problems that the Lords Select Committee and I raised, it is unclear what he proposes to do about it. He says the test is not enough, but then promises to bring in 'a British values test' as something new.

My concern arises from one difference that I have with the Home Secretary: I have sat the citizenship test and know it first-hand.

If Javid examines the test, he will see that it already does ask immigrants about 'the liberal, democratic values that bind our society together.' So, if he wants the UK citizenship test to do this, the good news is it already includes it.

It would be a mistake to rush towards launching a new values test or revising the current one without engaging with the public. There are concerns about immigration and how well it is managed that have remained strong for several years. An edict based on guesswork won't build confidence, especially for those most anxious about immigration levels. One problem shouldn't lead to something worse.

Now is the time to foster healing for a country divided many different ways beyond the Remain and Leave split. An advisory group, preferably led by a naturalised British citizen who understands the process first-hand, could play an important role in bringing citizens together to discuss what British values we have, what they mean to people and how they can help rebuild a post-Brexit immigration system. Such work could be done over a few months, serving as a useful means for fostering confidence while dispelling immigration myths that might remove some of the toxicity from the debate and move the conversation on.

But it would take courage to make such a new start – and we can only hope such a plan is in mind.

Fifteen facts that prove the Tory immigration system isn't fit for purpose [102]

While Parliament is gridlocked over Brexit, far more has happened beyond trying to work out how to move forward after

102 'Fifteen facts that prove the Tory immigration system isn't fit for purpose', *LabourList* (13 June 2019).

the EU referendum. During the current extended parliamentary session, there have been several surprising, even shocking, revelations hidden in unreported ministerial responses led by Shadow Immigration Minister Afzal Khan and Labour's frontbench team in the House of Lords. Labour's forensic investigation raises new concerns about how unfit for purpose the immigration system has become under the Tories.

1. *Identity checks haven't exposed anyone new to be unlawfully in the UK.*
Theresa May's hostile environment was justified by its supporters as a means to catch migrants residing in the UK unlawfully. New identity checks were introduced for anyone opening a bank account, getting a driver's licence or renting privately. It turns out that these checks have not, in fact, exposed a single person not previously known to be in the UK unlawfully. The checks are made against a list of persons already known. Nobody new has been discovered since the checks were introduced, but their use led to the Windrush scandal in which citizens were wrongfully threatened with deportation.

2. *The ex-lover report form flopped.*
The Home Office created a form for the public to help expose sham marriages. It asks for confirmation that a couple is no longer in a relationship. Not only did the Home Office fail to conduct any formal assessment as to whether this might have an impact on domestic violence, the Home Office is 'unable' to reveal whether it has ever received a form, nor whether any arrests or deportations have been made. It doesn't help that the form fails to say where it should be sent and does not ask for any contact information from the person submitting the form or the migrant being reported. Another example of how the hostile environment has been not only cruel, but ineffective.

3. *Most of the money earned from immigration fees pays for non-immigration services.*
The immigration system earns far more than it costs to run. Most of the income received is spent on non-immigration services. The public does not pay £1 for the immigration system. It is entirely self-funded from immigration-related fees, such as visa applications.

4. *No records are kept of how much is spent reimbursing the public for mistakes.*
Many documents are sent to the Home Office for processing in the post. Some of these go missing and applicants are reimbursed. A useful measure of how big a problem lost documents at the Home Office has become would be to count the cost of reimbursements paid out to the public as a result. But the Home Office does not keep records of what it has spent, so no such useful measure is available.

5. *The immigration health surcharge is based on non-health costs.*
The Government introduced an immigration health surcharge, which is supposed to cover the costs of migrants using the NHS. It has since been revealed that the costs used to set the health surcharge are not all health-related. This means migrants are effectively paying to plug spending gaps in the Treasury unrelated to any impact on the NHS. The Government has not yet decided whether to charge EU citizens after Brexit. Money paid in by a migrant does not follow that person to cover any additional costs of that person's use of the NHS in their locality. This is further evidence that the surcharge is about plugging non-migration related spending gaps rather than NHS costs.

6. *Cost of lost reviews are not kept.*
The Home Office loses over sixty per cent of appeals made against it. This will have significant administrative costs in contesting so many cases unsuccessfully. Unfortunately, the Home Office keeps no records of how much it spends in contesting these cases, though has suggested it might do at some point in the future.

7. *No guidance on what constitutes a 'complex' case.*
The Home Office is notorious for missing its targets, such as the timely processing of application forms. However, if an application is deemed 'complex', then it is not subject to any target and may take longer to process without negatively impacting on the Home Office's performance results. It conveniently turns out the Home Office lacks any guidance on when an application is deemed complex.

8. *No data on ethnicity, race or religion of people detained in enforcement operations.*
The Government is not keeping track of the race or religion of migrants caught up in its immigration enforcement operations. If it did keep such data, it would be easier to investigate allegations of discrimination. There are also no records kept of people who are survivors of sexual and gender-based violence and otherwise vulnerable under their Adults at Risk policy.

9. *Detained migrants are paid £1 per hour.*
Migrants held in immigration removal centres are paid £1 per hour and £1.25 per hour for 'specified projects.' There were 2,249,747 hours of such paid work from November 2014 to April 2017. Migrants are almost certainly being heavily exploited.

10. *Dad's Army border force is still being considered.*
To help an understaffed and under-resourced Border Force, the Government was rumoured to be considering launching an all-volunteer unpaid 'Dad's Army' of Border Force agents in all but name to close the gap. The Home Office is 'continuing the process of taking advice' and hasn't decided whether to implement the idea.

11. *Home Office is now making you pay to email them.*
The Home Office charges individuals £5.48 to email them from abroad. Non-UK-based phone calls are charged £1.37 per minute. Both are run by a private company Sitel UK Ltd. The Home Office refuses to say how much has been earned since it considers this information to be 'commercially sensitive.' This is supposed to make non-UK citizens pay for accessing Home Office services, but British citizens contacting the Home Office from abroad are also charged. The Home Office does not keep records of how often this happens.

12. *The Government knows it could restrict EU migration more, but has decided not to.*
The great myth of the EU referendum was the claim that EU citizens enjoyed free movement that is unrestricted, and that only by leaving the EU can EU migration be controlled. This is untrue. Like any freedom, the freedom of movement enjoyed by all EU citizens is subject to a number of restrictions. Nobody can go wherever they want, whenever they want, for as long as they want, without meeting set criteria to be enforced in each member state.

It didn't take long for the Government to admit that it has more powers to control EU migration than it chooses to use. There you have it: EU migration can be regulated more if the Government so chooses – without Brexit.

13. *Dual nationals are unchecked.*
The Government bases its policies around a commitment to reduce net migration. Yet net migration has never been higher than under the Tories. Nonetheless, it's important to get right the numbers. But dual nationals are unchecked. This means a US-UK dual national going to the US counts as an American citizen leaving, but as a British citizen when returning. As a result, the figures are deeply flawed.

14. *There are no plans to review the citizenship test.*
Six years ago, I published the only comprehensive report on the UK's citizenship test being like a bad pub quiz. I found errors, inconsistencies and a continuing failure to consult with old or new citizens alike to ensure the test was fit for purpose. Over two million tests have been sat, and there are still no plans to review or consult on what is best described as the test for British citizenship that few British citizens can pass.

15. *... but the citizenship test might be published in Cornish!*
In 2013, the Government stopped permitting anyone to take the UK's citizenship test in any language but English. It was previously available in Welsh or Scots Gaelic. Interestingly, there were no complaints at the time, including from nationalist parties.

Protected minority status was granted to the Cornish two years later. This gave the Cornish equal recognition with the Welsh, Scots and Irish in matters like the citizenship test – in which there is no mention of Cornwall, its patron saint or its famous pasty. When asked what plans the Government had to honour this new status, it revealed it would consider making the test available in Cornish. This is not, in fact, required by the granting of protected minority status.

All of the above contributes to the impression that the

Government's immigration system is unfit for purpose. May's hostile environment has not only been proven to be cruel towards the Windrush generation and others, but utterly ineffective.

These problems have been kept out of headlines so far, given continuing paralysis over Brexit, but no plans for leaving the EU will make these concerns go away without urgent, necessary root-and-branch reforms. The opposition frontbench deserves more credit for exposing these problems, which only a Labour government can put right.

Our immigration system is broken – and Javid's announcement shows he's hellbent on making it worse[103]

As Home Secretary Sajid Javid battles on to remain in the Conservative leadership race, we've seen two announcements on immigration. The first is Javid's promise to drop the net migration target if he gets to 10 Downing Street. The second, revealed only on Monday, concerns the means by which Javid plans to create a 'skills-based' immigration system for post-Brexit Britain.

Both are broadly welcome. The commitment to a net migration target that was not being met only kept eroding public confidence that the Government could take back control of our borders in any meaningful sense.

If Britain does leave the EU in October, then a new immigration system that could adapt to an end to freedom of movement will become necessary. A full consultation is longer overdue and public engagement much needed. Unfortunately, Javid's plans fall down at every hurdle.

103 'Our immigration system is broken – and Javid's announcement shows he's hellbent on making it worse', *The Independent* (19 June 2019).

The one key task for any post-Brexit system is how to address the different immigration status that EU citizens will have. It is estimated there are three million currently in the UK. EU migration accounts for about a third of all net migration each year.

Yet the Home Office has already closed its doors to hearing from those affected. Crucial groups like 3million are locked out of discussions with no representation at all. In fact, none of the five advisory groups address EU citizens specifically. Javid's review has failed this important litmus test at the start.

The five different groups launched – employers, the education sector, 'crossing the border', the national advisory group (ensuring a UK-wide system) and vulnerable groups – all speak to a system that sees the integration of migrants as a one-way street. There are few, if any, voices of migrants themselves or of naturalised citizens. The employer is engaged, but not the employee. This is a London-centric programme that is neither joined up or evidence-based.

When I became a UK citizen in 2011, I uncovered the many failings behind the Life in the UK citizenship test, which was like a bad pub quiz that few, if any, British citizens can pass. Part of the problem has been the test once justified as a means of testing integration has never been reviewed comprehensively until my report to see if it met its purpose. The voices of migrants and new citizens didn't matter – and as a result the test remains unfit for purpose.

Such issues were identified a year ago by a parliamentary select committee on citizenship – yet none of its proposals for improving a broken system are being taken seriously, such as the need for a UK-wide citizenship advisory group.

In continuing to ignore the views of EU citizens or indeed of families, the Home Office's engagement programme isn't addressing most of the migrants who come and live in Britain each year. This oversight seems intentional, but it could be addressed if new advisory groups on EU citizens and families are launched. Yet further fundamental problems will remain.

The overall programme promises a skills-based system, but yet only speaks to salary thresholds. Higher salaries are an inaccurate proxy of the skills we're in short supply of. It's an odd skills-based approach that makes no mention of any of the skills it claims drive it. Instead of a push for higher skilled migration, the raised salary cap appears more likely to see migrants barred from many highly-skilled jobs – in what has been described as a 'sucker punch' to business.

This view of migrants only as workers makes no mention of the families to which they belong or their positive contributions to their local communities.

Finally, the system is not what it says on the tin. The system does not actually treat EU and non-EU citizens alike, but will in fact treat individuals differently by their country of origin. Instead of being nationality-blind, the new system will be nationality-sensitive.

This means instead of a binary EU and non-EU system that already leads to a significant number of errors – most appeals against Home Office decisions are successful – we will instead have a far more complex system of several different streams by nationality accounting for each new trade deal. If the Home Office can't handle non-EU citizens as a single category, how can this improve if divided into a dozen or more without a huge increase in staffing?

A new immigration system built on consultation and evidence is needed. Unfortunately, this exercise is flawed at the start and likely to make a badly run system far worse.

This shameless profiteering from our cruel immigration laws needs to stop [104]

The Home Office has been heavily criticised for outsourcing immigration services 'on the cheap.' The chief inspector of Borders and Immigration, David Bolt, claimed that subcontracting services had become part of the Home Office's 'modus operandi' and he questioned whether the department had sufficient oversight to perform its duties. These criticisms are supported by the Law Society president, Simon Davis, who called Home Office subcontracting practices 'a can of worms from the very start.'

Last month, *The Independent* revealed the French firm Sopra Steria had earned millions for providing what lawyers branded a 'substandard service', forcing some applicants to pay high fees and travel hundreds of miles to submit their applications on time.

While this is shocking, it is not surprising, nor is it a recent development. In 2016, serious concerns were raised when it was revealed that many asylum seekers in Middlesbrough were identifiable by having homes with red painted doors. Despite complaints being raised since 2012, it took four years of repeated reports of asylum seekers being targeted before these problems came to national attention.

At the time, then Home Secretary Theresa May had launched her hostile environment campaign which some critics have blamed in part for stirring hostilities against migrants, especially asylum seekers.

The immigration minister James Brokenshire called for an urgent audit of the situation which he'd been unaware of – and

104 'This shameless profiteering from our cruel immigration laws needs to stop,' *The Independent* (17 July 2019).

this exposes the heart of the problem: the Home Office can try to outsource the delivery of its services, but it cannot outsource its responsibilities too.

As more services are handled externally, there has clearly been less oversight with ministers left unaware and ill-informed about how the immigration system they are supposed to manage is actually functioning.

The issue is not only the lack of oversight over immigration services, but also the rampant profiteering off immigration-related fees. As prime minister, May next moved to introduce a £5.48 fee for prospective migrants to send emails to the Home Office in a deal outsourced to Sitel UK. The Home Office has thus far refused to say how much has been paid or what profits earned

The Home Office already makes a hefty profit of up to nine hundred per cent on the processing of immigration-related fees. Not only are migrants paying the full costs for the delivery of immigration services, a large share of what is charged goes to non-immigration purposes including the profits of firms services are outsourced to.

While outsourcing services is not new, it has reached its greatest heights under the leadership of Theresa May as Home Secretary and then prime minister. This move has not improved the quality of the immigration services provided, has not increased its efficiency in handling applications and it has left a profit-heavy service cash-poor with chronic underinvestment in front-line services, immigration enforcement and integration projects, including English language classes.

Rolling back these agreements and taking services back in-house won't happen overnight, but they are a necessary direction of travel if a future government is going to have any hope at improving public confidence in the immigration system. Doing nothing and maintaining the status quo is not an option.

A first step in the right direction would be for the Home Office to establish the immigration system as self-funded and self-sustaining run entirely by the immigration-related fees raised. If the public understood that no public money supports or is needed to fund the immigration system as is the case, then this could go some way at countering popular misconceptions of migrants as a drain on public finances.

This should be launched with a commitment to spending most, if not all, earned on immigration-related services. That would help prevent the use of immigration fees for profiteering, diverting money out of a system that requires much more of the resources it receives to function properly. A new government wanting to break with May's legacy would do well to make this move and rebuild confidence in a system sorely in need of it.

Do you want to 'take back control' of the immigration system? This is what you should ask for [105]

The number one issue for pro-Brexit voters was immigration. Vote Leave's campaign slogan of 'take back control' came with a promise of stronger border controls, including an end to free movement of people and starting a points-based immigration system.

Since the 2016 referendum, the Government has made more problems than progress. This has damaged public confidence in the immigration system further: Brexit was supposed to improve things, but it's only making them much worse.

There are already serious concerns about a Windrush-like scandal engulfing some of the three million EU citizens living in the UK. Most

105 'Do you want to "take back control" of the immigration system? This is what you should ask for', *The Independent* (21 August 2019).

have not yet registered to continue their residency post-Brexit. While Home Secretary Priti Patel has promised an end to free movement on 31 October if there is a No Deal, this opens a Pandora's Box as the Home Office has no system in place for any such an eventuality – nor can one possibly be created within eight weeks.

10 Downing Street's plans to launch a points-based immigration system, focused on skills and not nationality, have been widely criticised for three reasons. First, the policy makes little mention of the 'skills' at the system's heart, instead proposing a minimum income threshold of £30,000 or more. There are many high skilled employees, including scientists and technicians, earning below this amount who are missed out.

Second, the policy states that nationality does matter because new trade deals may come with different immigration agreements – the new system will be more nationality-sensitive than ever before. Finally, the Government seems unaware it's reinventing the wheel as the UK has had a points-based system in place for non-EU systems for over a decade. I should know – I immigrated to the UK using the points-based system.

Brexit was supposed to help reduce net migration. Yet this figure remains at historic highs, exceeding any year under New Labour. While EU citizens continue to have free movement, their overall numbers have been decreasing year on year; it is non-EU migration that has been pushing these figures up – despite the fact that non-EU citizens are entirely under the Home Office's control.

Then there are the profits. In an exclusive report, *The Independent* found the Home Office earned £438.1m last year on visa operations after outsourcing them to a Dubai-based firm. Average profits per application rose from £28.73 to £122.56 in a single year. This extra funding has not gone to create a world-class service, hire extra border agents, or improve operational effectiveness. Instead, the cash is spent outside the system on non-immigration matters.

It is disappointing to see the Home Office prioritising profits over people – running a system that cares more for taking payments than supporting integration. So it's time to put this right.

Yes, the Government should 'take back control' of our immigration system. It can start by making the system self-funded on a sustainable basis. Immigration fees raise far more than the cost of operating the overall system. The immigration system is for immigrants and can be paid for entirely by immigrants. Taxpayers won't be able to see migrants as draining the public purse when no tax income is used to support the immigration system.

The fees are also excessive. Slashing average profits from £122.56 back to £28.73 can decrease the way in which the system exploits the vulnerable while still raising additional income to support hiring more staff and providing a more effective service.

If there is any extra income leftover, this might be spent in other governmental departments like education, health, housing or transport – but only with a big sign showing a project was funded by immigration fees. This could show people how their neighbourhoods have been improved through immigration-related contributions.

The Government has made a mess of the immigration system. Now is an opportunity for a rethink. Ending the shameless profiteering by the Home Office is a first step in the right direction.

Conservatives should know we've got an 'Australian-style' points-based immigration system [106]

While there are many uncertainties about what Brexit might look like, there is no question that the Tories want to use it to launch a points-based immigration system.

106 'Conservatives should know we've got an 'Australian-style' points-based immigration system', *The Independent* (6 October 2019).

First developed in Australia, this system awards points typically for qualifications, salary, skills and language proficiency. Those with higher salaries, more advanced qualifications or much-needed skills gain extra points in these areas. An applicant needs to earn enough points above a set target in order to immigrate. The system is designed to encourage immigration from highly-skilled and professional workers.

Priti Patel, the Home Secretary, told the Conservative Party's annual conference in Manchester that she would 'introduce an Australian style points-based immigration system' into the UK. This will be 'under the control of the British Government' and 'end the free movement of people once and for all' linking this system with leaving the EU. This is despite the UK having an opt-out on immigration policies anyway.

Patel's views echo those of most Brexiteers: the UK should end free movement and create a points-based system instead to help 'take back control.' In 2015, Nigel Farage and UKIP were calling for starting a points-based system. A year later, Boris Johnson and Michael Gove claimed introducing this system would help toughen immigration controls.

But despite the referendum's support for Leave, then Prime Minister Theresa May rejected the idea of having a points-based system immediately. This was partly because she was concerned about abuses of the system that, in her eyes, could let recent graduates qualify despite lacking sufficient English skills. But it was also because the system – as conceived in Australia – was designed to increase immigration while her government actively tried to cut it.

Perhaps unsurprisingly, Johnson hasn't only done a U-turn, but a full loop. First proposing it during the referendum, then saying he dropped it only to now lead a government in favour of introducing one. Then again, Johnson's tendency to switch sides and back again isn't a unique position for him on immigration, or Europe more generally.

From Johnson and Patel to Gove and Farage, the view of Brexiteers is clear: the UK should launch a points-based immigration system and this is what is needed post-Brexit. A big flaw in this argument exposing how little they seem to know about immigration is, well, the points-based system they want so badly is already in place. And thanks to Labour.

In 2008, Gordon Brown started a points-based system. It applied to non-EU nationals only and continues today. I should know – I was admitted through it.

While the official Gov.uk website carries information about the system and how to qualify, it's mostly something that only immigrants like me that have been through the system would know. The Home Office used to have an online points calculator. This would allow anyone to check and see if they qualified for a visa. I regularly forwarded the link to anyone interested in how a points-based system worked, especially to journalists in order to expose that it already existed.

However, the calculator has been taken offline since the EU referendum was held – perhaps in an effort to hide from the public that the system promised to them by Johnson and Patel is actually already in place.

The good news for the Prime Minister, Home Secretary and Nigel Farage is that the immigration system they want is already in place. It's time they stopped calling for its creation before more people realise their error.

The bad news for them is they should thank Gordon Brown for introducing it. If a points-based system is the future, they owe it to New Labour.

And the really bad news is that points-based systems increase immigration, create unnecessary complexity and can be difficult to manage.

This is a problem for anyone wanting a fairer, more transparent and accountable system. So the real issue isn't whether we should launch a system like this, but how we might scrap the one we've got. Yet this would require a Home Secretary who knew how the immigration system she wants to reform actually works.

And as someone who didn't migrate and has seemingly little understanding of the experiences of migrants like me who have, this gap between her promises and the reality will only grow larger. Maybe Patel won't take lectures from North London MPs, but perhaps she should sit in a class with a professor with expertise in immigration law.

Boris Johnson's immigration lies pale in comparison to his other deceits – and that's what's giving him a poll lead [107]

The Tories' current opinion poll lead over Labour is believed to be thanks to Tory campaign pledges on immigration. The only problem is – like many of Boris Johnson's Brexit promises – none of his immigration pledges are true.

Let's start with the first lie. Johnson is repeating the same old promise last heard when he asked the public to vote for Brexit in 2016: if the Tories win the general election, they will launch an Australian-style points-based system. It's claimed that this will bring highly skilled migrants the UK needs to support our economy.

The inconvenient truth is that the UK has had this points-based system for over ten years, launched by the Labour Party. It speaks volumes to see the prime minister make such a promise about an immigration system he clearly knows so very little about. Why else

107 'Boris Johnson's immigration lies pale in comparison to his other deceits – and that's what's giving him a poll lead', *The Independent* (20 November 2019).

promise the public a system we've already got, unless either the PM doesn't know or he hopes the public or media are easily fooled?

The Government even updated its guidance for our points-based system last Friday. Maybe someone should tell the Home Secretary Priti Patel, as she seems unaware of it too and it's her Home Office that runs it.

The second fib is that a vote for the Conservatives would bring an end to EU freedom of movement. This is false for two reasons. The first reason is simple: if Johnson wins and his MPs 'get Brexit done', this means they promise to pass a withdrawal agreement. Crucially, this also means the start of a minimum two-year transition period – where the agreement states that free movement will, in fact, continue.

When you remember the withdrawal agreement – not yet agreed – was supposed to take only two years, but has taken more than three, it is not hard to imagine the transition period might go on and on too.

The second reason is somewhat technical: EU freedom of movement isn't unrestricted. A regular mantra from both the left and right is an assumption that free movement means no limits. But there are limits – and every EU country expels EU citizens for violating EU free movement rules every month. Even the UK. Maybe the prime minister is again unaware of this, but it's true.

The third porkie is that EU nationals would be treated just like non-EU nationals and be required to have a job offer to work in the UK. That's not at all true either.

Non-EU nationals can work in the UK without a job offer. It's alarming to see this is apparently – yet again – unknown to the Prime Minister or Home Secretary. The easiest way is to apply for what's called a Tier 1 visa, but there can be other routes.

So while Johnson is clearly making much of this pledge, it's yet another promise he'll definitely break. And we know he will break this promise because there are no such changes for non-EU workers.

These three election pledges on immigration are helping the Tories in the polls. Yet each pledge promises a lie: a system already in place, freedom of movement will continue as per Johnson's Agreement terms and existing exemptions for non-EU citizens to work in the UK without a job contract will apply to EU nationals.

Such mass deception is as unwarranted as it is unprecedented. We now also see serious allegations that Brexit Party candidates may have been offered jobs to stand down as candidates to boost Tories at the polls – now under investigation. The public deserves to be treated – and respected – much better than this. We can start by exposing the facts.

Brexit or no Brexit, Labour must reset the immigration system[108]

The immigration system is needlessly complex and getting worse. The public has little confidence in it, and those who use it have even less. More than half of all appeals against immigration decisions succeed. Nearly all misconduct inquiries are about immigration, too. The system must become more accessible – and do a far better job of meeting public expectations.

Labour's manifesto will undoubtedly offer policies that can unite our party and country. But there are some urgently needed root-and-branch reforms that go to the heart of the problems with our current system. Why are we seeing such widespread confusion and so many administrative mistakes? A key reason is that new

108 'Brexit or no Brexit, Labour must reset the immigration system', *LabourList* (20 November 2019).

laws have been passed every year for over two decades – including fifteen in 2015 alone. And these laws are changed almost as fast as they're enacted.

The result is a patchwork quilt of different bits and pieces fitting together awkwardly, with no common purpose or overarching, systematic construction. It's no wonder both the public nor officials have difficulty navigating, let alone understanding, a system as broken as it is haphazard. Brexit or no Brexit, serious changes need to take place. Labour should give serious thought to adopting two key immigration reforms: a Royal Commission on immigration and a citizenship advisory group.

There is an urgent need for a Royal Commission to systematise current primary legislation into a more simplified, coherent new bill that restates the existing law. This would mirror the law commission's consultation, to which I gave written and oral evidence, on simplifying and rendering more accessible the smorgasbord that passes for secondary immigration rules. This would do much to improve public understanding of the law.

Then there is the task of improving wider public confidence. It has been about fifteen years since Sir Bernard Crick toured the country with an advisory group on citizenship. They engaged with the public to grasp its everyday understanding of British citizenship. Their findings led to the launch of the first citizenship test and citizenship ceremonies.

Nearly two decades later, over two million have sat the test – yet not one consultation has been conducted since then. One is needed to ensure that the process meets public expectations and fosters integration. My own research findings show that the test is like a bad pub quiz, and one that few British citizens can pass.

I have found that the current naturalisation process is expensive with arbitrary hurdles, and it acts against integration. This should be a cause for serious concern. The recommendation for a citizenship advisory group is supported by a House of Lords Select Committee on citizenship that the Government – to its shame – has yet to take seriously.

There is a crisis of confidence in an immigration system unfit for purpose, which is administratively dysfunctional and does not improve integration, nor meet public expectations. Failure to push for reform would condemn the system to continued dysfunction and disapproval, benefiting neither citizen nor immigrant alike. Labour has an opportunity to get this right – and improve fundamentals in the system.

While most of the focus may be on whether or not this election leads to a Leave or Remain final outcome, our political campaign manifesto will go beyond Brexit – and it simply must engage with immigration. The proposals outlined here would go a long way to getting this system right, whether or not Brexit happens – and failing to do so is choosing to make a bad situation worse. Labour must seize the opportunity to reset the system and create a more progressive, fairer immigration policy for all.

Reducing migration has little to do with Brexit – we've had a points-based system since 2008[109]

If Brexit is supposed to mean anything, it's that the UK will 'take back control', including a tighter grip on migration.

The one and only policy Boris Johnson has repeatedly proposed since the EU referendum is that Brexit means the UK can launch its own Australian-style points-based immigration system. Johnson has promised that this will mean a cut in immigration. But if Brexit

109 'Reducing immigration has little to do with Brexit – we've had a points-based system since 2008', *The Independent* (28 November 2019).

is stopped, then there can be no points-based system and migration will rise. This is a core campaign manifesto pledge that his appeal to voters rests on.

The problem with Johnson's only 'new' idea on immigration isn't that it's a house of cards, but a stinking pack of lies. It's time he was called out.

Let's start with the biggest fib of all. Johnson claims only Brexit can enable a points-based immigration system. The Tory manifesto clearly states that a post-Brexit 'future relationship' with the EU 'will allow' the UK to 'introduce' a points-based system.

Indeed, the Conservatives appear committed to starting a points-based system. Just before the election, Home Secretary Priti Patel asked the Migration Advisory Committee to consult on how such a system can be 'introduced.'

But the UK already has a points-based immigration system. It's even modelled on Australia's. Why would Brexit be required in order to have a system that's already in place? Britain's points-based system was launched over a decade ago in 2008 – by a Labour government.

But perhaps neither Johnson nor Patel understand how immigration policy works or what to do about it. If they did, they would know the Home Office has made several updates to its guidelines on how the points-based system we have in place works, including only a fortnight ago, and changing how it operates since Labour was last in power. It almost makes me feel bad for the chair of the Migration Advisory Committee who will eventually have to tell the Government they have literally asked them to reinvent the wheel.

This leads to the second big fib. Johnson promises that any points-based system would cut immigration. This is also completely untrue.

Australia launched its system specifically to attract an increase in migration: those who met the points threshold could live and work in the country.

The UK subjects only non-EU citizens to its points-based system. The Government could cut their numbers virtually to zero if they wanted: the fact is that non-EU migration reached the highest levels on record under Conservative Governments.

In the latest net migration figures, the Office for National Statistics confirms that not only is there a points-based system in operation but also that non-EU citizens coming to Britain through this system increased by eleven per cent over last year – 'the highest level since … the new system was introduced' in 2008.

The Prime Minister is lying to the public on every count. Brexit is unnecessary to launch a points-based system. His government will most definitely not start such a system since it's been in place (thanks to Labour, not the Tories) and its use will not help numbers fall.

The big problem here is not migration numbers (and I am a migrant). Migrants bring net benefits, such as paying taxes, contributing to the economy, fulfilling vital posts in education and the NHS.

Yet Tory prime ministers have a history of promising immigration targets that are never met – and never intended to be met. The manifesto pledge to cut migration to tens of thousands, for example, was an election promise that Tories loved to break.

Net migration isn't any one thing, but a collection of very different demographics – including British citizens and foreign students. Driving Brits out to meet an arbitrary goal is simply perverse. Labour is right to want it scrapped as it's been an unworkable focus for policymaking from the start. No wonder the Government has quietly abandoned it.

In this election campaign, Johnson's one and only 'new' policy idea to 'get Brexit done' isn't new and doesn't work as he intends. It shows how cynical the prime minister's propaganda machine must be, knowing they are deceiving people into voting for the opposite of what they've been promised.

But what is far, far worse is the long-term damage Johnson's personal ambition to hold power will do to public trust in our politicians and political system. For democracy's sake, he must pay an electoral price.

Here's how Boris Johnson can overhaul immigration post-Brexit, in seven easy steps[110]

A key part of the prime minister's election success was his repeated vow to 'get Brexit done', and a key part of that was 'shaking up the immigration system.' Boris Johnson's first one hundred days is a critical time for him to reshape a system desperately lacking public confidence. And if he wants to retain those new voters he has won, he'll need to appeal to the centre ground. By making good on his commitment to 'a more outward-facing' Brexit Britain, Johnson could allay the fears of those who have criticised his approach to date. But he'll only achieve that if he follows this seven-point plan:

1. *Scrap the net migration target*

'Net migration' includes all persons leaving and entering the UK for a year or more. It has never been met. Nothing would send a clearer signal of a clean break from Cameron and May than an end to this, as Johnson has committed his government to do – and he has been critical of this target in the past. Continuing to promise an undeliverable target will not improve public confidence. Not even the Office for National Statistics believes the figures are accurate, given serious problems with their data. An alternative approach is necessary and urgent.

110 'Here's how Boris Johnson can overhaul immigration post-Brexit, in seven easy steps', *The Independent* (25 December 2019).

2. *English must matter*

More can – and should – be done to ensure migrants speak English. The Government already demands only those in 'public-facing' public sector roles are fluent. The prime minister should go much further, making most, if not all, public sector staff meet this standard over the next five to ten years. Extra funding should be made available to end the postcode lottery of access to learning English. Integration is a two-way street: we must ensure adequate provision if we are to insist that migrants use it. These extra resources could support English literacy education for all tackling functional illiteracy that is a rarely reported but growing problem.

3. *EU citizens are welcome*

As the latest figures show, net migration of EU nationals has dropped by two-thirds since the 2016 referendum. Clearly, many EU citizens fear for their futures in the UK. They should be made to feel welcome, not be made pawns in any new trade deal with Brussels. The Government should commit to allowing all EU nationals currently in the UK the right to stay regardless of a deal (which should, in turn, help British citizens in Europe to keep their foreign residency).

4. *A system that works for Britain*

Post-Brexit Britain needs to be attractive to the world's brightest and best. It is welcome to see the Government committed to championing Britain for academics, scientists and other highly skilled workers. Yet the last immigration white paper promised a skills-based system that didn't mention the skills required, only the salary. High pay is not proof of highly skilled work. Our current points-based system in place since 2008 is overly complex and in need of an overhaul, and Johnson and Priti Patel, the Home Secretary, are right to want to reform it. But they must go further than economic value, to social value. This means extending the expertise of the Migration Advisory Committee (MAC), which gives independent advice to the Government on matters of immigration, beyond labour economics to law and social policy. No change to the MAC will lead to the same advice and continuing public frustrations.

5. *Focus on migration impact*

Public concerns about migration levels are linked to a perceived lack of proper border controls. Extra immigration officers must be put in place to tackle illegal working and expose sham marriages. The Migration Impacts Fund – a levy on immigration applications (I paid into it when moving to the UK) aimed at reducing the impact migration has on education, housing and transport, and which David Cameron closed in 2010 – should be reinstated, perhaps as part of Johnson's vow to reinvest in the north. The key to winning voter confidence is reducing the impacts of migration rather than an arbitrary, unachievable net migration target. Fewer migrants won't necessarily mean shorter A&E queues when migrants are more likely to be in A&E as doctors and nurses than as patients. The Government should take a wider perspective.

6. *Make the system self-funded*

Immigrants pay far more into the current immigration system than is required to run it; Home Office profits on application fees are two hundred per cent or more. The perception that immigrants are a drain on taxpayers can be overturned if Johnson made a system for immigrants that is funded only by immigrants. This would create space for a reduction in fees overall while maintaining the system's sustainability with adequate funding. Any extra income could be clearly earmarked as earned from migrants creating a new, more welcome image of migrants as the net contributors to our economy, which they are – a fact Johnson has previously celebrated.

7. *A national conversation*
Finally, it has been ten years since Sir Bernard Crick's advisory group recommending reforms to improving integration and fostering citizenship. My recommendations to bring this back and reform the Life in the UK citizenship test – a bad pub quiz, in my opinion – were supported by the House of Lords Select Committee on citizenship following my evidence to them. The new government should seize the opportunity to bring the country closer together through a UK-wide consultation on the kind of post-Brexit British citizenship the public wants. If the referendum taught us anything, it is that many people feel their voices have not been heard about the issues most important to them. A national conversation about Britishness is long overdue.

Immigration is a potential area of concern, as well as an opportunity. Thankfully for centrists, Johnson is unashamedly 'pro-immigration' – and now has a working majority to reform a system desperately in need of urgent change. How, and whether, he does this will shape and define his premiership.

Voters will see through Boris Johnson's pointless immigration plans in the end[111]

Since the EU referendum campaign, Boris Johnson made several promises he vowed to keep. Top of his list was launching a new Australian-styled 'points-based' immigration system. His winning election manifesto claimed that such a system is only possible if he could 'get Brexit done.' The benefit would be that he could make

111 'Voters will see through Boris Johnson's pointless immigration plans in the end', *The Independent* (19 February 2020).

good on his pledge to 'take back control' of the UK's borders and cut net migration.

Unfortunately, like much else he says, Johnson's promises are not based on facts. Whatever else it might achieve, Brexit was never necessary for introducing a points-based immigration system. For the very simple fact we've already had one since 2008, thanks to the last Labour government. If launching such a system is so fabulous, Johnson should thank New Labour for it.

Of course, the current points-based system only applies to non-EU citizens at present. When asked, the Migration Advisory Committee – which provides evidence-based independent advice to the Government – said Johnson should effectively roll out the current system to include EU nationals. (The chair went on to remind the Prime Minister that such a system was already in place, if such a prompt was needed.)

Today's policy statement by Priti Patel, the Home Secretary, claims that it delivers on promises made to voters. But making policy through slogans is no way to govern and these plans are deeply disappointing.

For example, the statement is an extended press release intended to give a highly misleading impression. It gives one table listing how the points will be allocated to immigrants. Everyone must have a job offer at the appropriate level plus speak English. But that won't be enough. There is a minimum salary to be met in light of whether someone has a PhD or fills a position where there is a shortage of applicants.

Tough looking stuff, but the appearance is only half the story. When turning from the one table to the details about how it actually works, a very different picture quickly emerges. First, you won't actually need a job offer to earn points but this has not been worked out yet. Secondly, the jobs shortage list is to be rewritten and commissioned soon.

Thirdly, you won't only get points for a PhD but other qualifications – or none, as relevant work experience will somehow be included too: except no details yet there either. In seemingly every area mentioned, the appearance of what's on offer is not the reality about how it will be put into practice – and still undecided. This deception will do little to earn back the public trust that will be lost when the truth is out by year's end.

The headlines focus on the door being closed to unskilled EU migrants. This will hit several industries hard, such as agriculture and construction. Businesses must adapt, but how and to what? There is no investment in place by government for a smooth transition, nor even an Immigration Bill for Parliament to consider. The law might not be passed until weeks before its needed, giving little time – if any – for businesses to adapt. This is not what taking back control should look like.

The existing points-based system doesn't allow for unskilled non-EU workers. The planned system extends this to EU workers. But this does not mean EU citizens can't work in unskilled jobs. Tucked deep into the statement is this gem: there are an estimated 170,000 'recently arrived non-EU citizens in lower-skilled occupations' that 'will continue to be available.' This is because they are allowed to work thanks to a family connection, such as being a spouse or dependent. There are no caps on numbers.

Unsurprisingly, the Home Secretary hasn't decided what to do about family routes to settlement except this won't be a part of the points-based system. This can be upwards of one in five of all non-EU citizens migrating to the UK. This means the door is only shut on EU unskilled workers having direct access to low paid work. They will all still have access through family connections. And again the Government hasn't decided what to do about it.

The system does seem to make it easier for professionals to work in the UK, taking the higher paid jobs. This group is the most mobile and best protected with lower salary thresholds to meet. With the cap removed on applications, their numbers could rise.

And, of course, the point of all other points-based systems is about increasing migration. Johnson should know. The highest ever recorded points-based immigration – of non-EU citizens presumably entirely in his Government's control – was noted during the last general election on his watch.

We can only conclude that the 'new' points-based system is pretty pointless. It makes an overly complicated system the Home Office can barely run, more complex – with most of the key features yet to be decided. Its main purpose seems to be to give a false impression, that will only disappoint voters even more, while damaging the economy overall. If this is the one part about Brexit the Government is agreed on, then I fear for what's next.

Ten new reasons why the Tory immigration system is broken [112]

With so much happening – not least growing concerns about the Government's handling of the Covid-19 pandemic – other matters pale in significance. Yet, there have been some startling recent revelations about just how truly awful the Tories' hostile environment has become. Over the last few months, parliamentary questions have discovered:

112 'The Tory immigration system is broken – and these ten new reasons prove it', *The Independent* (17 May 2020).

1. *As Covid-19 was coming to Britain, the Government said it was 'committed to increasing' the immigration health surcharge*
The comments were made on 15 January. The first Covid-19 case in the UK was confirmed two weeks later. Originally £200, the fee for non-EU citizens has trebled in a few years to £625 per year with a discount for students. The surcharge does not actually go towards increasing funding to the NHS, but to the Treasury instead. There is nothing extra to offset the added impact the surcharge was claimed to address at its launch. With many NHS doctors and nurses affected by this surcharge, the Government had been satisfied to allow these frontline key workers to pay extra – on top of their paying full tax – for their right to access the critically important health services they provide. Only after considerable pressure, the Home Secretary relented automatically extending visas waiving surcharge payments but only between March and October affecting about 3,000 (of 65,000 non-EU citizens working in the NHS).

2. *Net migration targets are almost a thing of the past*
Or in the words of the new Immigration Minister Kevin Foster: 'the Government is not in a numbers game in respect of net migration.' Awkwardly for the Tories, the 2019 manifesto they ran on promises to reduce overall migration. While the Tories have abandoned promises about tens of thousands, the general intent remains the same. But this is the first formal official confirmation the position is changing.

3. *The hostile environment isn't effective*
It was reported that the Government's National Community Engagement teams had the purpose 'to lure immigrants to advice sessions … persuading them to leave the UK.' However, it turns out the Home Office keeps no records of who shows up. Nor was there

any evidence that immigrants who met with these teams lacked a right to remain in the UK. So not only is the hostile environment unethical, it is ineffective too.

4. *The Government has been making compensation payments to Windrush victims, but won't tell us how much*
While this information was promised to be released, the Government is keeping quiet on how much it has begun paying out to Windrush victims. But we know payments are being made. Full details on claims submitted, the number of claims paid and total amount has been promised for about a year.

5. *The Home Office has no evidence its enforcing free movement limits*
Like most freedoms, EU freedom of movement has limits. The UK deports EU nationals every year, but the Home Office keeps no records on whether this is ever for breaching treaty rights. Nor did it have any records of deporting EU nationals who lacked a criminal record, but who might have still breached their treaty rights. For a Government that claimed it so desperately wanted to take back control of our borders, it continues to neglect through ignorance or choice its ability, if it wanted, to impose some restrictions on free movement. The (what I call) 'free movement myth' is, well, a myth.

6. *The Government decided to sit on a report into the EU Settlement Scheme until after the election*
The Chief Inspector of Borders and Immigration sent his report to the Government in late September exposing problems and making recommendations. The Government decided against publishing it until after the general election had concluded. This undoubtedly helped promote its narrative about how well the scheme was

working with this in-depth report kept locked away from public scrutiny.

7. The use of landing cards was ended too quickly

The Government admitted it had stopped using landing cards before completing a transition to a new digital system for managing arrivals was completed. This meant there was a known data gap about who was entering the country. This is picked up further in the Government's official (and much delayed) response to its landing card consultation. It acknowledges that it had received concerns (including from me) that there would be a loss of data until a new system was fully working and that 'a number of responses' indicated a preference to have no gap in the data collected. The Government went ahead anyway.

8. *Migrants granted asylum are subject to the two-child rule for Universal Credit*

This means that those who are successful in their applications for asylum based on the persecution they are experiencing abroad are treated punitively if caring for three or more children. If this family has a right of asylum that is accepted, there must be proper support for their being welcomed to the community and becoming settled.

9. *The Home Office admits mistakes in failing to follow its own guidance on asylum, but it has not reversed decisions*

This relates to reports that the Home Office had, contrary to its guidelines, refused asylum applications by including quotations from religious texts to test migrants. Yet despite admitting its failures in multiple cases, there is no evidence it has overturned a single case subsequently. It may give an impression that the conclusion reached may be more important than the supporting reasons or evidence behind it – and no doubt buoyed by facts like half of immigration appeals succeed.

10. *Only migrants with claims for asylum in the Home Office's system by year's end will be considered for family reunion cases*
This refers to the Dublin Regulation, an agreement between EU countries which the UK will exit after 31 December 2020 unless a new agreement is reached. Since it can take more than a few days to become entered onto the official system, there may be many cases of migrants making claims while the UK is still in the EU but not granted their full rights.

The UK continues to battle the current pandemic and most attention is rightly directed towards public health. So it is easy to miss the continuing failures over immigration perpetuated by the Government – and it has shown a remarkable ability to not learn from its many past mistakes. In these circumstances, it is all the more important that we do not lose sight that missing PPE targets are not the only problems of Boris Johnson's government.

Hopes can only be raised by the Labour Party gaining a new leader in Keir Starmer, who was formerly a Shadow Immigration Minister. I know he understands these issues as I have discussed many of them with him. With such a knowledgeable leader and experienced team, the Government's immigration policies are likely to be scrutinized in an evidence-based way like never before. This can only be welcome news after more than a decade of broken promises and counterproductive policies.

The Tory immigration bill is no way to offer thanks to our NHS workers [113]

The Prime Minister returned to work only a few weeks ago. His top team – chief advisor Dominic Cummings, Health Secretary Matt Hancock, Chief Medical Advisor Chris Whitty and top civil servant Sir Mark Sedwill – had all tested positive for Covid-19. While they recovered at home, Boris Johnson required hospitalisation and was treated in intensive care.

After leaving hospital, Johnson praised NHS staff for the 'brilliant care' he received, saying: 'I can't thank them enough. I owe them my life.' He went further, naming the nurses who saw to him personally, including an EU national. As millions across the country take time out each Thursday evening to clap and show their thanks to key workers, not least NHS staff and care workers, it would seem Johnson has extra reason to show appreciation.

But Johnson's first actions following his return to 10 Downing Street are a slap in the face to many of our frontline key workers, who are risking their lives to save others and protect the health of everyone in our country. The Government has rushed to pass a new immigration bill that would end the current rights of EU nationals to continue working in the UK. And it seeks to end their current rights, creating a hole before the new immigration system takes its place.

There are 180,000 EU nationals working as NHS staff and care workers. Our health and social care system relies on their bravery, courage and dedication now more than ever. Shadow Home Secretary Nick Thomas-Symonds was right to say that it is not in the national interest to seek parliamentary approval for kicking

113 'The Tory immigration bill is no way to offer thanks to our NHS workers', *LabourList* (21 May 2020).

out key workers while they are on the frontline fighting a global pandemic.

The Prime Minister is hardly showing thanks to those NHS workers to whom he says he owes his life. A calculation has presumably been made that the public would rather prevent the NHS working at full capacity, by ending EU rights as quickly as possible, than prevent a rising Covid-19 death toll. Under this Tory government, Brexit is more important than protecting public health.

Labour was right to set a three-line whip against the immigration bill on Monday. As Shadow Immigration Minister Holly Lynch said: 'To those workers in our NHS who have had their visas extended for a year, the Government did not do you a favour. You did us a favour.' It is deeply disappointing the current Tory Government can show such a callous disregard to many tens of thousands of the heroes who have helped keep us safe and make our country work.

Keir Starmer's call for NHS and care workers to become exempt from the immigration health surcharge is especially welcome – and already gaining cross-party support. Over five years ago, I wrote for *LabourList* that this surcharge was 'an election stunt.' It is built around a fictional guesstimate of average use of all public services, including citizens, and not the additional impact of any migration. Funds raised from the IHS neither go to a local health authority nor even to the NHS. It is non-hypothecated and goes straight into a Treasury blackhole. With some application fees already up to nine hundred per cent above their cost, this is yet another cash-raising ruse that does not improve the immigration system or the health service. It's time the plug was pulled.

Things look set to go from bad to worse. While the Government claims its plans for a new points-based immigration system rewards skills over salaries, the white paper only recommends points based on how much someone earns. This is set above what many highly-skilled workers earn in the NHS or in health-related research, and so it is likely to have a negative impact on a system already under significant pressure. Thomas-Symonds said it suggests to anyone earning less than £25,600 that they are 'unwelcome' by the Government – highlighting again that salaries, not skills, are what counts most in these Tory plans.

More than ever, we need a Labour Government. The current leadership under Keir Starmer should continue to hammer home the message that the Government is making a political choice – prioritising Brexit now over public health, as if a global pandemic and mounting death toll aren't happening. The sooner a change in priorities, the better. Labour must continue to show the leadership so lacking in Johnson's Government.

The hostile environment for migrants is unjust – and doesn't work anyway [114]

Since 2010, the Conservatives have promised again and again across four general elections that they would slash immigration. A key part of this promise to voters was a 'hostile environment' policy, launched by then Home Secretary Theresa May, designed to expose and remove those residing unlawfully while hardening border controls.

Much is written about why this policy is unfair and unjust. It's easy to see why. Migrants are subject to scapegoating and the painful Windrush scandal continues. Meanwhile, the Government presses on seemingly unaware or unconcerned about the injustices adding up. As Kenan Malik remarks: 'The ignorance is as shocking as the rules are cruel.'

---

114 'The hostile environment for migrants is unjust – and doesn't work anyway', *LabourList* (3 June 2020).

This is about more than ethics. There will be differences of opinion about whether the means can justify the ends. And this is why it's important to be clear that not only is the hostile environment the wrong means – it's not achieving its ends either. Even if someone thought this unjust policy was a price worth paying, it doesn't do what it says on the tin.

Despite the many efforts of successive Tory governments to make the UK a more unwelcome place for immigrants, they have failed. The highest net migration levels ever seen at or above three hundred thousand were all under Tory Governments. Their pledge to cut this by over two-thirds is one campaign promise we hear less and less about for good reason.

When we drill further down, we can see why. In 2014, identity checks were introduced for anyone renting private accommodation, opening a bank account or obtaining a driver's licence to ensure that they had a right to live here. The reason for these checks was to expose people unlawfully resident and create a deterrent.

But these checks have proved a total con. Not a single individual has been newly exposed for living in the UK unlawfully from these checks, though many have encountered discrimination as a result of them. The checks are impotent because they look to confirm whether anyone known residing unlawfully is still around. Nobody unknown is ever discovered.

Deportations aren't working out either. The latest findings from the Office for National Statistics last week revealed that deportations are actually at the lowest levels 'since records began.' It seems many of the individuals singled out for removal – like the Windrush generation – are those with a legal and moral right to stay.

Recently, the Government U-turned on an element of the immigration health surcharge policy following significant pressure from Keir Starmer at PMQs. It's wrong that NHS and care workers who are risking their lives at this time of crisis must pay hundreds of pounds on top of their taxes to access a system that they keep running for our benefit. As a former Shadow Immigration Minister, Starmer understands this principle.

But the surcharge is even worse than that. It was originally promoted as a means to stop so-called 'health tourism' and make migrants 'pay their fair share.' However, two facts about the charge are almost never raised.

The first is that the health surcharge is not determined in light of actual use of the NHS or care services by migrants. It is a guesstimate of any use of public service far beyond health care – despite the fact that most migrants have no recourse to public funds anyway, a point recently lost on the Prime Minister.

The second is that money raised by the health surcharge is neither earmarked for the NHS and care services, nor does it go to the localities where migrants live. If the whole point is to make migrants pay – above and beyond their taxes – for their impact on the health service, it makes no sense that not one penny is earmarked to do any such thing. The migrant health surcharge is an extra tax on migrants but not for any services rendered or received.

Perhaps the most shameful of the policies rarely reported is the Home Office's form for reporting ex-lovers. This is a printable Word document for telling the Government that a relationship is over – presumably with the intention that the former partner might now be deported.

The possibility of this being used by abusers is significant, and yet no risk assessment was conducted before launching it in 2016. At last count, the Home Office has no record of receiving a single form. It's probably little wonder since the website doesn't say where they can be sent.

The sheer incompetence is staggering. It is a mistake to see the hostile environment as only morally wrong. On virtually every count, it has made things worse – and often with results that break every promise.

The Government now seeks to push through new laws launching a points-based immigration system – forgetting that Labour already did this in 2008. Even the Government's own independent migration advisory committee felt it needed to remind the Home Secretary that the system exists and already does much of what she wants it to achieve.

Instead of announcing more gimmicks, what we need is an evidence-led and spin-free plan. Speaking in jargon where down means up and 'fair' creates more inequality will only damage public confidence even further. The Home Secretary needs to start an honest, national conversation to better understand public expectations as a first step towards a system more fit for purpose.

Priti Patel's new immigration rules put us in a terrible position for a post-Brexit world[115]

Today the Home Secretary Priti Patel has published the Government's latest plans for immigration reforms with the underwhelming subtitle of 'further guidance.' A more appropriate name would be 'further disappointment' as much remains unknown, to be decided some other time. Less than five months from leaving the EU, this is a very poor position to be left in. If only the Home Office's passion for overblown press releases were as strong as its focus on delivering improved performance.

As someone who contributed to the Law Commission's report on simplifying the immigration rules, I am delighted to see its

115 'Priti Patel's new immigration rules put us in a terrible position for a post-Brexit world', *The Independent* (13 July 2020).

recommendations will be accepted although it remains unclear how far the Government is willing to go.

However, one change that will not simplify matters is introducing minimum salary thresholds subject to a 'going rate.' So it's not enough to meet a general minimum – salaries must be within eighty per cent or more of the one-size fits all 'usual going rate.' So a veterinarian on £22,900 would make above the published general minimum of £20,480, but would still be barred because she'd actually have to earn eighty per cent of £32,500. This means that the simple-looking three bands of income thresholds and points will actually differ for every profession – instead of three categories, there would be three for every role in the country whose amount would change regularly. The complexity and problems surrounding the new system will reach new heights. Adding such significant confusion will not help boost Britain as open for business and risks turning away top talent.

The guidance increases uncertainty. Start with the claim that offenders with a custodial sentence of at least twelve months will be barred. Sounds simple, but how will this work? This is talking about prison in a different country for crimes that might not be illegal here in the UK. Criminal background checks have been patchy and need to be improved to meet this standard, and there needs to be clarity about whether someone with a suspended sentence of a year or more, who does not spend one day in prison, would be barred. All of this is to be confirmed later.

We remain none the wiser about how much of the system will work. For example, there already is a points-based system for non-EU migrants that has been around since 2008. It's deliberately misleading to make no reference to the fact that the 'new' system is a revision of what Labour introduced over a decade ago. This message should be repeated again and again until the Government acknowledges it.

When we look at our existing points-based system, we can see it does not include a route for family visas and reunification. While the Government seemed keen to change this, they wisely took the advice from the Migration Advisory Committee to avoid it. However, this major route for migration affecting about one in five remains undecided and to be confirmed later. This is an area of real change where the can has yet again been kicked down the road.

The guidance claims it has learned the lessons from Windrush. But a key problem was that there were people with right of continuing residency, and often citizenship, who did not have documented proof from the Home Office in hand. This was a problem under the hostile environment where such proof was required from private landlords, to register with a GP or open a bank account. However, there's nothing in the further guidance about guaranteeing that EU citizens with similar rights to residency or citizenship, such as in the Windrush cases, will receive their documented proof – and the law creating the hostile environment will remain unchanged. Together, these factors suggest lessons have not been learned, only compensation paid. This is not good enough.

The Home Office makes much noise about how it will be restricting immigration only to those with a working knowledge of English. There are exceptions they aren't mentioning, like for artists, athletes, musicians and 'religious workers.' So contrary to its public announcements, there is actually more 'business as usual' in these guidelines than the Government acknowledges. Again.

Then there's the money. The 'NHS surcharge' is misnamed. The price reflects estimated uses of public services not limited to the NHS. The original rationale is the impact of migrants using the NHS would be offset by the money raised. But the money is not actually linked to a migrant's local health authority and instead goes into a large pot – and so not fulfilling its original purpose. People are paying money on top of taxes that isn't going to where it is needed. And it's scandalous the Government refuses to rule out an exemption for health and care workers given the sacrifices made this year fighting Covid-19.

The fees and income continue to rise and rise. The Government has raised student visas from £348 to £475 and skilled worker visas from £1,220 to £1,408. Those with UK ancestry see their fees doubled from £516 to £1,033. While the Home Office collects ever greater profits, there is no plan for this ensuring a better service for applicants, businesses or families. The profiteering is already at nine hundred per cent in some cases. It's wrong that immigrants are exploited so blatantly and, worse, that much of the funding raised is sent elsewhere and not to improve a system lacking strong public confidence. For this government, migrants' only value seems to be what they can be charged, not what they can contribute.

This is an opportunity delayed. We do not know all categories that will earn points. While we know that experience can earn points in addition to qualifications, we do not have the full guidance on either. It seems most of how this system will work is to be decided – and whether or not there is a deal with the EU could change these decisions yet again.

What I think many of us had hoped was that we get a clearer picture about how each of the pathways worked so that individuals and businesses can plan. The Government seems to be leaving this to the wire – and while they make up their minds, businesses will have to wait and delay their plans which does nothing for an economy needing all the help it can get.

The law is sometimes referred to as a patchwork quilt. What we have here is a few pieces but nothing stitched together yet – we are not as far forward as we should be as the clock towards Brexit continues to tick.

Priti Patel's immigration reform is a confusing mess that will leave us worse off[116]

The latest net migration statistics published on 27 May are a snapshot of England and Wales. The Office for National Statistics notes that new data from the year up to June 2019 should be viewed with some caution as Covid impacted its data collection. Nonetheless, these new figures raise serious questions about the future plans for immigration reform announced by the Government earlier this week.

The latest data shows drops in all areas from EU and non-EU citizens alike. Visits to England or Wales for work or study for three months to a year fell from 160,000 in June 2018 to 100,000 by June 2019. The only category where migration rose was in British citizens seeking work abroad. This doubled from 30,000 to 60,000 over the same period.

The picture being painted is clear. Most did not see England and Wales as a place welcoming global talent, with a greater number of citizens looking elsewhere for opportunities. The trend continues in estimates up to this spring, where work-related visas were down by over one third on last year, with more than two thirds due to falls in intra-company transfers.

While there should be some caution regarding these estimates, they show that in the run-up to 1 January 2020, those seeking work and study opportunities were looking elsewhere and this was before the pandemic arrived. It seems all but certain that this is the start of an unfortunate trend that the Government may want to address urgently.

Since 2010, the Conservatives have made election manifesto promises to cut net migration to the tens of thousands. One regular

116 'Priti Patel's immigration reform is a confusing mess that will leave us worse off', *The Independent* (29 May 2021).

criticism is that net migration has not, in fact, been higher than under the Tories. This highlights how their rhetoric does not match reality. Talking tough has not translated into results.

A second frequently raised concern is about the use of net migration for setting policy. Net migration counts all individuals entering or leaving over the year regardless of their nationality and mostly estimated using passenger data, making it more guesswork than science.

It has been noticeable for years that net migration would actually be higher if British citizens – who are more likely to leave for abroad than return – were discounted from the figures.

Earlier this week, Home Secretary Priti Patel vowed to strengthen the UK's digital border and introduce 'greater accuracy', avoiding hypothetical guesstimates of how much migration is actually happening. It is a shocking indictment that it has taken the Conservatives more than a decade to finally commit the Government to getting a more accurate count, although no such system will be in place until 2025.

Paradoxically, the Tories have said they will not make any promises on migration reductions as they strive towards better accounting. This comes after making promises to cut numbers when the figures were known to be problematic for policymaking.

This move towards improved accuracy is a part of Patel's new plan for immigration, which sets out how she will fix the 'broken immigration system' that her government has overseen for eleven years. While Patel won't say whether the new plan would lead to more or less immigration, it is clear she wants to position these plans as radical and positive changes. But in short, does it matter?

Her plans include a much-heralded points-based system. What Patel leaves out is that the 'new' system was actually already in place since 2008, when launched by New Labour. Patel's plans mean that the already complex and confusing system will be changing for the worse.

For example, there is no one size fits all approach to a minimum salary needed. Instead, what is required and the number of points earned will depend on what occupation someone is in and the latest annual report on what the average salaries happen to be at that time, subject to regular changes that will cause major confusion in calculating whether someone can or cannot apply.

Given that the system was already in place for non-EU citizens in 2019, these changes do not appear likely to encourage global talent to work in the UK.

Patel also plans to reform the appeal process for rejected applicants. While she cites too many 'repeated unmeritorious appeals and claims' as justification, Patel is silent on the large number of successful appeals against the Home Office.

If the Home Secretary wants a fairer and more transparent system, she can start by ensuring her department does a better job at enforcing their own rules in the first place. This proposal is also unlikely to lead to any beneficial changes. The latest figures for this spring show a drop of more than forty per cent in grants of asylum, mostly because far fewer applications have been processed, leading to a record-level rising backlog.

Finally, a major aim of the new plan is to reform the UK's asylum and refugee policy. Patel proposes to cut numbers by diverting some to apply on new economic migration pathways, which simply involves counting the same individuals, but in a different way.

None of these proposals address the core issues. Global talent is mobile, but the Government fails to make a case for why more of the most talented should choose to relocate to a country where its immigration laws are becoming more complex, confusing, too often wrongly applied and in a continuous state of flux, where policies are aimed at making headlines and not evidence-led.

A more thorough, publicly engaged review is needed to ensure the system is fit for purpose and has public confidence. Until then, Patel's plans may only fuel the unfortunate trend we see in these latest migration statistics. It will be yet another failed government strategy, that leaves us all worse off.

Law and Disorder

The first awakening of my interest in UK legal matters was when Jack Straw floated proposals to curtail the use of trial by jury. Growing up in the United States where the Bill of Rights – including trial by jury – are widely seen as having a divine authority, I had taken this right for granted. It was a comment and barely developed theory by nineteenth century German philosopher G. W. F. Hegel which struck a chord with me: without a jury, the trial becomes a conversation between legal professions using a technical vocabulary largely inaccessible to the public. The only way the defendant, if not a lawyer, could be held to have a reasonable chance of understanding the relative weighting of available evidence and any grounds for conviction were if a group of similarly situated non-lawyers from the public could be so convinced. Anything less, would leave the law – and public justice, for that matter – a 'possession' by a professional class. And so my two decade interest in the law and legal philosophy began.

These essays cover a wide range of topics. These include the launch of digital courts long before the Covid outbreak and up to the Supreme Court case ruling the Prime Minister acted unlawfully in prorogating Parliament for weeks unnecessarily. They also include an idea whose time, I hope, has come: the launch of a hate crime register.

In different ways, what unites these concerns is the crisis of trust – in our courts, in our trials, in the lawful actions of the government and of the rising hate crime in our communities – with some suggestions for what might be done about it.

Defence of the jury is an open and shut case[117]

If we abandon trial by our peers, we abandon the transparency essential to a robust legal system.

Why should we have a right to a trial by jury? An increasing number of academics and politicians, not least Tony Blair, argue that the use of jury trials should be curtailed, if not ended. It is estimated that scrapping them would save the Treasury at least £120 million a year and its detractors flatly deny that such a move would entail a loss of liberty.

After all, why entrust justice to twelve randomly selected members of the public rather than a professionally trained judge or magistrate?

Consigning jury trials to history seems to make good economic sense and further the cause of justice, they argue. But we would be wise to reject such claims. The right to trial by jury is a curious right with a long history, but it is a right worth defending.

Justice must not only take place, it must be seen by the public to take place. This idea is at the heart of any defence of the jury trial. If they were scrapped, the vital transparency of the legal process would be lost.

Law is a public good that serves and protects the rights of all. We believe that it is necessary for persons to be found fit for trial before it commences. They could then be expected to understand the charges brought against them and the reasons justifying their

---

117 'Defence of the Jury is an Open and Shut Case', *Times Higher Education Supplement* (2 March 2007): 14.

conviction. Why would we think a defendant would understand the reasons he or she is on trial and the justification of sentencing without a jury trial? They force legal professionals to discuss public justice not merely among themselves, but with the rest of us. The public must be persuaded beyond reasonable doubt that a defendant is guilty. Most of us are not trained in law and its increasingly technical vocabulary. It is not unreasonable to suppose that a defendant of modest intellect might not sufficiently comprehend court proceedings.

One safeguard against this problem is our guarantee of legal counsel. However, the best safeguard is a jury. Not only do they ensure that trials are not held in private and, thus, defended publicly, they also ensure full transparency in forcing legal professionals to speak the public's language in the public interest, deciding matters of justice in accordance with the rule of law.

If juries often reached mistaken verdicts, as their critics argue, then we would expect them to acquit defendants out of line with how judges decide similar cases. While there has not been enough recent research on jury deliberation, the evidence we have is clear and to the contrary: juries do not decide cases out of line with judges. This is true even in fraud trials, despite the routine efforts of politicians to criticise jurors for their 'inability' to handle such difficult cases.

Of course, a jury's ability to arrive at verdicts is not best enabled by denying them transcripts or from taking notes as is currently the case.

They should not be prevented from using such tools to help them render verdicts, unlike judges or magistrates who are not constrained in those ways.

There is one final consideration. Even if I am correct to argue that juries render verdicts in line with magistrates and judges and that they ensure transparency, critics of such trials argue that jurors are susceptible to intimidation in trials involving paramilitary groups or organised crime. Of course, a defendant would have to intimidate not one but three jurors against his conviction to ensure a 'not guilty' verdict. They would need only intimidate one judge to get the same result.

I do not for a moment believe judges are subject to such treatment. Nor do I fear for mistaken verdicts due to jury intimidation. We hear these claims regularly and yet the evidence is scant. In fact, if juries are subjected to intimidation, then it seems to clearly be a case for greater police protection not the scrapping of the institution. It is not an argument against the use of juries: they should be afforded the same protections offered to judges and magistrates.

We increasingly hear critics deride the jury as a poor body to decide cases. But their claims that there is nothing to lose and we will make substantial monetary savings if we follow their advice are pure nonsense.

Curtailing the use of juries will lead to greater cynicism of the judicial system.

In fact, juries enjoy wide support among the public, with citizens far more likely to vote after jury service than before. The system is therefore a great public good worthy of special protection, not degradation. If we abolish jury trials, the province of law will be a realm from which the public will be excluded, preventing us from participating in our own political life.

Paper-hungry courts put on digital diet[118]

The UK courts are to be dragged into the twenty-first century with a £160 million investment to help them go digital. Announcing its

118 'Paper-Hungry Courts put on digital diet', The Conversation (4 July 2013).

plans, the Ministry of Justice revealed that the courts get through a staggering 160 million pieces of paper every year (the equivalent of fifteen Mount Snowdons). They will be weaned off this diet with a host of new technology.

Court cases of all kinds require a huge amount of paperwork. Now, instead of lugging suitcases full of documents in and out of court as they currently do, legal teams will be able to access files related to the case electronically. The aim is to enable them to access the files stored on their own systems back in their offices too – handy if your overstretched team has left something behind. This might seem trivial but the cost of adjourning a court case, sending away jurors, lawyers and defendants, makes the introduction of digital technology a potentially very important development.

Courtrooms will also be fitted with WiFi and evidence screens to further modernise the system while police will be encouraged to participate in proceedings via video link rather than spending their time waiting around at the Old Bailey for their turn to give evidence.

The investment should be taken as good news. Our laws change over time and so should the way we use information.

Cutting back on these paper mountains is not just good for the environment. There are wider implications, one of which is control. If more information is only available in digital form, there will be fewer paper documents that could fall into the 'wrong' hands – a serious matter when justice is at stake. Information could be better contained through more rigorous control. I say 'could' because there will certainly be issues surrounding the security of communications.

A digital court could lead to better managed control of information but we all know how important it is to keep networks secure to avoid the loss of sensitive data. WiFi-ready courtrooms have great potential to speed up the system but satisfactory assurances will need to be made about security first.

Costs are another concern. The history of government IT projects might be summed up as 'promise low, deliver high' and I would be very surprised if the actual costs are not much higher than the £160m promised this week. The Ministry of Justice is facing substantial cuts and we might be concerned about how well any future overspend will be funded. Its budgets for prisons and vital services like legal aid are already being squeezed and further cuts of ten per cent are due in 2015–16.

Then comes the challenge of integrating different bodies to make the system work. The idea that information should be shared more easily and efficiently is compelling, but sometimes much easier said than done. In any big IT system like this, organisations with often incompatible systems and different approaches to data collection must be brought together somehow.

In the court system, this means a marriage between public sector organisations and private law firms. Each holds information that they want to share with the other parties but also information that they don't. After all, prosecution and defence are competing against each other once a case is in motion. These problems are not reasons to shy away from creating the digital court, but they do highlight the challenges to be faced.

The Government is right to argue the court should be modernised for the twenty-first century. My only fear is that it might not be completed before the start of the twenty-second.

Our courts are no enemies of the people – they are champions of our liberties[119]

'Enemies of the people' declared the tabloid press. They were not referring to Isis or some terrorist organisation, but our judges. Their crime was to apply the rule of law – and the widespread misunderstanding of what this meant.

The concern for many Brexit campaigners was that giving a Parliament a say meant that the High Court was denying the referendum result. This anxiety that a long-cherished goal of seeing the UK leave the EU could be thwarted led to some of the most extraordinary accusations. They didn't make a mountain out of a molehill, but took leave of reality as well as their senses.

The case was about whether the Government or Parliament could trigger Article 50 of the Lisbon Treaty launching Britain's exit from the European Union.

The Government argued that this was about treaties – and whether we are a part of them. The Government is able to make such agreements subject to any expressed view of Parliament. The Prime Minister's argument was that triggering Article 50 concerned a treaty and so the Government had the right to trigger Britain's Brexit at its pleasure.

This argument was rejected by the High Court because this power – like all freedoms – has strings attached. One crucial issue is that if the Government got its way then it would effectively cancel out an Act of Parliament, namely the European Communities Act 1972 which incorporated EU law into UK domestic law. Only Parliament has the power to do that and so MPs must have a vote.

119 'Our courts are no enemies of the people – they are champions of our liberties', *The Journal* (27 January 2017): 31.

The Government was then quick to appeal to the Supreme Court. Their argument was little more than trying to re-run the same line of argument they tried unsuccessfully before. The result was the same with an 8–3 verdict that the Government could not trigger Britain's Brexit when it wanted, but must gain Parliament's approval.

Pro-Brexit campaigners should see nothing to fear. There is no concerted will of a majority in Parliament to stop the referendum result. The question was primarily constitutional and it has been answered emphatically.

Our courts are no enemies of the people – they are champions of our liberties. Some argued the people spoke and Brexit should happen immediately. However, we live in a parliamentary democracy where Parliament is sovereign. Those who wanted Parliament to take back control have their wish – and should celebrate the courts putting Parliament first.

We do not live in an elected dictatorship nor a tyranny of the majority. Just because a majority want something doesn't mean it is anything goes. We live under a rule of law that affords protections to all – and the rule of law is one of Britain's most cherished and ancient values.

Leavers have an enemy though – a barrier to achieving their Brexit goal – and that's this government. The Supreme Court made clear that the Government deserves some blame for the constitutional mess it has created.

The Supreme Court noted that the Act of Parliament creating the referendum we held last June was not especially well thought out. That Act said there would be a referendum, but gave no provision to what would happen if the public voted to leave.

If the legislation said something like a Leave vote meant Parliament authorised the Government to start the UK's Brexit, then this matter would be resolved from the start. It is the Government's poor planning that has meant extra delay and confusion. But it does not stop there.

The Conservative Party's manifesto for the 2015 general election does not say what it would do in government about the referendum result if there was a vote for Brexit.

Honouring the result can mean many things. While some Leave voters wanted controls on immigration, the EU free movement rules are separate from the EU – countries like Norway have free movement as members of the single market while not being an EU country.

Campaigners arguing Brexit meant no EU free movement get wrong how free movement works or its legal basis. You'd expect leading parliamentary campaigners to get this right, but there you are.

If the Tories made clear their intentions on what any Brexit might mean in their manifesto, then this would help bind the hands of the House of Lords. But because they didn't, it is unclear what any vote in the House of Lords might look like.

It is also the case that the Government could have had its Brexit bill by now if it had not been going down the route of taking this to the courts. When it so soundly lost in the High Court, it should have then moved to get a bill through Parliament so it could meet its March deadline.

This now looks very difficult and it is only because of the Government's continued poor handling of the referendum and its aftermath.

Even now we still struggle to make sense of what Brexit means. This is not what the public voted for.

While Britain will leave, its terms and negotiating position must be carefully considered. The Prime Minister will continue involvement in different EU organisations – such as on security – and a full withdrawal from all such associations is not on the cards.

A second referendum is unnecessary, but a vote in Parliament is required – and it should not be rushed as Britain embarks on the biggest change in political course in generations.

We need to do more to stop hate crime – that's why Britain needs a Hate Crime Offenders Register[120]

Hate crime isn't something new. But its continuing rise is a serious problem that must be tackled. Doing nothing or being complacent are not options.

Individuals become hate crime victims where their being a victim is a result of their offender's prejudice against them because of their race, religion, sexual orientation, disability or because they are transgender.

The main idea is that offending is a public wrong whoever the victim might be. If a victim was targeted as a result of their simply having certain characteristics – such as having a disability or appearing to be a member of an ethnic minority – this is considered to be a more dangerous public wrong. A key problem here is that the victim could have been anybody: a hate crime is a crime targeting a group. Bad enough that a crime has happened, but even worse than that when it could have been anybody – what a person is counts for more than who the person is. Hate crimes are offences we can all do without.

Sadly, hate crimes are on the rise. While they have been happening long before Brexit, there has been a noticeable increase in hate crimes reported to police since the controversial referendum result.

---

120 Could a register of hate criminals be the solution?' *The Journal* (24 February 2017): 27.

Over the last year, about seventy-five per cent of all police forces in England and Wales reported record numbers of hate crimes. Some areas had increases by fifty per cent. Durham saw a rise of sixteen per cent and Cleveland rose by nearly a third.

There are several factors relevant. Police forces are getting better at recording reported hate crimes. More work has gone into engaging with communities to support victims coming forward and addressing concerns. This is very welcome and continuing.

The Crown Prosecution Service is getting better at prosecuting hate crimes, too. I've had the pleasure of serving on a CPS North East Community Involvement Panel and the efforts put into getting this right by the CPS are genuinely commendable. Of course, procedures and systems must be routinely monitored and improved – but hate crimes are squarely on the radar. Law enforcement and prosecutors are very much on the case even if there is always further work to be done.

These efforts at better recording hate crimes and prosecuting them may explain why more are being reported, but go nowhere near the major increases we've seen over the last year. If we're to make more progress on tackling hate crimes, we need to do something different.

Locking more people up for longer – without the right support within prisons in place – is both highly expensive and ineffective. When the US state of California brought in – by popular referendum – a 'Three Strikes and You're Out' law that saw anyone convicted for a third felony offence sentenced to life in prison, several things went wrong and most especially the cost of incarcerating everyone affected went through the roof and a significant chunk of the state's annual budget was going to prisons instead of to schools and health care. Studies found that any deterrence effect was negligible: the hugely expensive – and at the time popular – reforms became a failed experiment.

So we need to do something different to help bring down rising hate crime.

Let's launch a Hate Crime Offenders Register. It would work much like a register for sex offenders. We already know what are sexual offences. In addition to any sentencing, there are further restrictions – a ban on working with children and vulnerable people, limits on ability to go near certain locations. Plus it is subject to review to remove it under certain conditions satisfying a high threshold.

We should act similarly with individuals convicted of hate crimes. They should be restricted from working with similar groups and face similar kinds of restrictions on movement relating to the kinds of hate crimes they committed – all of it subject to future review so that those who make amends and turn their lives around for the better are not labelled hate crime offenders any longer than necessary.

We already know what are hate crimes. We already use a similar kind of register. There is already precedent in how cases are reviewed. Such a model could be launched quickly and potentially effectively.

No law will make everyone avoid criminal behaviour. I don't believe for a second that a Hate Crime Offenders Register – or any other such proposal – will stop all hate crimes from happening.

But that is no reason to do nothing. We have crimes against committing murder – but murders still happen. We criminalise theft and people still steal. These are not reasons to legalise murder and theft. Instead they give us cause to think again how the laws we have can be improved – as well as the support many offenders (and the wider public) too rarely receive.

No register will stop hate crimes, but it can bring hate crimes down. It is a way of our society making a more vocal declaration that hate crimes will not be tolerated. Crime is bad enough, but to be fuelled or caused by hatred towards people on what they are is even worse.

If we're not comfortable with hate crime offenders teaching young children or working with vulnerable adults, then a Hate Crime Offenders Register is one way of making that happen.

A Hate Crime Offenders Register can be a tool used fairly quickly to send out a clearer signal to help stop the rise of hate crime in our region and nationally.

In the absence of better alternatives, it may be an idea whose time has come.

As a law professor, I can see Boris Johnson hasn't committed a crime – he's done something far worse than that[121]

Three years ago, Boris Johnson argued Britain should vote Leave, taking back control and 'freeing' the UK from the European Court of Justice to make the British Supreme Court its top judicial body. Today, that same Supreme Court has given Johnson the most devastating verdict issued in a generation, and it's left his premiership in tatters.

Johnson's government prorogued Parliament for five weeks. They argued that the extended suspension was simply needed to put together a new legislative agenda for a Queen's Speech next month, and that this was a political decision beyond review of the courts, meaning that any such intervention would be an act of judicial interference.

In its landmark decision, the Supreme Court has found the

121 'As a law professor, I can see Boris Johnson hasn't committed a crime – he's done something far worse than that', *The Independent* (24 September 2019).

government wrong on all points. Its damning, unanimous verdict is that 'it is impossible for us to conclude on the evidence ... that there was any reason – let alone a good reason – to advise Her Majesty to prorogue Parliament for five weeks.' Lady Hale, president of the Supreme Court, declared that Johnson's actions were 'unlawful, void and of no effect.'

The legal implications are clear: when Black Rod came to the House of Commons to suspend it, the order was a mere 'blank piece of paper' as its words had no lawful effect. Parliament was not technically suspended, and should now be reconvened immediately in a manner to be determined by the speakers of each house.

The repercussions of this verdict are profound, and given the unanimous verdict, they will run deep. The prime minister has been declared to have made an unlawful request to the Queen to silence Parliament in order to pursue a policy agenda that Parliament was trying to block. This is not simply undemocratic in that it gags Britain's elected representatives; it's also unconstitutional.

Amongst lawyers and legal commentators, it was widely expected the Government would lose. The executive simply cannot avoid unwelcome scrutiny by Parliament, to which it is accountable, by suspending it in order to get its way by other means. The UK may have an 'unwritten' constitution insofar as its central rules and conventions are not set out in one document as they are in the US, but its rules and conventions are no less real and form the basis for the rule of law.

So what now? There is a clear convention to be followed by senior government officials when they have been found to have breached the law: to resign immediately. Johnson may not have committed a criminal offence, but in committing an offence against our constitution and the rule of law, he has arguably done something even worse – not only damaging the office of the prime minister, but dragging the Queen into his Brexit mess.

Johnson's time is now up. He has made a serious error of legal judgement, and he must face the consequences. Clinging onto his office will not improve his position, whether in Parliament or in trying to represent the country abroad as he tries to secure a new Brexit deal.

Whether one supports Leave or Remain is irrelevant; the rule of law was always going to prevail. In spite of the prime minister's constitutional vandalism, it has done so triumphantly. Johnson must now pay the price and become the UK's shortest serving occupant of 10 Downing Street. And the sooner, the better.

Priti Patel, if you're serious about tackling racism in Britain then put offenders on a hate crime register[122]

Nearly one month ago, George Floyd's on-camera killing by a white police officer in the United States gave new life to the Black Lives Matter campaign, and helped to spread support for the cause in this country, too. As Will Smith observed, racism isn't getting worse, it's getting filmed. A moral stain such as this cannot so easily be ignored when it's circulating across social media.

The problem with racism in the structures and institutions of our society is well documented. There are reviews aplenty confirming racial bias in the criminal justice system (exposed by the Lammy Report), in the workplace and highlighting the underachievement of white working-class children in schools. While these reports pile up, the injustices continue. The need for action is now visible on the streets of our towns and cities as the public demand change.

122 'Priti Patel, if you're serious about tackling racism in Britain then put offenders on a hate crime register', *The Independent* (19 June 2020).

We've seen Theresa May's 'race disparity audit' providing further evidence of shameful inequalities from access to health care to housing and beyond. She described this work as 'holding a mirror up to our society.'

If the Government is now looking at itself, they should be ashamed at what they see. So many promises made with little or nothing to show for it. No wonder there remains little faith in words alone. Government plans for yet another new half-hearted review neither they nor campaigners want will hardly heal a deepening divide.

What's needed now is an urgent policy sending a clear signal that there is no turning back. The public need to have confidence the Government is ready to tackle racism – and all forms of discrimination – head on.

An important symbolic first step in this direction would be made if Priti Patel, the Home Secretary, immediately seeks to launch a hate crime offenders register.

Hate crimes are defined by the Crown Prosecution Service as offences motivated by hostility or prejudice based on a person's real or perceived ethnicity, disability, gender identity, nationality, race, religion or sexual orientation. When someone is convicted of a hate crime, it can already be a factor in a more severe punishment. But once time is served, it's over – hate crime or not.

We need to treat hate crimes differently to fraud, theft and other forms of criminality. By harming somebody simply for who they are, hate crimes are more dangerous and of greater public concern.

A hate crime offenders register could be launched relatively quickly. We already have a working definition of what constitutes a hate crime and have high thresholds for securing criminal convictions.

As I've recommended in written evidence to the Home Affairs Select Committee, a register for hate crime offenders could work similarly to those used for sex offenders. An individual must be convicted of a crime punishable by a year or more.

Being on the list would carry consequences. Head teachers, doctors, landlords and youth leaders may be notified when such an offender is in their area. There may be restrictions imposed, preventing offenders from working with children or vulnerable adults. Any foreign travel would require permission prior to departure and a valid address must be maintained each year. Perhaps registration for some could be for a fixed-time, allowing time for re-education, but those convicted of more serious hate crimes might remain on the list long-term.

The aim of a hate crime offenders register is to send a message that these offenders will carry much greater consequences – perhaps long after the initial punishment is over. Hate crime won't be seen like any other offence and it will have an impact – as well as create a more effective deterrent to help reduce future offences.

No register is going to end racial injustice. The criminal justice system should be a last resort. But the value of a register is in making clear – and urgently – that hate crimes won't be tolerated. It is only a beginning, but an important symbolic move that can help set us all on a path to much more changes to come.

The problem of racial injustice and other forms of discrimination are deep-rooted. It will take a long-term, collective commitment to eradicate prejudice and promote understanding. A tougher stance against hate crimes can help move us in this direction.

King Alan's Court

Nearly a decade ago, the *Times Higher Education* commissioned a semi-autobiographical essay from me on the topic of what motivated an American to come to live, work and build a career in the UK. An important part of my US identity is my being from the New Haven area in Connecticut. I am a native New Englander. Since 2004, I have also lived in the North East moving between Newcastle upon Tyne and Durham. Or as I sometimes say, I'm from one North East and now live in another.

In addition to discussing some of the history of my former and current homes, I draw on Mark Twain's novel *A Connecticut Yankee in King Arthur's Court*. This is a story about someone from my native US state waking up in a different time and place – where he quickly becomes at home.

This perspective of the outsider becoming an insider is one that resonates more with me today than it did then. The outsider immigrant in me notices differences, little details about how a system works or assumptions made that can be easily missed. Meanwhile, the insider citizen in me better understands how these differences came to be – and pathways to their being transformed.

All of this is built on presuppositions based on trust – and this is increasingly in short supply.

A Connecticut Yankee in King Alan's court[123]

Where we are from often informs who we are. I traded life in the American Northeast for life in the North East of England. New Haven – the site of America's first public tree-planting programme, earning it the nickname 'Elm City' – is famous for the great Patriot Nathan Hale, the cotton-gin inventor Eli Whitney, and for Sally's Apizza, a legendary pizzeria. As such, it is rather different from Newcastle, or 'Geordieland', which counts footballer-turned-pundit Alan Shearer and politician and tea-godfather Charles Grey, the 2nd Earl Grey, among its most famous sons.

Yet it is a trade I would make any day. Let me explain why a Connecticut Yankee would prefer life as a Geordie-in-training.

First, it is necessary to explain what a 'Connecticut Yankee' is. Perhaps the best-known example is found in Mark Twain's 1889 novel *A Connecticut Yankee in King Arthur's Court*. Twain (real name Samuel Clemens) settled in Connecticut after many years travelling across the US and Europe, coming to rest in Hartford, the state capital, where he wrote many of his most famous works, *The Adventures of Tom Sawyer* (1876) and *The Prince and the Pauper* (1881) among them.

A Connecticut Yankee tells the tale of Hank Morgan, who receives a crushing blow to the head that knocks him out cold. When he wakes, he finds himself under an oak tree and discovers that he is no longer in nineteenth century Connecticut; he has somehow been transported to the sixth century and to King Arthur's England.

The novel is an insightful satire about social and political thought from the perspective of a stranger in a strange land. Hank uses his knowledge of Victorian science to dispel the false magic of

123 'A Connecticut Yankee in King Alan's Court', *Times Higher Education* (7 July 2011): 44–6.

Merlin, win favour in King Arthur's court and reform society from within, contributing to a more egalitarian and republican state. While he holds in contempt the public's confidence in the Church and the aristocracy, Hank soon discovers that he 'was just as much at home in that century as I could have been in any other.'

He builds close friendships and has a family. The story ends with his transportation back to modern Connecticut, where, in his dying moments, he is heard mumbling of his longing for his long-dead wife and lost life.

Twain's Hank is the archetypal New Englander of his time: highly educated, pragmatic and resourceful, with a general distrust of institutional authority.

He has a deep commitment to egalitarianism, which was also not uncommon: New Haven was the scene of a famous court case favouring the abolitionist cause against slavery that was later retold in the movie *Amistad* (1997). Hank is described as 'a Yankee of the Yankees' and his Connecticut roots serve as a fitting background. (How much more 'Yankee' can you get than a man from a state whose song is Yankee Doodle?)

It wasn't a blow to the head that sent me to England, but the allure of further study. I don't mean to say that the experience was not disorienting. My preconceptions were blown out of the water on day one, when I discovered that, contrary to expectations, not everyone in the UK speaks like John Cleese – least of all in the North.

It is often assumed that moving to the UK must be fairly easy for an American, or at least easier than the other way around. After all, how could an Englishman or woman survive in a country where kettles, decent chocolate and knowledge about the finer points of queuing etiquette are hard to come by?

I confess that the first time I saw a sign telling customers in a sandwich shop where to queue, my first thought was that a 'queue' must be some sort of culinary offering: something containing eggs, I imagined.

The differences in everyday life are to be found all around. Take driving, for example. In the US, we park on driveways and drive on parkways. In the UK, by contrast, we park in car parks and drive on motorways. This clearly makes more sense.

But it is not all so straightforward. It makes less sense to use a white circle with a diagonal black stripe through it to denote a speed limit, far less so when this sign – representing the national speed limit – means different things to different drivers, depending on the type of vehicle you are driving, whether you are towing anything and the conditions of the road. Oh, and the signs are sometimes posted on the left, sometimes on the right, and they come in different sizes. Surely it is far more sensible to follow the US model of stating the speed limit for all in numerical form on the same-sized sign and the same side of the road?

But if my UK driving test had me in knots, it had nothing on the curiosities arising from the citizenship test. This involves an examination based on the *Life in the United Kingdom: A Journey to Citizenship* document and is a requirement for 'Indefinite leave to remain' visas as well as citizenship.

The first oddity is that you do not become a citizen by passing the test. Instead, you must first receive indefinite leave to remain and then wait at least a year before applying for citizenship. The second is that you quickly discover that no British citizen seems to know the answer to most of the questions. The third is that those questions that may seem of most importance to any immigrant – such as British history or basic facts of law – are not part of the test. Instead, it grills applicants on whether the British government restricted immigration from Australasia in the 1960s, the percentage of young people in higher education, and whether '1 April is a day when people play jokes on each other.'

My test included the following question:

Q: Which two places can you go to if you need a National Insurance number?

A. Department for Education and Skills

B. Home Office

C. Jobcentre Plus

D. Social security office

Readers who answered C and D can give themselves a pat on the back because they are, apparently, the correct options. But it is worth pointing out that two of the answers (A and D) no longer exist. This is because the *Life in the United Kingdom* textbook was last updated in April 2007. To pass the citizenship test in 2011, you must answer questions as if you were living in the past. It is hardly surprising, then, that so many fail the test.

To return to Hank's story, it is fair to say that his journey was very different from mine. He travelled backwards in time, whereas I often feel as if I have gone forwards, given the many advantages of life in the UK over that in the US.

Healthcare is a clear example. In the UK, even the Conservative-led Coalition Government supports a strong NHS, even if there is serious disagreement about the best way this might be secured. But in the US, members of the conservative Republican Party condemn healthcare systems such as the NHS as 'socialist' and even 'communist' (to translate this for the non-paranoid reader, this means 'very bad' and 'much worse').

While capital punishment was abolished decades ago in the UK, many Americans still believe that the only reason why even more of their fellow citizens don't murder each other is the fear of lethal injection.

Oh, and several million Americans believe they have been abducted by aliens.

But this is not to say that I have somehow 'gone native' and delight in denigrating all things American. Far from it. In fact, there is much about my Connecticut roots that fills me with pride.

For example, Connecticut launched the first municipal public library in 1659. It has the oldest continuing newspaper, *The Hartford Courant*, first published in October 1764. Connecticut also has a distinguished history in higher education, being home to Yale University and the Litchfield Law School, founded 1784 – the first law school in the US. In addition, the state gave birth to everything from the corkscrew and friction matches to the cotton gin. Famous Connecticut citizens include the showman P.T. Barnum, the composer Charles Ives, the politician Ralph Nader, the author and abolitionist Harriet Beecher Stowe, the lexicographer, author and political reformer Noah Webster, and Jonathan Trumbull, the only colonial governor to support American independence: not too bad for a small state of about three million in a country of more than 300 million people.

One of the reasons I feel at home in the North East of England is the fact that the local population – at about 2.5 million, it is similar in size to Connecticut's – are just as proud of their region. There is a rich Roman heritage, and it is home to Lindisfarne, a 'cradle of Christianity' in England, where St. Aidan founded his Anglo-Saxon monastery in AD 635. The area is awash with castles – Bamburgh, Bishop Auckland, Durham, Newcastle and Tynemouth: indeed, the land was once the home of the Northumbrian Kings. And then there is the city of Durham and its cathedral, which my compatriot Bill Bryson described as 'the best cathedral on planet Earth', urging readers that if they hadn't visited it yet, 'go at once; take my car.'

It is also interesting to compare the mysterious origins of the words associated with both places. The word 'Connecticut' is believed to derive from the native Mohegan word Quinnehtukqut, meaning 'Long River Place.' But what of the origins of 'Yankee'?

One account is that English settlers referred to Dutch settlers in New Amsterdam as 'John Cheese' (or 'Jan Kaas' in Dutch) because they were known as cheesemakers. If true, it is a curiosity of history how and why a derogatory term for early immigrants to what is now New York City has come to refer instead to the citizens of New England.

Similar questions hang over the origin of 'Geordie.' One account is that it refers to Newcastle upon Tyne's support for George II during the Jacobite Rebellion of 1745, but there is much debate over its true origins.

Today, both 'Yankee' and 'Geordie' mean different things to different people. If you are not from New England or Newcastle, the terms are used as catch-alls – and not always in a positive way. But if you are from New England or Newcastle, you would never refer to people from anywhere else as Yankees or Geordies, and the terms are used with pride.

Mark Twain's Hank finds England a land of opportunity, and my experience has been the same. I'm often asked why I left the Greater New York area. You could say that I discovered the American Dream, but discovered it elsewhere: in the United Kingdom.

The US is often thought of as a friendly country, but much of that friendliness is of the plastic variety typified by such platitudes as 'Have a nice day' and 'Have a good one' ('What "one"?' I'm always tempted to ask). By contrast, I am constantly reminded of the genuine friendliness of the people I have met in the UK, not least the North East (Newcastle is not known for its nightlife for nothing).

Another aspect of the country that has a major hold on me is the history. Anyone who enjoys visiting castles and cathedrals half as much as I do would be in heaven in the North East. Perhaps Twain's Hank shared this fascination. While Connecticut has buildings dating from the early seventeenth century, they are mere buildings. There is something altogether different about castles and cathedrals, something more magical and enchanting, not unlike finding oneself transported back in time to King Arthur's court.

The UK today strikes me as a land of wonder, in which villages retain their charm and cities their unique personality. The same is not always true for the modern US. I find it much easier to find inspiration in the Northumberland coastline than I do in the shoreline along the Long Island Sound.

My family left England for New Haven in the eighteenth century and have remained there ever since. As such, I consider my return to our original home long overdue and while I will always be a Connecticut Yankee, the fact is that my life is here now. Is Britain best for me? Why aye, man.

Building the Future

We live among the ruins of a quiet revolution created by a crisis of trust – in our political leaders, our public institutions and even each other. This change did not happen overnight, but is a product of many years of creating a narrative where politicians should never be trusted, public institutions only inflexibly serve a status quo justifying their own existence at rising taxpayer expense and a growing distrust in our fellow citizens to be honest and patriotic.

Each has plenty of fuel to build its destructive fire. Too many politicians make promises to further careers with little chance of delivering their claims. Our institutions require renewal – but are also too often unable to defend themselves in the absence of leadership within organisations or government. Plus, newspapers don't sell us stories about hope, but fear about our communities. Together, these forces paint a misleading picture that turns us against each other – favouring leaders who pitch themselves as 'strong' and 'doers' ready to tear up the rules – and, to their critics, the rule of law.

Such views must be challenged if we no longer want to live in a world without trust. This shift requires a greater openness, more transparency and accountability. This is more difficult than it sounds because it means creating a target. If opponents say one thing and do another, then they are more difficult to rebut than someone who aims for clearer consistency. It will take courage – and conviction.

But if we fail to act how we believe we should, then no one may do it for us. Our leaders and institutions must take that risk of being the politicians and public bodies we should have, and make hope a reality.

Crucially, this work is not something for somebody else to do. It is too easy to say Prime Ministers should do a better job or that the world could be different. We must become the change we believe it. Principles and ideals do not exist in the heavens, but through us and what we do. There is no better substitute for selling a vision of hope than to embody it.

This is not only a task for politicians or civil servants but for every one of us. It is through our actions that we must challenge ourselves to become tomorrow's leaders – and to hold others to the high standards we set for ourselves.

We need to be trusted – and for this we must be trusting. This means opening ourselves up to criticism. It's about becoming more vulnerable, and more human. People need to believe in one another again. This will be a slow process much as the quiet revolution seeing trust ebb further and further way is a product of more than a decade. Now is not inevitable.

I'm realistically optimistic that we can build a brighter future. The election of Joe Biden in the United States and Labour's election of Keir Starmer gives me hope. We need to learn from the mistakes highlighted throughout this book and be a part of the solution. Just as we transitioned into a political crisis, we can also get out of it. Taking seriously trust – *the trust factor* – will be at the heart of the next revolution. I'll see you there.

Index